Retirement System Risk Management

Retirement System Risk Management

Implications of the New Regulatory Order

EDITED BY

Olivia S. Mitchell, Raimond Maurer, and J. Michael Orszag

OXFORD
UNIVERSITY PRESS

OXFORD
UNIVERSITY PRESS

Great Clarendon Street, Oxford, OX2 6DP,
United Kingdom

Oxford University Press is a department of the University of Oxford.
It furthers the University's objective of excellence in research, scholarship,
and education by publishing worldwide. Oxford is a registered trade mark of
Oxford University Press in the UK and in certain other countries

First Edition published in 2016

Impression: 1

Published in the United States of America by Oxford University Press
198 Madison Avenue, New York, NY 10016, United States of America

British Library Cataloguing in Publication Data
Data available

Library of Congress Control Number: 2016945378

ISBN 978–0–19–878737–2

Printed in Great Britain by
Clays Ltd, St Ives plc

Preface

In the wake of the Global Financial Crisis of 2008–10, regulators and policymakers around the world sought to restructure the environment within which financial institutions operate. The goal was to make more transparent and more consistent the regulations and monitoring infrastructure of institutions such as banks, insurers, pension funds, and asset managers. The financial sector meltdown also spurred efforts to reassess how accounting systems handle reporting of assets and liabilities, particularly for long-term promises such as pensions.

In this, our newest volume in the Pension Research Council/Oxford University Press series, we take stock of these changes and consider how they will alter how both banks and nonbanks will operate in the future. We also evaluate what the possible unintended effects may be for other markets and segments of the economy as well. Lessons from the international experiences are germane, since there is still no fully global harmonization of regulations and practice. Our volume will interest employees and retirees, consumers and researchers, and financial institutions working to design better retirement plan offerings.

In the process of preparing this book, many people and institutions played key roles. Co-editors Raimond Maurer and J. Michael Orszag contributed numerous helpful suggestions as we designed and structured the analysis presented herein. We thank our Advisory Board and Members of the Pension Research Council for intellectual and financial support. Additional support was received from the Pension Research Council, the Boettner Center for Pensions and Retirement Research, and the Ralph H. Blanchard Memorial Endowment at the Wharton School of the University of Pennsylvania. We also offer deep appreciation to Oxford University Press, which publishes our series on global retirement security. The manuscript was expertly prepared and carefully edited by Donna St. Louis and Joseph Brucker.

Our work at the Pension Research Council and the Boettner Center for Pensions and Retirement Research of the Wharton School of the University of Pennsylvania has focused on aspects of pensions and retirement well-being for over sixty years. This volume furthers our effort to generate excellent research and engage lively debate on pension and retirement security policy around the world.

Olivia S. Mitchell
Executive Director, Pension Research Council
Director, Boettner Center for Pensions and Retirement Research
Wharton School, University of Pennsylvania

Contents

List of Figures

List of Tables

Notes on Contributors

Javier Alonso works for BBVA Research in Madrid. Previously, he was Research Economist in the Foundation for Applied Economics in Spain (FEDEA), Financial Expert at Novartis in Madrid, and professor at the University Complutense de Madrid. Javier Alonso received his Ph.D. and BA in Economics from the University Complutense de Madrid.

Alfonso Arellano works for BBVA Research and Institute BBVA of Pensions in Madrid. He is also a part-time Associate Professor at University Complutense of Madrid. Previously, he was a post-doctoral researcher at the Foundation for Applied Economics (FEDEA) and visiting professor at the University of Alicante. Alfonso Arellano received his BA in Economics at University Complutense of Madrid, his Masters in Economics and Management at University Pompeu Fabra, and his Ph.D. in Economics at University Carlos III of Madrid.

Andrew G. Biggs is a Resident Scholar at the American Enterprise Institute where he analyzes Social Security reform, state and local government pensions, and public sector pay and benefits. He received his Bachelor's degree from Queen's University Belfast in Northern Ireland, Master's degrees from Cambridge University and the University of London, and his Ph.D. from the London School of Economics.

Joseph Busillo is a Senior Strategist for SEI's Institutional Group, where he works closely with defined-benefit clients in providing strategic advice. He is responsible for the development and application of SEI's global liability-driven investing strategy, and he has deep experience in the investment industry.

Asli Demirgüç-Kunt is the Director of Research at the World Bank. After joining the Bank as a Young Economist, she has held various positions including Director of Development Policy, Chief Economist of Financial and Private Sector Development Network, and Senior Research Manager. Her research and advising focus on financial sector and private sector development issues. She received her MA and Ph.D. in economics from the Ohio State University.

Catherine Donnelly is Associate Professor at the Department of Actuarial Mathematics and Statistics of the School of Mathematical and Computer Sciences of Heriot-Watt University. Her academic interests include proposing and analyzing ways in which a group of people can share their risks, with a focus on sharing investment and mortality risks. Her other interests include annuities, life insurance, pension funds, life-cycle investment (portfolio optimization), and quantitative risk management. She received her MA in Mathematics from Trinity College, University of Cambridge, her M.Sc. in Mathematics and Foundations of Computer Science from Keble College at the University of Oxford, and her Ph.D. in Mathematics from the University of Waterloo.

Peter A. Fisher is a Partner with Tapestry Networks where he leads the firm's practice in financial services, comprising bank and insurance governance, private equity, asset management, and new business development. His interests are financial services, strategic new business development, new product development, and thought leadership. Previously he was managing director at Pyramis Global Advisors where he focused on long-term business strategy and global expansion initiatives; he also led the design and launch of the Fidelity Research Institute and the Strategic New Business Development group. He also was affiliated with Bain & Company and National Economic Research Associates (NERA). He received his BA in economics from Northwestern University, and his MA and Ph.D. in business economics from Harvard.

Montserrat Guillén is a Professor and Director of the Riskcenter, the Research Group on Risk in Insurance and Finance, at the Universitat de Barcelona. Her research focuses on actuarial statistics and quantitative risk management. She is an Associate Editor for the *Journal of Risk and Insurance* (the official journal of the American Risk and Insurance Association), a Senior Editor of *Astin Bulletin* (the official journal of the International Actuarial Association), and Chief Editor of *SORT-Statistics and Operations Research Transactions*. She received her M.Sc. in Mathematics and Mathematical Statistics and Ph.D. in Economics from the University of Barcelona, and her M.Sc. in Data Analysis from the University of Essex.

Thomas Harvey serves as Director of the Advisory Team within SEI's Institutional Group where he delivers ongoing strategic advisory services to institutional clients, and he also serves as an adjunct professor of finance at Penn State University. Previously he was an investment banker and Director with Wachovia Capital Markets. He earned his BS and his MBA in finance from the University of Michigan. He maintains his FINRA Series 7, Series 63, and Series 24 licenses.

Bryan Hoffman is a Senior Portfolio Strategist within the SEI Investment Management Unit. Working with the Research and Development team, he is responsible for the development and maintenance of SEI's capital market assumptions and quantitative asset class modeling; he also conducts asset allocation research in support of SEI's multi-asset models and funds with emphasis on risk-based allocation methods. Bryan earned his BBA in Finance and Economics from the University of Notre Dame and he is a CFA charter holder.

Leora Klapper is Lead Economist in the Finance and Private Sector Research Team of the Development Research Group at the World Bank. Her research interests include entrepreneurship, banking, financial access, corporate governance, bankruptcy, and risk management. She has been instrumental in developing ways to measure financial inclusion (Global Findex). Previously she worked at the Board of Governors of the Federal Reserve System, the Bank of Israel, and Salomon Smith Barney. She earned her Ph.D. in Financial Economics from New York University Stern School of Business.

Raimond Maurer is the Chair of Investment, Portfolio Management, and Pension Finance at the Finance Department of the Goethe University Frankfurt. His research focuses on asset management, life-time portfolio choice, real estate, and pension finance. Previously he visited the Wharton School, and he serves in several professional capacities including the Union Real Estate Investment group, the Society of Actuaries (academic chairman of AFIR), the Association of Certified International Investment Analysts (academic director and member of the International Examination Committee). He earned his Habilitation, Ph.D., and Diploma in business administration from Mannheim University, and he was awarded an honorary doctorate from the State University of Finance and Economics of St Petersburg. He also serves on the Senate of the Goethe University.

Olivia S. Mitchell is the International Foundation of Employee Benefit Plans Professor, as well as Professor of Insurance/Risk Management and Business Economics/Policy; Executive Director of the Pension Research Council; and Director of the Boettner Center for Pensions and Retirement Research, all at the Wharton School of the University of Pennsylvania. Concurrently she serves as a Research Associate at the NBER; Independent Director on the Wells Fargo Advantage Fund Trusts Board; Co-Investigator for the Health and Retirement Study at the University of Michigan; Member of the Executive Board for the Michigan Retirement Research Center; and Senior Scholar of the Centre for Silver Security at the Sim Ki Boon Institute of Singapore Management University. She received the MA and Ph.D. degrees in Economics from the University of Wisconsin-Madison, and the BA in Economics from Harvard University.

Jens Perch Nielsen is Professor of Actuarial Science at the Cass Business School of the City University of London. He has worked as an appointed actuary and led various product development departments before specializing in research and development. Previously he worked as an entrepreneur and he is still co-owner and board member of Copenhagen-based ScienceFirst and Fredensborg Advisor. He received his Masters in Actuarial Science from Københavns Universitet, his Ph.D. in Statistics from the University of California, Berkeley, and a Danish Doctorate in Actuarial Science, Finance, and Statistics from Københavns Universitet.

J. Michael Orszag is Global Head of Research at Towers Watson, a global actuarial consulting firm. His research interests include pensions, personnel economics, risk management, and insurance. He is a founding editor of the *Journal of Pension Economics and Finance* and co-editor of the *Oxford Handbook of Pensions and Retirement Income.* He earned his Ph.D. from the University of Michigan in economics and his AB from Princeton University in economics.

Georgios A. Panos is a Reader in Finance at Adam Smith Business School at the University of Glasgow, where he focuses on the intersection between financial and labor economics. Previously he taught economics at the University of Stirling and the University of Essex Business School, and he has consulted with the World Bank. He earned his Ph.D. in Economics from the University of Aberdeen.

Brian Reid is Chief Economist at the Investment Company Institute, where he leads the Institute's Research Department and oversees all Institute statistical collections and analysis of the mutual fund industry. Previously he was a staff economist in the Monetary Affairs Division of the Federal Reserve Board. He received his BS in economics with honors from the University of Wisconsin-Madison, and the Ph.D. in economics from the University of Michigan.

Ralph Rogalla is an Assistant Professor in the School of Risk Management, Insurance, and Actuarial Science at St John's University. Previously he taught at the Goethe University Frankfurt and Frankfurt University of Applied Sciences, and he served as the Metzler Visiting Professor at the Wharton School, University of Pennsylvania. His research focuses on pension finance and household portfolio choice. He earned his Ph.D. in Finance and his Habilitation from Goethe University, and he holds a diploma in economics from Technical University Berlin.

Ivonne Siegelin is an actuary in product development for Generali Life Insurance in Frankfurt, Germany. Her research focuses on policyholders' utility and insurer risk in participating life annuities. She earned her Ph.D. in Finance from Goethe University.

David Tuesta is a Chief Economist for BBVA Research in Madrid; he is also Research Associate at the Center for Competitiveness and Development of University San Martin de Lima. He collaborates on joint projects with the World Bank, Inter-American Development Bank, and the OECD. Previously, he worked for the Ministry of Finance of Peru and the Peruvian National Regulator of Energy. He received his Ph.D. in Economics from the Catholic University of Peru and his Master's in Public Affairs from the University of Minnesota.

Karel Van Hulle is a Lecturer at the Business and Economics Facility of the Katholieke Universiteit Leuven and the Economics Faculty of the Goethe University of Frankfurt, where he is a member of the Executive Board of the International Centre for Insurance Regulation. He participates in the Master Study Program in Actuarial Science and Financial Mathematics at the University of Abomey-Calavi in Benin. He is also an academic member of the Insurance and Reinsurance Stakeholder Group of EIOPA and he was recently nominated as a member of the Public Interest Oversight Board which oversees the standard-setting activities of the International Federation of Accountants. He is a lawyer by training, studying law at the KU Leuven and then undertaking a postgraduate degree in American Business Law at the Marquette University Law School in Milwaukee, Wisconsin.

Dan Waters is Managing Director of ICI Global. Previously he served as Asset Management Sector Leader at the UK Financial Services Authority (FSA) where he led the FSA's regulatory and supervisory policy for the asset management industry. Waters also represented the United Kingdom in the International Organization of Securities Commissions Standing Committee on Investment Management, and led the Investment Management Standing Committee of CESR (now ESMA) where he worked on significant revisions of the UCITS Directive (UCITS IV). Waters also served as UK Director of Enforcement at the Investment Management Regulatory Organization and he headed international enforcement at the US Commodity Futures Trading Commission. He received his BA from Boston College and Law degree from Harvard Law School.

1

Introduction: Implications of the New Regulatory Order for Retirement System Risk Management

Olivia S. Mitchell, Raimond Maurer, and J. Michael Orszag

Responding to the worst financial crisis since the Great Depression, the US Congress in 2010 passed the Dodd–Frank Wall Street Reform and Consumer Protection Act, thereby altering the playbook for how banks and other financial institutions must manage their risks and report their activities. The European System of Financial Supervision (ESFS) has also worked diligently to build a coherent framework to supervise regulated financial sector institutions including banks, insurers, pension funds, and asset managers. The implosion of the financial sector also prompted calls for change to the accounting system from many seeking to better understand how assets and liabilities are reported.

While initially banks were seen by many as the most important focus for regulatory reform in the wake of the 2008–10 financial meltdown, other institutions are now attracting policymakers' purview and reform efforts. On the one hand, there is logic to this in terms of managing systemic risk and ensuring a level playing field that avoids arbitrage between institutional structures. On the other hand, the nature of pension and insurer liabilities is so different from those of bank liabilities that careful attention is needed in drafting appropriate rules. The new rules are having both direct and spillover effects on retirement systems around the world, including insurers and personal and employer-based occupational pension schemes. The first half of this volume undertakes an assessment of how global responses to the financial crisis are potentially altering how insurers, pension plan sponsors, and policymakers will manage risk in the decades to come. The second half evaluates developments in retirement saving and retirement products, to determine which and how these might help meet shortfalls in retirement provision.

Global Risk Assessment for Pensions and Annuities

Understanding how national, regional, and local regulations are changing post-financial crisis requires an assessment of the supervisory and regulatory environment for retirement systems and insurers. In his chapter, Peter Fisher (2016) takes on this task along with an examination of the effects of supervisory changes on market structure, conduct, and performance. In most cases, the supervisory structures overseeing insurance and pensions are complex and relatively untested. For instance, in the US and Canada, supervisors are mainly state-based, augmented by the National Association of Insurance Commissioners (NAIC). Federal actors have also recently entered the field, including the US Federal Reserve, which now supervises insurance companies representing about one-third of US insurance industry assets, the International Association of Insurance Supervisors (IAIS), and the Financial Stability Board (FSB). These regulators influence private-sector activity mainly by establishing requirements to achieve policy objectives including financial stability and enhanced consumer welfare.

Nevertheless, these policies often involve tradeoffs and have unintended effects on other markets and segments of the economy as well. For example, to ensure financial stability, some countries require global insurers to maintain elevated levels of capital, often at the subsidiary level within the country administering the measures. This reduces capital mobility across national borders. The lack of coordination across geographic markets may lead to capital inefficiencies, and higher operating costs can lead to higher product prices and potentially reduced competition as firms withdraw from certain markets. Moreover, while regulators could curtail market risks for investors, this could exacerbate the impact of other factors including longevity risk.

Life insurance companies are also coming under more scrutiny in the wake of the financial crisis, in part because they have traditionally used accounting techniques that smooth changes in values of firm assets and liabilities. By doing so, they transfer surpluses in good years to cover benefit payouts in bad years. On the one hand, some criticize these techniques for making it difficult to assess insurers' true financial status as such approaches most frequently use discretion rather than fixed rules, leaving them open to possible manipulation. Smoothing permits losses to be deferred, but when assets must be sold to pay the benefits—and losses must be realized—large reductions in benefit payments may be triggered and firm solvency may be challenged. On the other hand, opponents of fair market value (FMV) reporting contend that mark-to-market (MTM) reporting is misleading for assets held to maturity, may not be reliable if based on model prices, and could lead to undesirable firm actions. But smoothing also defers gains, and when the gains are realized, benefits can increase due to the larger value of the contingency reserve.

In their chapter on this topic, Raimond Maurer, Olivia S. Mitchell, Ralph Rogalla, and Ivonne Siegelin (2016) show that smoothing can actually add value to both annuitants and insurers. This means that curtailing smoothing might undermine the market for long-term retirement payout products.

The particular product the authors examine is the participating payout life annuity (PLA). To illustrate how payout smoothing works, the authors construct a stylized model of a life insurer selling single premium participating life annuity contracts. These are patterned after the TIAA Traditional Annuity offered by the Teachers Insurance and Annuity Association-College Retirement Equities Fund (TIAA-CREF). This product provides retirees with lifetime guaranteed benefits plus non-guaranteed surplus payments. The authors conclude that accounting smoothing in the PLA context values assets at historical cost rather than at fair market value, and the practice helps to shield insurer balance sheets and income statements against capital market volatility. Surpluses shared with policyholders are conventionally computed using realized gains and losses.

Turning to mark-to-market accounting for corporate defined benefit pensions, the chapter by Joseph Busillo, Thomas Harvey, and Bryan Hoffman (2016) notes that most plan sponsors utilize Generally Accepted Accounting Principles (GAAP) for their pension plan valuation. These shield the plan from market fluctuations, which can be sensible in stable markets. Yet in a crisis such as the 2008–10 event, many plans lost money and ended up with a large pool of unamortized losses that had to be recognized over time. The mark-to-mark approach by contrast exposes the balance sheet and income statement to real-world volatility. In practice, many equity analysts and rating agencies 'unwind' the pension funds' status in comparative calculations. In fact, a study examining share price movements over a five-day period surrounding the announcement of an accounting change to MTM indicated that companies experienced no statistically significant changes in share prices as a result. Moreover, companies adopting pension MTM have not tended to alter their pension asset mix in response, for the most part remaining with a traditional mix of 60/40 equities/fixed-income strategies. This is similar to that followed by corporate pension plans utilizing traditional GAAP pension accounting methods.

Risk disclosure in the insurance context is the subject of Karel Van Hulle's (2016) chapter, where he discusses the evolution of European policy starting with the Solvency I regulatory regime developed during the 1970s. He argues that there was little incentive for insurers to be risk sensitive in those days, whereas Solvency II rules under development will require harmonized insurer information available at the EU-wide level. Nevertheless, occupational pension funds will still not be required to provide information to the public at large about the risks they bear. Hence, though transparency in the insurance sector will be enhanced, he concludes that there is still no level playing field between highly regulated insurers and pension funds subject to less disclosure. What remains to be done is to better align systemic risk management with better reporting and regulation, and to more carefully assess whether pension funds should, and could, be held to the same standards as are insurers.

One concern voiced by many in the pension field today is that regulators may be throwing the proverbial baby, pensions and insurers, out with the bathwater, namely the poorly performing banks that brought the financial system to near-ruin. In their chapter, Brian Reid and Dan Waters (2016) describe what systemic risk is, how bank-oriented models and rules have influenced thinking about systemic risk, and how this thinking has affected the subsequent regulatory focus on pensions as well as the funds and products in which they invest. They also question current theories of how asset management products could pose risks to the financial system.

As the authors note, the US Financial Stability Oversight Council (FSOC) has been established to identify threats to financial stability and promote market discipline. In Europe, the European Parliament created the European Systemic Risk Board (ESRB) to coordinate and oversee risks within the European Union. Internationally, the Financial Stability Board (FSB) has taken on the role of identifying sources of global systemic risk. Some studies exploring the connections between banks and nonbank financial institutions drew parallels between bank and nonbank intermediated credit, and thus some in the literature began referring to nonbanks as 'shadow banks' and their activities as 'shadow banking.'

Nevertheless, the authors disagree with this view because they argue that capital market financial intermediation is fundamentally different from bank-based financing. Banks normally finance their investments by issuing short and medium-term debt and deposits, which create a fixed set of claims on banks. At the same time, banks hold portfolios of loans and marketable securities, the values of which rise and fall over time. This can create a mismatch driving the need to hold capital to help protect bank depositors and creditors from losses. Banks' heavy reliance on debt to finance their balance sheets magnifies the effects on their capital when asset prices change. Among the largest US banks, the average balance sheet leverage ratio is 9:1. If asset prices fall and depositors pull money out, banks may have to quickly dispose of their assets, spurring a downward cycle. By comparison, asset managers deliver services through publicly or privately offered funds and do not own the underlying assets nor do they guarantee a set rate of return. Therefore asset managers and the products and services they provide are structurally different from those provided by banks, and they should be regulated differently.

Regulators have expressed concern that some fund structures, namely those that buy back an investor's shares on a daily basis, could confer a 'first mover advantage' on fast-moving investors, potentially posing systemic risk. For instance, if investors redeemed their bond funds during a period of financial market stress, the funds might not be able to sell their assets to meet these orders, or their actions could cause prices in the bond markets to fall sharply. Yet US fund managers are required to mark their funds' portfolios to market on a daily basis, using forward pricing and fair valuation methods to avoid predictable price movements. Using a bid- or mid-price passes some of the trading costs along to the investor leaving the fund because this pricing method values the shares near to what the fund would receive if it needed to sell assets to accommodate the redemption. Another way that funds manage costs is by imposing redemption fees on investors who leave a fund within a certain window of time after investing in the fund. In addition, most funds also reserve the right to redeem shares in kind if investors with particularly large trades want to quickly redeem their shares, so that rather than receiving cash the investor is paid with a slice of securities. Pooled products such as mutual funds or collective investment funds often have the option to redeem in-kind if the retirement plan sponsor has not given sufficient warning that it is removing the plan from the fund. Yet global regulators seem to be close to designating asset managers and their funds, possibly including large pension funds, as global systemically important financial institutions (SIFIs). If the FSOC were to designate some set of US funds or asset managers as SIFIs, this could cause a small group of funds and their investors, including pension plan participants, to bear significant costs.

Developments in Retirement Saving and Retirement Products

The second portion of this volume turns to an examination of where and how people save for old age, whether they are saving enough, and whether new risk management approaches as well as investment vehicles might enhance retirement saving efforts. The breadth and scope of these topics illustrate the challenges that face regulators and policymakers in the pension arena. To be successful, retirement income programs must be inclusive and involve as many members of society as possible. Yet at the same time, investments need to be appropriate to the timescale of savings, and may include more than the traditional liquid investments such as bonds and equities. Finally, it is important to set appropriate goals in an environment where even widely accepted notions, such as the replacement ratio, have a degree of ambiguity. This section grapples with each of these difficult issues.

The chapter by Asli Demirgüç-Kunt, Leora Klapper, and Georgios A. Panos (2016) discusses global patterns of saving for old age and inclusion using an invaluable new dataset, the World Bank's Global Findex. This includes information from many thousands of individuals interviewed around the world, providing a new set of insights into the individual and country-level factors associated with old-age asset accumulation. One of the useful aspects of this survey is that it asked about 'unbanked' persons, or those who save outside the formal banking system. The chapter shows that people report saving mainly for old age, education, or to a start a business, and globally, about 25 percent say they are saving for old age. This rate rises to about 40 percent in high-income OECD countries and the Asia Pacific region, though it is lower in poorer economies. There is also some difference in saving propensities by gender, in that men tend to save more, as do the better educated. Financial inclusion is also strongly and usually positively correlated with old-age saving. Finally, the authors find little evidence for public/private 'crowd-out,' in that the probability of people saying they save for old age privately is not significantly associated with the existence or generosity of pensions.

The next chapter, by Andrew Biggs (2016), examines new ways to think about old-age retirement system payouts. Financial advisors and policymakers often use the term 'replacement rate' to judge the adequacy of peoples' retirement savings, where the term refers to a comparison of anticipated retirement income benefits to pre-retirement earnings. As a summary statistic though, the replacement rate notion has a myriad of calculation and interpretational attributes implying it can have profound implications for policy as well as individual outcomes and decisions. This chapter takes up three key questions: (1) should policymakers use replacement rates based on *stylized* workers, or should they use administrative or microsimulation data; (2) should the denominator of the replacement rate calculation—pre-retirement earnings—be adjusted for the growth of prices or the growth of economy-wide wages; and (3) should replacement rates incorporate family-size adjustments to account for how having children affects parents' need to save for retirement?

The impact of these methodological choices is illustrated using a microsimulation model of Social Security benefits and employer-sponsored pensions. The author concludes that much of the disagreement over whether Americans face a 'retirement crisis' stems not from disagreements over how much retirement income American retirees *will have*, but from how much income they will *need*. Biggs argues that a replacement rate of 100 percent is unnecessary, since retirees pay lower taxes and have fewer work-related costs. Moreover, many have paid off their mortgages and completed their retirement saving. The author points out that taking these factors into account greatly reduces measured estimates of those likely to experience shortfalls in retirement.

Managing retirement risk is also taken up by Catherine Donnelly, Montserrat Guillén, and Jens Perch Nielsen (2016) in their chapter analyzing strategies for an investor with a retirement saving plan. Previous research has found that fees paid for managing investment funds and for mitigating longevity risk substantially erode pensioners' wealth. Moreover it can be difficult to communicate the concept of uncertainty to consumers. Their chapter, by contrast, offers a retirement investment approach with both an upper target which their wealth should not exceed, and a lower bound below which their wealth must not fall. Establishing upper and lower bounds on retirement wealth can help the returns of pension savers in the sense that managerial fees can be reduced while controlling risk.

In the final chapter by Javier Alonso, Alfonso Arellano, and David Tuesta (2016), the authors explore what shapes pension funds' decisions to invest in infrastructure. Though financial regulators in many countries do allow pension funds to invest in infrastructure, relatively few do so. This is of interest given that pension funds need to consider all possible investment options so as to improve outcomes for members and that infrastructure investment tends to be long-term in nature and hence can be aligned with pension fund objectives. Yet at the same time, infrastructure investment requires a substantial degree of governance and expertise that few pension funds have. While countries differ with regard to financial investment regulations, the degree to which their capital markets allow such investments, and the pension funds' technical capability to access direct or indirect infrastructure financing, the authors conclude that regulatory restrictions on pension funds to invest in infrastructure are less important than the institutional framework in which they operate.

Nevertheless, infrastructure investing is complex, requiring the alignment of many different stakeholder interests including shareholders, financial institutions, regulators, insurance companies, contractors, project operators, raw materials suppliers, and of course the end-users of the output. Moreover, numerous risks characteristic of such huge projects include construction delays/cost overruns/technical failures, operational risks, financial market surprises, market fluctuations, and political challenges (e.g., expropriation, political turmoil, regulation). As infrastructure investment is not marked to market frequently and often involves large projects of political importance, it is also a source of significant governance concerns. In view of these, pension funds must develop deep expertise in these fields and make sure that their governance arrangements are sufficient for the complexity involved. Some countries such as Australia and Canada permit pension funds to invest with enormous flexibility, and there the pensions have apparently successfully invested intensively in infrastructure.

Conclusion

The global financial crisis had immediate and detrimental impacts on pension and insurance company assets intended to finance millions of peoples' retirement. Since that time, regulators and policymakers have turned to increasingly focused efforts to alter how pensions and insurers manage and report the risks they take on. In many cases, US and European regulators have been influenced by their views of how the banking system needed to be strengthened. Nevertheless, pension funds, asset managers, and insurers differ in fundamental ways from banks, and this volume illustrates several ways in which retirement risk management should be conceived of differently from bank practice. Finally, the volume discusses a wide range of issues that regulators should consider, making clear that pension regulation requires that those involved have both breadth and depth, so as to complement what will inevitably be complex legislation and regulations to protect member interests.

In sum, our assessment of regulatory responses to the financial crisis shows that the playing field is changing for insurers and pension plan sponsors. We also discuss developments in retirement saving and retirement products, to determine which and how these might help meet shortfalls in retirement provision.

References

Alonso, J., A. Arellano, and D. Tuesta (2016). 'Pension Fund Investment in Infrastructure and Global Financial Regulation,' in O. S. Mitchell, R. Maurer, and J. M. Orszag, eds, *Retirement System Risk Management: Implications of the New Regulatory Order*. Oxford: Oxford University Press, pp. 186–213.

Biggs, A. G. (2016). 'Retirement Replacement Rates: What and How,' in O. S. Mitchell, R. Maurer, and J. M. Orszag, eds, *Retirement System Risk Management: Implications of the New Regulatory Order*. Oxford: Oxford University Press, pp. 154–70.

Busillo, J., T. Harvey, and B. Hoffman (2016). 'Mark-to-Market Accounting for United States Corporate Pensions: Implementation and Impact,' in O. S. Mitchell, R. Maurer, and J. M. Orszag, eds, *Retirement System Risk Management: Implications of the New Regulatory Order*. Oxford: Oxford University Press, pp. 51–67.

Demirgüç-Kunt, A., L. Klapper, and G. A. Panos (2016). 'Determinants of Saving for Old Age around the World,' in O. S. Mitchell, R. Maurer, and J. M. Orszag, eds, *Retirement System Risk Management: Implications of the New Regulatory Order*. Oxford: Oxford University Press, pp. 121–53.

Donnelly, C., M. Guillén, and J. P. Nielsen (2016). 'Fundamentals of Cost and Risk that Matter to Pension Savers and Life Annuitants,' in O. S. Mitchell, R. Maurer, and J. M. Orszag, eds, *Retirement System Risk Management: Implications of the New Regulatory Order*. Oxford: Oxford University Press, pp. 171–85.

Fisher, P. A. (2016). 'The New Insurance Supervisory Landscape: Implications for Insurance and Pensions,' in O. S. Mitchell, R. Maurer, and J. M. Orszag, eds, *Retirement System Risk Management: Implications of the New Regulatory Order*. Oxford: Oxford University Press, pp. 13–39.

Maurer, R., O. S. Mitchell, R. Rogalla, and I. Siegelin (2016). 'Accounting-Based Asset Return Smoothing in Participating Life Annuities: Implications for Annuitants,

Insurers, and Policymakers,' in O. S. Mitchell, R. Maurer, and J. M. Orszag, eds, *Retirement System Risk Management: Implications of the New Regulatory Order*. Oxford: Oxford University Press, pp. 40–50.

Reid, B., and D. Waters (2016). 'Pensions, Risk, and Global Systemically Important Financial Institutions,' in O. S. Mitchell, R. Maurer, and J. M. Orszag, eds, *Retirement System Risk Management: Implications of the New Regulatory Order*. Oxford: Oxford University Press, pp. 95–118.

Van Hulle, K. (2016). 'Risk Disclosure in the European Insurance Industry: Implications for Occupational Pension Funds,' in O. S. Mitchell, R. Maurer, and J. M. Orszag, eds, *Retirement System Risk Management: Implications of the New Regulatory Order*. Oxford: Oxford University Press, pp. 68–94.

Part I

Global Risk Assessment for Pensions and Annuities

2

The New Insurance Supervisory Landscape: Implications for Insurance and Pensions

Peter A. Fisher

The supervisory landscape for insurance is becoming considerably more complex and influential in the wake of the global financial crisis. New authorities have been created, new powers granted, and the scope of oversight broadened. The intent of the new apparatus is to ensure greater financial stability, improved market conduct, and greater standardization across legal jurisdictions—and many of these benefits have been realized. At the same time, the connections and rules of engagement between supervisory authorities are frequently unclear, supervisory mandates sometimes overlap, and the intended policy objectives can be pursued despite significant unintended consequences and negative effects on other dimensions of social welfare.

This chapter first outlines the new supervisory landscape in North America, Europe, and globally, with a particular focus on insurance oversight and implications for pension policy. It then explores a series of specific supervisory issues that have received special attention since the financial crisis and identifies recent supervisory developments. The effects of supervisory activities on market structure, conduct, and performance are then examined, with follow-on identification of potential effects on several dimensions of social welfare. A series of specific examples is used to illustrate connections between immediate policy objectives and sometimes ambiguous effects on net social welfare. Finally, a forward-looking view is provided, identifying future challenges and issues on the horizon.

Current Supervisory Landscape

The supervisory structures overseeing insurance and pensions exist at multiple geographic levels: provincial, national, regional, and global (see Figure 2.1). This supervisory apparatus is responsible for implementing and overseeing regulations to ensure adequate solvency, good market conduct, financial stability, and effective governance and risk management.

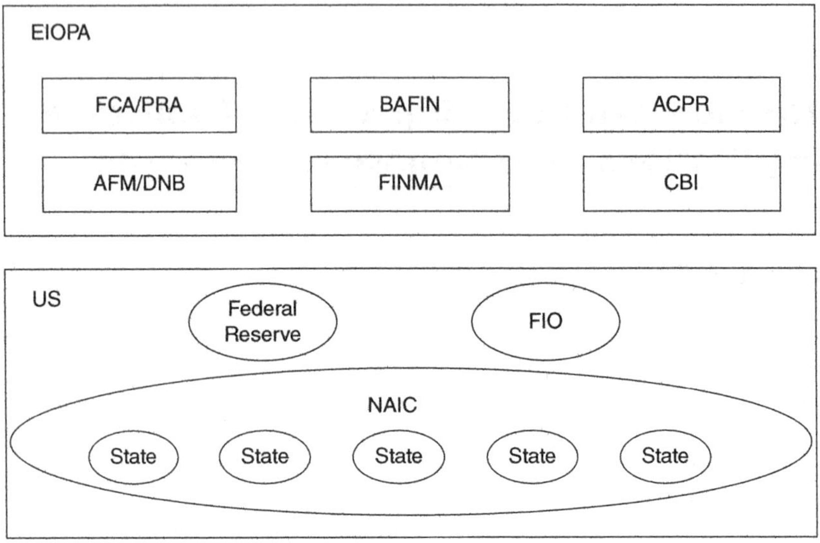

Figure 2.1 Insurance regulatory/supervisory structures

Notes: For additional detail and explanation, please see the 'Glossary of Terms.'

Source: Author's contribution.

International overview

North America

The US supervisory structure is foundationally state-based. Each state has a dedicated insurance commissioner overseeing insurance market activity within its own borders, and each commission has primary oversight over insurers domiciled within its state. State-level commissioners have a dual supervisory mandate to ensure the solvency of insurers and the protection of policyholders. Unlike many other country-level systems, the state-based US system does not directly address group-level issues but focuses instead primarily on state-level and subsidiary-level oversight and policy. Augmenting the state-level system is the National Association of Insurance Commissioners (NAIC), which acts to coordinate and, to some extent, standardize, the state-level activities of individual commissioners. The NAIC is the US standard-setting and regulatory support organization created and governed by the chief insurance regulators from the 50 states, the District of Columbia, and five US territories. Through the NAIC, state insurance regulators establish standards and best practices, conduct peer reviews, coordinate their regulatory oversight, and represent the collective views of state regulators domestically and internationally. The NAIC's mission includes protecting the public interest, ensuring competitive markets, protecting insurance consumers, and promoting the financial stability and solvency of insurance institutions. The NAIC is a voluntary coordinating organization, without explicit legal authority over individual state supervisors. While its members are the insurance commissioners of each state and territory, the NAIC is a non-governmental organization that concerns itself with insurance regulatory matters but does not actually regulate. In particular, the states have not delegated their regulatory authority to the NAIC. It also acts as one of the primary points of engagement for other elements of the US and global supervisory structure, including the US Federal Reserve, the International Association of Insurance Supervisors (IAIS), and the Financial Stability Board (FSB).

At the federal level, there are three primary entities: the Federal Reserve, the Federal Insurance Office (FIO), and the Financial Stability Oversight Council (FSOC). At the national level, the Federal Reserve oversees any insurer that contains a bank holding company (BHC), has been designated as systemically important by the Financial Stability Oversight Council, or is a US domiciled insurer that is considered an Internationally Active Insurance Group (IAIG).[1] The newly created Federal Insurance Office, a part of the US Treasury, does not currently have legal jurisdiction over any element of the US insurance market, but it is an influential analyst and evaluator of the current composite framework. The FIO is currently the US representative at the IAIS, but it has no parallel domestic supervisory authority. The FIO, in its recently published modernization report, provided detailed recommendations for supervisory activities that should ideally be administered at one or more of several levels, including the individual states, the federal level, and the international level (FIO 2013). Finally, the FSOC has the authority to designate insurers as systemically important financial institutions (SIFI), depending on their size, complexity, and range of activities. If designated a SIFI, a new host of regulations then becomes active and primary supervisory oversight transfers to the Federal Reserve.[2]

The Canadian supervisory oversight resides primarily within the Office of Superintendent of Financial Institutions (OSFI), an independent agency that reports to the Minister of Finance. In addition to regulating banks, it is the primary regulator of insurance companies, trust companies, loan companies, and pension plans in Canada. In this capacity, it oversees matters of solvency, conduct, and financial stability at the national level and as a point of engagement with international initiatives.

Europe

The European supervisory structure has two principal dimensions: one at the country level and the other at the European regional level. Within each country there typically exists one of two structures: (1) a single integrated supervisor covering conduct, prudential, and systemic oversight; or (2) a 'twin peaks' structure that bifurcates conduct and prudential regulation into two entities, as a structural response to supervisory lessons learned from the financial crisis. An example of the twin peaks structure is the Prudential Regulatory Authority (PRA) and the Financial Conduct Authority (FCA) in the United Kingdom. Other country-level entities include Federal Financial Supervisory Authority (BAFIN) in Germany, the Autorité de Contrôl Prudentiel (ACPR) in France, the Autoriteit Financiele Markten (AFM) in the Netherlands, and the Swiss Financial Market Supervisory Authority (FINMA).

The primary regional authority for Europe is the European Insurance and Occupational Pension Authority (EIOPA), a European Union financial regulatory institution composed of representatives from the insurance and occupational pensions supervisory authorities of the European Union. It was created following the financial crisis to help ensure a more level playing field across the EU and to reflect increasingly integrated financial markets. EIOPA carries out a number of significant functions including strengthening supervisory colleges and enhancing the prudential regime within the European Union through the drafting and oversight of the Solvency II Directive. It is at this level that pan-European regulations and supervisory oversight are defined, implemented, and enforced.[3]

Global

At the global level, the primary organizations with significant influence over supervisory functions are the Financial Stability Board (FSB) and the International Association of Insurance Supervisors (IAIS). The FSB was created in the wake of the financial crisis to monitor and oversee financial institutions and activities to ensure global financial stability; it consists at its core of central banks and treasuries of the G20 countries. This core is augmented by a variety of additional executive, regulatory, and supervisory institutions. The IAIS, established in 1994, represents insurance regulators and supervisors of more than 200 jurisdictions in 140 countries, constituting 97 percent of global insurance premiums. It has three pillars of activity, consisting of standard setting, implementation, and financial stability for the global insurance sector.

Most recently, the IAIS and FSB have collaborated closely to develop new standards around group-level global capital standards and requirements; group supervision; corporate and risk governance; designation criteria and supervisory models for global systemically important insurers (GSIIs); recovery and resolution planning; and macro-prudential standards.

Supervisory issues

Policy objectives of the many supervisory structures span a broad range, including financial stability, market conduct, solvency, organizational governance, and supervisory coordination.

Financial stability and systemic risk

Ensuring global financial stability is a top priority within supervisory mandates in the wake of the financial crisis, and it is being addressed at the global and national levels through consideration of organizational size, complexity, interconnectedness, and type of activities.[4] Much of the supervisory mechanics for overseeing systemic risk are in very early stages of development. These include designation criteria and evaluation process; oversight of capital, leverage, and liquidity requirements; development of more intensive supervision standards; and creation of resolution and recovery plans. Designation and supervision of systemic organizations are progressing simultaneously at the global and national levels, with considerable uncertainty regarding how the range of national and global supervisors will standardize and coordinate their many designation decisions, oversight activities, and overlapping mandates.

Conduct/consumer protection

A second top priority emerging from the financial crisis is to develop a more intensive supervisory focus on the market conduct of financial institutions so as to ensure adequate consumer protection. In several countries, this renewed focus has led to the creation of a new conduct-focused supervisory body separate from prudential and stability oversight, in order to avoid potential loss of focus and mixed objectives of an integrated organization. Examples include the FCA in the UK and the Consumer Financial Protection Bureau (CFPB) in the US. The conduct mandate has frequently been defined very broadly to extend across both retail and institutional markets, and it has in some cases been defined to include all manner of conduct and elements of culture within the internal workings of financial institutions.

Solvency/funding

One of the most fundamental policy objectives for supervising both insurance and pensions is assuring adequate levels of solvency and funding of supervised organizations in meeting their expected future liabilities.[5] Significant recent activity in this area includes the finalization, early implementation, and drive toward equivalence of Solvency II in Europe under the direction of EIOPA, and the NAIC's related Solvency Modernization Initiative in the US. Each has developed new approaches to accounting standards, treatment of assets and liabilities in solvency measurements, and standards for information sharing and organizational governance.

Governance

One of the many contributors to the financial crisis—as identified by supervisors—was incomplete oversight and capabilities of boards and directors. Supervisors have therefore renewed their focus on the capabilities of individual board members; the collective capabilities of the full board; committee structures, responsibilities, and composition; the specific governance of risk through the creation of new risk committees and Chief Risk Officer (CRO) roles; adequate independence of board members from the Executive; and more intensive oversight by the board regarding supervisory matters related to risk, capital, conduct, and solvency.

Coordination

With the multitude of new supervisory authorities at the national, regional, and global levels, there is a renewed focus on coordinating the many overlapping mandates. This has met with some success through the activities of supervisory colleges under the auspices of the NAIC, IAIS, EIOPA, and other institutions. However, much important work remains to be done. Supervisory colleges have improved communication and awareness among the many supervisory authorities to enhance coordination and standardization, but the degree of substantive coordination, mandate clarification, and agreement on key areas of policy is still very limited.

Recent Developments

The supervisory structure for insurance has become much more complex since the financial crisis, as authorities work to ensure greater financial stability and enhanced consumer welfare. Commentators have pointed to a variety of potential supervisory failings during this period including unclear supervisory mandates, regulatory arbitrage, non-standardized supervisory definitions and approaches across jurisdictions, a 'light-touch' stance on oversight of financial institutions, and less-than-vigorous supervision of interactions between buyers and sellers of financial products. Many of the recent supervisory developments are meant to address these perceived shortcomings.

United States

The supervisory landscape within the US has been evolving rapidly since the financial crisis. The traditional state-based supervisory system has been augmented by new federal entities with either direct supervisory authority or with important influencing roles. These include the Federal Reserve, the FSOC, and the FIO. In particular, the FSOC has designated three insurers as systemically important (AIG, Prudential Financial, MetLife), thereby transferring primary supervisory authority for these institutions to the Federal Reserve and establishing enhanced capital, liquidity, resolution, and governance requirements. The potential for being designated systemically important has also influenced the business behavior of remaining large insurers with respect to size, engagement in 'non-traditional, non-insurance activities' (NTNIA), and interconnectedness. As one example, the provision that authorizes Federal Reserve oversight over any insurer with a bank holding company within its structure motivated MetLife recently to shed this element of its operations. In addition, many insurers have largely exited the market for credit default swaps, considered NTNIA.

The advent of new federal supervisory authorities and new regulations has injected a degree of tension between state and federal authorities and somewhat blurred the scope of authority at these two levels. As an example, the FIO released its long-awaited reports on modernization and improvement opportunities within the state-based system in December 2013 (FIO 2013) and on the general state of the insurance industry and its oversight in September 2014 (FIO 2014). In its modernization report, the FIO recognized certain 'limitations inherent in a state-based system of insurance regulation' and concluded that 'the proper formulation of the debate at present is not whether insurance regulation should be state or federal but whether there are certain areas in which federal involvement in regulation under the state-based system is warranted' (2013: 11). Specifically, 'In all events, federal involvement should be targeted to areas in which that involvement would solve problems resulting from the legal and practical limitations of regulation by the states, such as the need for uniformity or the need for a federal voice in US interactions with international authorities' (2013: 12).

The report goes on to identify 18 areas which the FIO recommends for near-term reform by the states, relating to capital adequacy and safety/ soundness, insurer resolution practices, and marketplace regulation. The modernization report also identifies nine areas where it recommends direct federal involvement in insurance regulation. The NAIC has vigorously opposed greater federal involvement in insurance supervision, citing the effectiveness of the state-based system in meeting local needs and providing local oversight, and the beneficial coordinating function of the NAIC.

The NAIC has responded to greater federal supervisory participation by enhancing its governance structures, solvency standards, and engagement with federal, regional, and global supervisory authorities.

The supervisory trend within the US appears to be toward greater federalization of oversight, with the expanded authority and footprint of the Federal Reserve, influence of the FIO, and engagement of global supervisory authorities by national (vs. state-level) US entities. Growing federal oversight has at least two parallels within existing insurance markets. First, the movement toward federal oversight (relative to state-based supervision) is analogous to the group-level management and capital structures used by diversified insurers in the US to aggregate and allocate resources at the group level as they are needed locally. Second, movement toward federalization within the US in some ways parallels the evolution within Europe from country-level supervisors to more standardized approaches at the pan-European level through EIOPA and Solvency II standards. The recent FSB peer review of US insurance supervision added even greater energy to the supervisory landscape, with its findings of greater need within the US market for (1) regulatory uniformity; (2) enhanced insurance group supervision; (3) modernization of solvency requirements; and (4) governance and funding reforms (FSB 2013).

Within the next few years, several concrete issues could arise that directly challenge the evolving structures, with the possibility for one supervisory entity to establish a clear mandate on a specific issue, or to strike a compromise that keeps amorphous rules of engagement intact. Examples include the willingness of US federal and state authorities to implement and enforce standards of capital, liquidity, and governance established by the global IAIS/FSB entities. Specifically, how do IAIS directives get enforced within the US (the world's largest insurance market), and to the extent they are not enforceable, can a global standard be achieved without substantive participation by the US? Also important are disagreements between the FSOC and the IAIS/FSB on systemic designation of US domiciled insurers. Specifically, if the systemic label applied to MetLife recently via the FSOC were to be overturned, MetLife would remain systemically important by the FSB designation. So how then would US authorities carry out the requirements of a global authority in situations where the domestic process produced a different conclusion regarding systemic importance? Additionally, there are concerns about the divergent developmental pace between the Federal Reserve's creation of capital standards for firms it supervises, and that of the IAIS/FSB's crafting of the Insurance Capital Standard (ICS) for internationally active insurers, which include several firms the Fed also supervises. Another topic of discussion is the layering of local capital 'add-ons' above the level of the ICS standard established by the IAIS, resulting in a patchwork of local capital standards, undermining the benefit of a single global standard and creating an uneven competitive field. These may all be manageable supervisory confrontations, but each would immediately test the ability of overlapping supervisors to agree, establish a clear mandate, or compromise on important elements of financial sector performance.

How this supervisory mosaic will settle in steady-state is very unclear at the moment. What is clear is the greater energy around federalization, centralization, and standardization across multiple supervisory jurisdictions across both North America and Europe. One possibility is that individual states may be left with oversight of conduct, policyholder protection, product approvals, rate-setting on required insurance, and solvency considerations to protect local policyholders; with the remaining supervisory responsibilities aggregated at the national level through the Federal Reserve, an evolving FIO, and other federal entities.

At a higher level of generalization, the complexity and possibility of unintended consequences arise from simultaneously developing important new policies and regulations (e.g., Solvency II, group capital standards, global capital standards, SIFI designations) while also implementing these policies through a supervisory structure that is itself being restructured (e.g., greater federalization within the US). Accordingly, ambiguity arises both around the substance of the new policies as well as where authorities lie to interpret and implement them.

Europe

Considerable regulatory and supervisory change is under way within Europe. The recent agreement to final standards of Solvency II regulation, with implementation beginning in early 2016, has taken center stage for much of the past few years. There are many points of intersection and potential conflicts between established Solvency II statutes and other policy areas, including the development of global capital standards for systemically important and internationally active insurers (i.e., BCR, HLA, ICS), accounting standards, valuation methodologies, asset risk-weighting measures, and liability estimation. Any degree of incompatibility between established Solvency II standards and emerging global standards will likely create confusion, additional compliance and reporting burdens, and possibly excessive levels of required capital. Alternatively, it is also possible that the implementation of global capital standards could be an opportunity, if designed in compatible ways, to effectively standardize around Solvency II norms, thereby advancing multiple policy objectives. Finally, there is some concern, particularly within European countries, that the emerging global capital standards may effectively act as a capital floor, with local supervisory authorities instituting 'add-on' requirements that raise the local de facto standard (e.g., Early Warning Indicators in the UK). This would result in a non-level competitive field, but it may also increase the likelihood and extent of base-level standards adoption.

A second area of significant supervisory change is conduct regulation and policy. In select European markets such as the UK and the Netherlands, conduct supervisors were instituted following the financial crisis, and they have taken self-described aggressive stances in redefining the distribution of rights and responsibilities between buyers and sellers of financial products. Although the most intense focus has been on retail markets, the purview of many conduct authorities extends both into institutional markets and into internal organizational behaviors of financial institutions. In the UK, conduct authority actions have included (1) examining long-dated 'back books' within the insurance sector, (2) instituting a requirement for 'fit and proper' that enables authorities to reject company selections for top board and executive management posts, (3) creating a requirement that new directors and executives take a personal oath to uphold the interests of consumers above other business objectives, and (4) participating in the recent policy change of removing required annuitization for designated portions of accumulated pension pots. Compared to supervision of systemic stability and prudential concerns, there has been very little international coordination of conduct supervision and regulation. In particular, conduct seems to persist as largely a local authority protecting the interests of residents within the domicile of the supervisor. There are, however, early movements toward a degree of international standardization and coordination on issues of conduct, initially promulgated through ComFrame and the IAIS subcommittee on market conduct, which is drafting issues papers and constructing frameworks on policyholder protection policies and devising model approaches to conduct supervision (IAIS 2015). The US Federal Reserve is also beginning to examine areas of conduct policy for those firms under its mandate.

Global

The most important global development is the direct, coordinated engagement of the FSB and IAIS in overseeing issues of global financial stability and the effective oversight of global insurance firms at the group level.

Financial stability

The FSB, established after the financial crisis, has the direct decision-making authority over designations of GSII firms, and the development of required capital, liquidity, and resolution regulations for those firms. However, it has delegated much of the data gathering, methodology development, and analysis of these issues to the IAIS, which then makes recommendations to the FSB for final decision and implementation.[6] Early development of methodology, designations, and oversight has begun via the FSB/IAIS process, such as GSII designation and the Basic Capital Requirement (BCR). However, other elements of this process are in very early stages of design, including the development of Higher Loss Absorbency (HLA) requirements for GSII firms, the creation of an Insurance Capital Standard (ICS) that will apply more broadly to all internationally active insurance groups (IAIG), and methods for recovery and resolution of systemic firms. As such, GSII firms exist in a state of suspended animation, knowing that their supervisory and competitive landscape will be changed significantly, but not knowing how or when these changes will occur. This creates degrees of uncertainty for boards, management teams, policyholders, prospective customers, and investors that can immediately influence significant near-term decisions.

Mandates and enforcement

A fundamental unknown at the global level of supervision is the extent and mechanism for enforcement of standards after they are defined and implemented. The FSB and IAIS do not have legal authority over insurers within any national jurisdiction. It will be incumbent on the national member of the FSB (e.g., central bank, supervisory authority) to implement and enforce the FSB/IAIS standards. Under this structure of local jurisdiction, there will be significant scope for local deviation from global standards, which creates a great deal of uncertainty for firms in the sector. Additionally, many of the specific statutes will be defined and implemented over a lengthy process, extending under current plans through 2019. Consequently, global firms are encountering lengthy periods of supervisory engagement, organizational preparation, future uncertainty, and business model redesign. This uncertainty extends significantly into the designated firms' experiences with policyholders, decisions on product design, long-term strategic direction, organizational structure and legal entity status, and capital market required rates of return.

Within the relatively fragmented US supervisory structure, there has been greater uncertainty and organizational positioning around which elements of the American system can best engage with global supervisory structures. The FIO and, to some extent, the Federal Reserve have each been positioning to become the US voice in international supervisory bodies, with the NAIC acting as the consolidated body within the US to represent state-level views. The NAIC's view, by contrast, is that it should be the primary voice representing the US in international supervisory bodies.

Currently the FIO sits on the Executive Committee of the IAIS and is represented within the IAIS Technical Committee developing the ICS. The Federal Reserve has applied for membership to both the IAIS and its influential Executive Committee. Some have speculated that the Fed may eventually take the place of the FIO within the Executive Committee if it is not granted membership directly.[7] The NAIC is a member of the IAIS and has observer status at the various committee levels (conferring the opportunity to comment in detail on developing standards), but it is not a member of the Executive Committee. More recently, the IAIS has proposed ending the observer role at the IAIS, effectively distancing the NAIC from IAIS activities, which the NAIC has vigorously opposed (Woodall 2014). Finally, the Federal Reserve has attempted to unify the US voice in international venues by 'acting on the international insurance stage in an engaged partnership with our colleagues from the FIO, the state insurance commissioners, and the NAIC. Our multi-party dialogue, while respectful of each of our individual authorities, strives to develop a central 'Team USA' position on the most critical matters of global insurance regulatory policy' (Sullivan 2014: 7).

At both the US and global levels, there is also significant uncertainty regarding the implications of systemic designation. Currently nine firms have GSII designations and three US firms have been designated locally as systemically important. However, the specific requirements for capital, liquidity, risk governance, and supervisory oversight have not yet been fully articulated, so firms find themselves in the uncomfortable situation of being members of a select group under specific criteria, but not knowing what the long-term requirements or implications will be.

Global capital standards

A very active area globally is the development of new global capital standards. The IAIS/FSB recently released the first element in this series, known as the Basic (or Backstop) Capital Requirement (BCR) for systemically important insurers. This is meant to be a standardized capital floor, upon which an HLA capital add-on will be layered for systemically riskier activities. The HLA is currently under development, with focus on both the add-on methodology and the base set of activities on which it will apply. Parallel to that effort is the development of the more broadly applied Insurance Capital Standard, which will apply to all IAIGs, approximately 50 of the largest global insurers.

The ICS will have much more extensive effects, given its broader span of jurisdiction and application to all internationally active firms. It is also meant to be a more sophisticated measure of capital adequacy relative to the BCR, which was developed very rapidly, meant to be quite basic (at the lowest capital level), and therefore considered a somewhat simple but necessarily quick measure. In particular, the BCR did not incorporate the beneficial risk reduction inherent in asset-liability matching practices and diversification across geographies, product lines, and customer segments; it assumed flat-line discount rates beyond a 30-year time horizon; and it instituted an operational risk charge of 12 percent of gross income flowing from asset management operations. The industry concern now is less with the shortcomings of the BCR and more with the possibility that much of the ICS will be modeled from the BCR, retaining some of its more primitive features. The ICS, if retaining these more primitive characteristics, would then have the capability of (1) adding significant new capital charges; (2) shortening industry time horizons to within 30 years of operations; (3) discouraging insurer involvement in the asset management sector; and (4) possibly motivating insurers to change legal organizational structure to fall outside the scope of IAIG designation and thereby not be subject to ICS requirements. However, a significant benefit of a well-designed ICS would be global standardization and comparison of required capital, a presumed reduction in risks of systemic instability and insolvency, and reduced scope to pursue regulatory arbitrage.

Effects on Market Structure, Conduct, and Performance

The ultimate influence of new regulations and supervisory structures on the markets for pensions and insurance depends on their propagation through a network of product manufacturers, distributors, consumers, and supervisory bodies at the local, regional, and global levels. In the first instance, policymakers usually establish requirements on product manufacturers and distributors to achieve a desired policy objective (e.g., financial stability, enhanced consumer welfare). The ultimate effect of the policy, however, depends on the action–reaction cycle between each element in the system until a new equilibrium has been achieved.[8] When the market settles, the initial policy objectives may be achieved (or not), and there may be many side effects that were either anticipated or not, both in their existence and magnitude. Much of the current policy debate within evolving insurance and pension markets centers on the identification and quantification of these general equilibrium results, whether the initial policy objectives will be achieved, and the resulting social welfare outcome.

Policy objectives are advanced through many levers controlled by supervisory and regulatory authorities, including capital definitions and requirements, risk-weighting of assets, regulation of product design, pricing, governance practices, and conduct oversight. Yet policy authorities do not exert direct control over desired outcomes. Financial institutions and others respond to policy actions through the levers they control, including product set decisions, product design, pricing, target customer segments, geographic presence, chosen domicile, legal entity structure, underwriting practices, risk selection, and investment portfolio decisions. It is the complex interplay between policy actions, market responses, and ongoing action–reaction responses that determine whether policy objectives are met and how social welfare is affected. This complex interplay is depicted in Figure 2.2.

New policy measures are likely to enhance financial stability, improve market conduct, standardize capital measurement and requirements, and align required levels of capital with measures of assumed risk. It is also possible for a series of potentially unintended consequences to unfold, including (1) reduced capital fungibility across geographies and businesses; (2) lower product availability, altered product structures, and rising product prices to reduce exposures to newly capital-intensive products; (3) reduced firm size for systemically designated institutions and likely exit from some products, geographies, and customer segments; and (4) reduced availability and rising prices of income-generating insurance products that are very

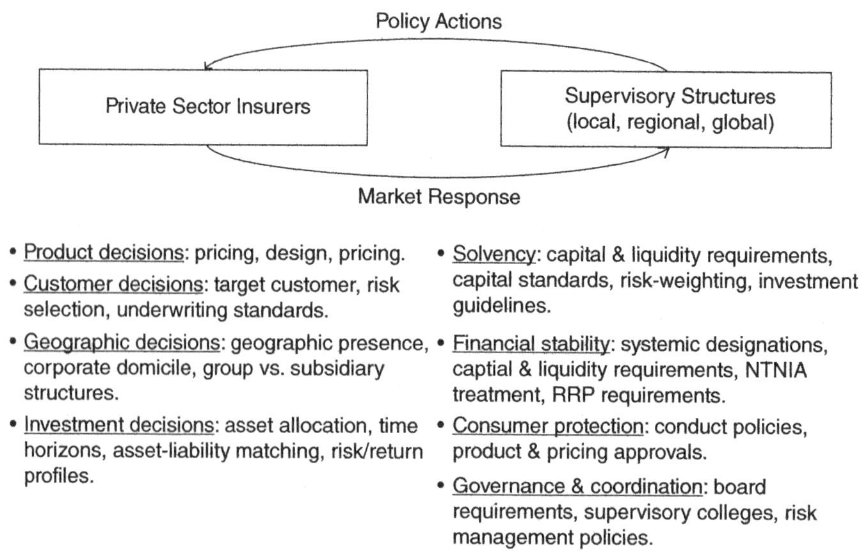

Figure 2.2 Industry–policy feedback loops determine social welfare outcome

Source: Author's contribution.

useful in shifting longevity and market risk from individuals to risk-efficient institutions and investors.

Social Welfare Dimensions and Tradeoffs

Much of the regulatory and supervisory structure within the financial service sectors is attempting to improve one or more dimensions of social welfare, including (1) financial stability; (2) individual firm solvency; (3) macro-economic growth; (4) adequate returns to investor capital; and (5) direct consumer welfare (which can be further decomposed into market coverage, product quality, and price). A simple depiction of social welfare elements and connections is shown in Figure 2.3.

In the abstract, a central policy challenge is identifying the 'best' social welfare outcome and then achieving it. A more realistic approach involves recognizing that there is not a single 'best' outcome, because each member of the system (e.g., conduct authorities, prudential authorities, consumers, financial sectors) values elements differently: what is best for one may be inferior for others. What can be achieved, however, is the set of possible outcomes where no member of the system can be made better off without making other members worse off (Pareto efficiency).[9] All agree that

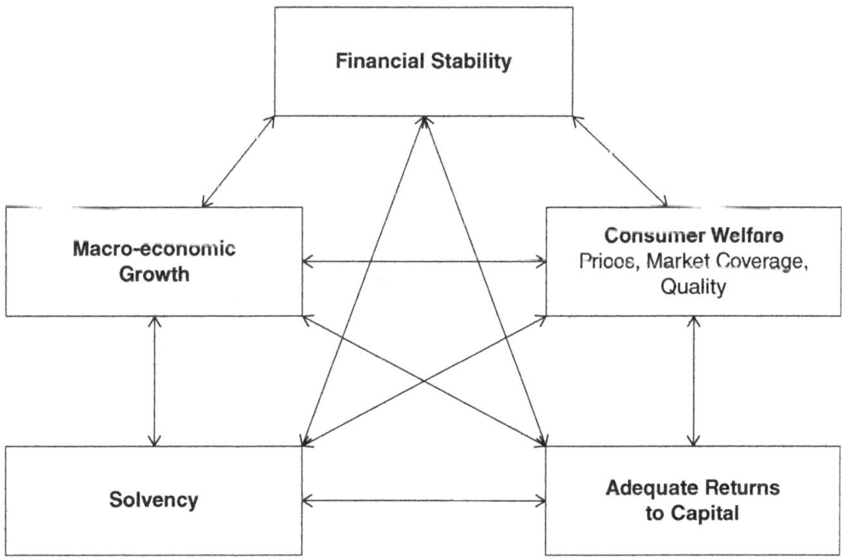

Figure 2.3 Social welfare considerations

Source: Author's contribution.

avoiding the inferior outcomes and achieving a Pareto-efficient outcome where 'no money is left on the table' is in the interests of all.

This is more elusive than it may seem. Frequently, members of a complex system lack awareness of the system's scope, do not appreciate the extent of system reactions in response to actions, and do not realize how beneficial intentions can sometimes propel the system into detrimental outcomes as a result of unanticipated dynamics. Specifically, in the markets for insurance and pensions, there are many challenges within the supervisory structures that complicate attempts to improve social welfare.

Geographic scope

Virtually every supervisory entity has limited geographic scope, either at the provincial, state, or regional levels. Welfare implications that lie outside the scope of geographic oversight rarely receive significant attention.

Supervisory mandates

All supervisory bodies have a limited range of activities or outcomes over which they govern. A very recent example is the separation of prudential and conduct oversight into separate supervisors at the national level in several jurisdictions. While this may sharpen the focus of supervisors on their assigned mandate, it runs the risk of lowering policy awareness and consideration of important interactions between the pursuits of each policy mandate.

Uncertain side effects

It is frequently difficult to identify and quantify the unintended side effects that may result from policy actions. Consequently, it is sometimes expedient for supervisors to acknowledge the possibility of unintended consequences and to consider opportunities to minimize them, but ultimately to assign little weight to collateral effects, relative to achievement of the more proximate policy objectives.

Social welfare tradeoffs

It is difficult for any supervisor to ascertain and implement possible social preferences for tradeoffs between multiple dimensions of social welfare. For instance, if greater financial stability is obtained at the cost of reduced sources of guaranteed retirement income, at what point are these multiple objectives in proper balance with respect to maximizing social welfare? It is easiest for supervisors to press forward with the social welfare dimension for which they are responsible, largely discounting the possible negative effects on other dimensions as an unquantified, collateral effect.

Proximate vs. general equilibrium effects

The proximate effects of a new supervisory or regulatory action can be quite different from the ultimate equilibrium effects after all participants within the industry networks have acted and reacted to the new order and the system has reached a new equilibrium with different characteristics.

Examples of Possible Market-Wide Effects

There are many examples where actions taken to advance proximate policy goals result in significant social welfare consequences in other market dimensions. In no case is it clear that the initial policy is not worthwhile, all things considered, since that type of analysis is not conducted here. Rather, these examples illustrate the general equilibrium connectedness of policy actions and the possibility of material consequences elsewhere in the system.

Financial stability and capital allocation

Enhanced supervisory measures at national and global levels to ensure financial stability have required elevated levels of capital of insurers. In addition, many countries are requiring that the higher capital levels be effectively held at the subsidiary level within the country administering the measures. For global insurers, the result is both higher required capital levels and reduced capital mobility across national borders. These measures certainly enhance financial stability and local solvency, but at a considerable cost in terms of required cost structure and reduced fungibility of capital across geographies and markets. The risk-pooling benefit of deploying capital where it is needed most is largely lost. And higher operating cost structures can result in elevated product prices and potentially reduced competition as firms exit or trim their market presence. Finally, some globally active firms, when faced with reduced benefits from global operations through economies of scale and capital fungibility, may choose to change legal structures, breaking into several locally domiciled entities to avoid being subject to global requirements.

The earliest capital requirements for systemically important insurers were developed quickly to minimize the period where the system was still vulnerable. The Basic Capital Requirement was the first developed, and, to expedite the process, it was allowed to be somewhat primitive in its formulation.[10] While the tradeoff between sophistication and speed may have been worthwhile for the first element of the new capital structure, now the concern is that some primitive characteristics may be carried forward into longer-term, more broadly applied measures of required capital such as the Insurance Capital Standard, which will be applied to all internationally active insurance groups. If this transpires, there could be severe detrimental effects resulting in non-level competitive fields between international and domestic insurers. This may motivate some insurers to disintegrate, changing legal organizational structure in order to bypass capital markets levied on IAIGs. The social welfare risk is that market structures will be dramatically altered, risk diversification benefits will be lost, and systemic risk will not be significantly reduced.

Conduct policies and market coverage

Conduct authorities in some countries have become very assertive in articulating the obligations of product sellers and the rights of product buyers in financial markets. Some commentators have concluded that the lines governing the relative distribution of responsibilities between buyers and sellers have moved significantly away from the traditional principle of *caveat emptor*. As a result, some product providers have decided to exit product markets, withdraw from serving less profitable customers, or alter product features and pricing to avoid market conduct risks. The recent UK experience in advice markets highlights the direct connection between safeguarding the interests of consumers and ensuring that sufficient market coverage remains with high-quality products and services that benefit most consumers.

Prudential vs. conduct policies

In a few instances the supervisory responsibility for prudential oversight has been separated organizationally from the conduct and consumer protection mandate. Although structures do exist to ensure connections between the two policy objectives (e.g., cross-membership on supervisory boards), each supervisory organization will be primarily concerned with the policy area it oversees. Consequently, prudential goals tend to be advanced with less regard for conduct implications and vice versa. Examples include the implications for firm solvency from sizeable conduct fines, and the elevated cost structures, higher product prices, and market exits created by very conservative prudential policies.

Product risks and provision

Under the current methodology adopted by the IAIS/FSB for annuity products with guarantee features, firms offering these products are likely to be designated as systemically important and have more stringent supervisory capital requirements. Both policies result in higher cost structures for firms participating in the guaranteed annuity market, causing collateral effects, including market exit, product redesign, repricing to account for higher costs, withdrawal from lower profit customer segments, and higher industry concentration. As the developed world's population ages and defined benefit structures taper, the consumer need for alternative sources of guaranteed income is rising. The enhanced financial stability accomplished through higher capital requirements for these products may very well be fully warranted given some inherent risks, but it also generates a reduction in other dimensions of social welfare through adverse effects on product markets and reduced retirement security.

Resolution methodology and capital efficiency

The regulations and supervision for orderly recovery and resolution of systemically important insurers is still a work in progress. Two of the most complex aspects of developing a credible resolution plan are identifying and enforcing the rights of the group supervisor (usually located where the firm is domiciled) to act as a 'single point of entry' in the resolution process. This lead supervisor status confers the exclusive right to oversee the distressed organization and make decisions about the uses and location of available capital, and it is crucial to an orderly resolution process. The alternative approach, multi-point resolution, allows multiple supervisors with limited oversight of the firm to seize capital wherever they may find it. Local supervisors with mandates to protect local policyholders and investors then have an incentive to secure as much capital as possible immediately, setting off a rapid-fire competition across supervisors to lock down resources in periods of distress. In resolution accords, although a single point of entry mechanism is desirable and usually officially adopted, many supervisors doubt that the resolution protocols would be strictly enforced in the event of distress. As a result, many supervisors require locally-held capital to protect the interests of local constituents, effectively raising total capital requirements and creating multiple local pockets of trapped capital. These dynamics raise insurer costs, reduce the benefits of global risk diversification, and have downstream effects on consumer welfare in the form of pricing policy, product availability, and higher market concentration.

Regulatory policies and investment pro-cyclicality

Globally, insurance companies and pensions funds manage $50 trillion in assets (Bank of England 2014). The asset allocation and investment decisions of these institutions have decisive influence on the cost of capital of many sectors of the global economy. By extension, the regulatory, supervisory, and accounting policies that influence these institutions' investment decisions have significant second-order effects on capital market pricing and cost of capital.

Currently there are substantive differences between European and US accounting policies with respect to balance sheet valuation methods for investment assets.[11] European conventions largely follow mark-consistent methods, requiring that balance sheets and capital calculations incorporate recent market experience and pricing. American conventions differ in significant respects, although there is much recent examination of reconciling US standards to conform more closely to European practices. A middle ground that has been suggested by some observers would adopt 'mark-to-funding' standards, using the asset prices and returns that would be realized if the owner held the investment asset to full maturity (in the case of fixed income) (Persaud 2008).

Mark-to-market pricing conventions combined with current regulatory capital requirements, while beneficially reflecting current market values in balance sheets and regulatory capital measurements, can also create self-reinforcing pro-cyclical policies.[12] These dynamics can be magnified during periods of capital market disruption and distress. As asset prices drop, insurers' calculated assets in riskier investments decline, potentially triggering the need to bolster capital through asset sales of riskier assets (and purchase of low-risk assets to bolster capital positions) into a market already under some degree of stress. The added selling activity further depresses prices of riskier assets and increases prices of risk-free assets. The reduced yield on risk-free assets can then feed back into higher estimated liability streams. The final result is regulated institutions selling large blocks of risky assets into distressed markets. The mirror image of these feedback loops can occur during market upturns, raising capital positions during more frothy markets and encouraging greater risk-taking during market peaks.

One suggested antidote to pro-cyclical policies is to heighten capital requirements during market upturns and to exercise some measured degree of supervisory forbearance during market downturns. While potentially beneficial, these policies can also be troublesome. In particular, the frequency, incidence, and degree of supervisory forbearance can introduce moral hazard in situations where weaker or poorly managed firms are given special leniency, or where the riskier activities of some firms are forgiven through ad hoc flexibility granted during downturns.

Application of bank-oriented prudential standards within insurance sector

Many of the newly established supervisory entities for insurance are institutions with legacy oversight of the banking sector, including the US Federal Reserve, central banks in European countries, and the UK Financial Stability Board (with many central bank constituents). Although similar in some respects, the insurance and banking sectors have very important differences in the structure of their balance sheets and attendant risks. Prominent highlights include (1) the very different nature of assets within banking (e.g., outstanding loans) and insurance (e.g., investments in a variety of asset classes); (2) differing types of liabilities within banking (e.g., deposits) and insurance (e.g., uncertain future contingent payouts); and (3) the differing degrees of friction and length of time horizons for significant movements in assets and liabilities during periods of distress (e.g., depositor runs in banks vs. policy lapses/cancellations in insurance). In the early stages of newly established supervisory oversight, bank-oriented policymakers and supervisors may be inclined to apply identical or largely similar approaches from the banking sector to the insurance sector. This can result in very broadly applied designations of systemic importance and ensuing capital requirements that ensure a very high degree of system safety, but at the cost of high capital intensity and elevated cost structure that can motivate exit from product and geographic markets.

Systemic risk methodology, international capital standards, and firm structure

At the global level, the methodology for identifying and overseeing systemically important insurance firms is determined partly by size, international activity, interconnectedness, and presence in non-traditional, non-insurance activities (NTNIA). For more broadly applied supervisory tools, such as the Insurance Capital Standard, the full set of internationally active insurance firms is within scope, regardless of systemic importance. If the tools and terms for overseeing such firms are sufficiently onerous, some insurers may prefer to decouple their currently integrated operations into separate legal entities by country, thereby bypassing the more intensive oversight. This disintegration of firm structure can result in more locally dedicated capital, loss of scale and scope economies, and lower risk diversification. The net social welfare consequences are not fully known, but significant negative spillover must be considered.

Risk-weightings applied to sovereign debt and systemic risk

Much of the risk-weighted capital calculations in current supervisory models applies a zero weighting to the risk from sovereign bonds issued by developed countries. As such, the risk-weighting applied to different sovereigns would be invariant with respect to macro-economic health, debt burden, debt servicing requirements, current budget deficits or surplus, and currency strength. The rationale for this regulatory shortcut is that sovereigns are unique borrowing entities relative to private organizations that may have existential threats, and that applying differential risk weights across countries would be fraught with political risk that could unnecessarily complicate financial oversight. Capital markets, however, recognize significant differences cross-sectionally and longitudinally in the risk premiums embedded within the market pricing of sovereign debt.

Insurers and other regulated institutions effectively must hold large quantities of low-risk fixed income investments to match the time horizon of their liability streams and to satisfy supervisory requirements, and so are effectively bound to hold large investments in sovereign debt. If all sovereign debt has zero recognized risk under supervisory regimes, but sovereigns exhibit actual return variation in capital markets pricing, it can be tempting for financial institutions to invest disproportionately in some of the riskiest sovereign debt, earn higher returns, and benefit from 'zero-risk' recognition by their supervisors. This outcome introduces three types of systemic risk: (1) institutions create large allocations to some of the riskiest sovereign debt and are effectively motivated by supervisory standards to do so; (2) firms' strategies become more highly correlated as many institutions move in the same direction, exposing the financial system to amplified negative consequences in response to certain types of shocks; and (3) national governments and domestic financial institutions are more likely to experience significant negative shocks simultaneously and become more dependent on each other for mutual success or possible failure, thus increasing the 'interconnectedness' of public and private institutions during periods of distress. This is a rare example of a scenario where attempts to reduce systemic risk through specific policies can actually cause the probability and severity of systemic events to rise.

Future Challenges

The ways in which insurers are regulated and supervised across products, geographies, customer segments, and policy objectives matter very significantly for ultimate effects on broad measures of social welfare. The transmission mechanism flows initially from the implementation of measures meant to achieve proximate policy objectives. It then has both direct effects on achieving those objectives (often recognized) and indirect effects on other social welfare measures either directly or through the second-order responses of supervised institutions (frequently unanticipated or less acknowledged by policy authorities). Additional challenges arise from incomplete mandates of supervisory authorities, resulting in either lack of recognition or less concern about the effects that materialize outside of official policy mandates. A final challenge is created when multiple supervisory authorities with intersecting mandates engage in actions that have negative action–reaction cycles between supervisory authorities and with the supervised financial institutions.

There are several worthwhile areas where new approaches to policy implementation could be developed and pursued.

Supervisory coordination across geographies

Supervisory colleges across multiple geographies are an important vehicle for better communication, coordination, and allowance for the multitude of effects flowing from supervisory actions. Global structures such as the FSB and IAIS can be very effective mechanisms for coordinating and harmonizing the implementation of policies. One model approach to improving social welfare outcomes starts with the Common Framework (ComFrame) approach taken by the IAIS for instituting supervisory and regulatory standards, which can then be interpreted and modified at more local levels.

Supervisory/regulatory clarity

Achieving greater clarity in the intent and implementation of supervision and regulation would be very beneficial both to supervised institutions and to the achievement of higher social welfare. Greater clarity can be realized in articulating desired future end states, paths to achieve them, and negative scenarios to avoid. At a more tactical level, significant improvements can be made in greater standardization of supervisory approaches, coordination across multiple authorities, reduced duplication of effort, stability of the supervisory structures, and movement toward a more level competitive landscape across geographies.

Improved understanding of outcomes

All participants within the networked financial system would benefit from greater understanding of the interconnectedness of their actions:

TABLE 2.1. Implications for insurance/pensions/retirement security

- Annuity provision, pricing features, guarantees, innovation, availability
- Capital market pricing volatility and stability
- Market coverage of products, customer segments, geographies
- Financial advice provision and coverage
- Transfer of longevity risk
- Pension settlement

Source: Author's contribution.

policymakers, regulators, supervisors, financial institutions. In particular, enhanced understanding of network dynamics can occur in several areas: (1) first-order responses to actions; (2) second-order effects that arise from an action–reaction cycle among members of the network; and (3) consequences that lie outside supervisory mandates.

Broader allowance for several dimensions of social welfare

Finally, it would be very helpful, although admittedly challenging, for policymakers, regulators, and supervisors to acknowledge and allow for effects of their actions on dimensions of social welfare that may have a more complex causal chain and that lie outside their official mandates. This is particularly important for connections to long-term financial and retirement security that depend on adequate returns to capital, financial stability, macro-economic growth, the ability to pool and diversify risks efficiently, and reliable, low-cost sources of guaranteed income (see Table 2.1).

Conclusion

The next decades will be decisive in determining whether the large aging population cohort in developed countries will be able to navigate a new retirement system that relies both on adequate levels of financial resources and the ability to pool and allocate specific risks efficiently across institutions and society. The supervisory structures and policies overseeing the insurance, asset management, and pensions sectors will be a significant contributor to whether and to what extent this navigation is successful.

Glossary of Terms

ACP	French Autorité de Contrôl Prudentiel
AFM	Netherlands Authority for Financial Markets

BAFIN	Germany Federal Financial Supervisory Authority
BCR	Basic Capital Requirement
BHC	Bank Holding Company
CBI	Central Bank of Ireland
DNB	Dutch National Bank
EIOPA	European Insurance and Occupational Pension Authority
FCA	Financial Conduct Authority, UK
FINMA	Swiss Financial Markets Supervisory Authority
FIO	Federal Insurance Office, US
FSB	Financial Stability Board
FSOC	Financial Stability Oversight Council
GSII	Global Systemically Important Insurer
HLA	Higher Loss Absorbency
IAIG	Internationally Active Insurance Groups
IAIS	International Association of Insurance Supervisors
ICS	Insurance Capital Standard
NAIC	National Association of Insurance Commissioners, US
NTNIA	Non-Traditional, Non-Insurance Activities
OSFI	Office of the Superintendent of Financial Institutions
PRA	Prudential Regulatory Authority, UK
RRP	Recovery and Resolution Plans
SIFI	Systemically Important Financial Institutions

Endnotes

1. The regional Federal Reserve office in which the insurer is domiciled becomes the primary overseer of that financial institution.
2. Voting members of FSOC include Secretary of the Treasury, Chairman of the Board of Governors of the Federal Reserve, Comptroller of the Currency (OCC), Director of the Consumer Financial Protection Bureau (CFPB), Chairman of the Securities and Exchange Commission (SEC), Chairperson of the Federal Deposit Insurance Corporation (FDIC), Chairperson of the Commodity Futures Trading Commission (CFTC), Director of the Federal Housing Finance Agency (FHFA), Chairman of the National Credit Union Administration (NCUA), and an independent member with insurance expertise who is appointed by the President and confirmed by the senate for a six-year term. Non-voting members include the Director of the Office of Financial Research (OFR), the Director of the Federal Insurance Office (FIO), a state insurance commissioner designated by the state insurance commissioners, a state banking commissioner designated by the state banking commissioners, and a state securities commissioner designated by the state securities commissioners.
3. See, for instance, Van Hulle (this volume, Chapter 5) for coverage of Solvency II regulations in greater depth.

4. See, for instance, Reid and Waters (this volume, Chapter 6) for in-depth coverage of issues of financial stability and systemic risk.
5. Regulatory issues around solvency are addressed in greater depth in Van Hulle (this volume, Chapter 5).
6. The IAIS is also a member of the FSB, constituting a formal connection between the two organizations.
7. 'The Executive Committee currently has three U.S. members, two from the NAIC and one from Treasury's Federal Insurance Office (FIO). The North American region is limited to five seats on the Executive Committee. Canada and Mexico each have one' (Festa 2013).
8. This is sometimes referred to as a general equilibrium outcome, and the before-versus-after comparison as comparative statics.
9. Pareto efficiency, or Pareto optimality, is a state of allocation of resources in which it is impossible to make any one individual better off without making at least one individual worse off.
10. This included not incorporating (1) the risk-reducing benefits of asset-liability matching; (2) risk diversification advantages of deploying capital across uncorrelated geographies, product lines, and customer segment; and (3) levying a simple capital surcharge based on 12% of income generated from asset management operations.
11. See, for instance, Maurer et al. (this volume, Chapter 3).
12. The Procyclicality Working Group defines procyclicality along two dimensions:

> First, in the short term, the tendency to invest in a way that exacerbates market movements and contributes to asset price volatility, which can in turn contribute to asset price feedback loops. Asset price volatility has the potential to affect participants across financial markets, as well as to have longer-term macroeconomic effects; and
>
> Second, in the medium term, as a tendency to invest in line with asset price and economic cycles, so that willingness to bear risk diminishes in periods of stress and increases in upturns. A tendency by insurance companies and pension funds to invest procyclically in the medium term might deepen the troughs and exaggerate the peaks of asset price or economic cycles in a way that is potentially detrimental to financial stability and long-term economic growth (Bank of England 2014: 2).

References

Bank of England (2014). *Procyclicality and Structural Trends in Investment Allocation by Insurance Companies and Pension Funds: A Discussion Paper by the Bank of England and the Procyclicality Working Group*. London: Bank of England. <http://www.bankofengland.co.uk/publications/Documents/news/2014/dp310714.pdf>.

Federal Insurance Office (FIO) (2013). *How to Modernize and Improve the System of Insurance Regulation in the United States.* Washington, DC: US Department of the Treasury. <http://www.treasury.gov/initiatives/fio/reports-and-notices/Documents/How%20to%20Modernize%20and%20Improve%20the%20System%20of%20Insurance%20Regulation%20in%20the%20United%20States.pdf>.

Federal Insurance Office (FIO) (2014). *Annual Report on the Insurance Industry.* Washington, DC: US Department of the Treasury. <http://www.treasury.gov/initiatives/fio/reports-and-notices/Documents/2014_Annual_Report.pdf>.

Festa, E. D. (2013). 'Fed to Join IAIS to Help Guide Global Insurance Supervision,' Lifehealthpro.com (updated 26 Sept. 2013). <http://www.lifehealthpro.com/2013/09/26/fed-to-join-iais-to-help-guide-global-insurance-su>.

Financial Stability Board (FSB) (2013). *Peer Review of the United States: Review Report.* Basel: Financial Stability Board. <http://www.financialstabilityboard.org/wp-content/uploads/r_130827.pdf>.

International Association of Insurance Supervisors (IAIS) (2015). *IAIS Newsletter,* Jan.

Maurer, R., O. S. Mitchell, R. Rogalla, and I. Siegelin (2016). 'Accounting-based Asset Return Smoothing in Participating Life Annuities: Implications for Annuitants, Insurers, and Policymakers,' in O. S. Mitchell, R. Maurer, and J. M. Orszag, eds, *Retirement System Risk Management: Implications of the New Regulatory Order.* Oxford: Oxford University Press, pp. 40–50.

Persaud, A. D. (2008). *Regulation, Valuation and Systemic Liquidity.* Paris: Banque de France. Financial Stability Review, No. 12.

Reid, B. and D. Waters (2016). 'Pensions, Risk, and Global Systemically Important Financial Institutions,' in O. S. Mitchell, R. Maurer, and J. M. Orszag, eds, *Retirement System Risk Management: Implications of the New Regulatory Order.* Oxford: Oxford University Press, pp. 95–118.

Sullivan, T. (2014). Statement to the US House of Representatives, Subcommittee on Housing and Insurance, Committee on Financial Services. Washington, DC, Nov. 18, 2.

Van Hulle, K. (2016). 'Risk Disclosure in the European Insurance Industry: Implications for Occupational Pension Funds,' in O. S. Mitchell, R. Maurer, and J. M. Orszag, eds, *Retirement System Risk Management: Implications of the New Regulatory Order.* Oxford: Oxford University Press, pp. 68–94.

Woodall, L. (2014). 'IAIS Warned over Plans to Shut Members Out of Committees,' Risk.net (updated Aug. 22, 2014). <http://www.risk.net/insurance-risk/news/2361596/iais-warned-over-plans-to-shut-members-out-of-committees>.

3

Accounting-Based Asset Return Smoothing in Participating Life Annuities: Implications for Annuitants, Insurers, and Policymakers

Raimond Maurer, Olivia S. Mitchell, Ralph Rogalla, and Ivonne Siegelin

Insurance companies offering variable life annuity products have been permitted to report asset values in their income statements at historical cost instead of fair market values, under current accounting standards.[1] They are also allowed to report their liabilities using actuarial smoothing, rather than marking them to market. Little is known about the economic consequences of these practices, despite the fact that the accounting rules play a key role for understanding the life insurance industry. They are important since smoothing allows insurers to defer losses; of course when they sell assets to pay benefits, the losses must be realized, which can trigger large reductions in benefit payments. Smoothing also allows them to defer gains, such that when gains are realized, benefits can increase due to the firms having a contingency reserve.

These practices have come under criticism of late, in view of the persistent low interest rate environment and the loss of transparency that such practices imply (e.g., Jorgensen 2004; Bleck and Liu 2007; Ng and Schism 2010). Yet moving to fair market valuation of insurer assets and liabilities would introduce new volatility into the insurers' balance sheets, which could undermine profitability and decimate the appeal of retirement annuities. This chapter outlines the conditions under which smoothing can be beneficial for policyholders who hold *with-profit* or *participating payout life annuities* (PLAs). These are bought by retirees expecting to receive a guaranteed benefit for life, along with variable non-guaranteed payments that depend on investment returns and mortality experiences of the insurance pool (Maurer et al. 2013b). Our objective is to show how accounting smoothing affects the risk and return profiles of PLA payouts as well as insurer profitability. We investigate these patterns using a model of a participating life annuity that draws on the TIAA Traditional Annuity.[2] We demonstrate that such accounting techniques can actually be welfare-enhancing, since risk-averse consumers can benefit substantially when insurers smooth asset and longevity surprises.

A Brief Overview of Life Insurance Accounting Smoothing

Under US Generally Accepted Accounting Principles (US GAAP), company-held assets can be categorized as those held to maturity, those held for trading purposes, or assets available for sale (Herget et al. 2008). Assets held to maturity should be valued at amortized cost when acquired (historical cost valuation, or HCV); in this instance, asset price changes are recognized as gains or losses only when the instruments are sold. Assets held for trading purposes are to be reported at fair market value (FMV), so price changes immediately affect insurer profits (whether they are realized or not). Under US GAAP, this is the default for valuing stock holdings. Assets available for sale are also reported at FMV, but unrealized gains and losses resulting from market price fluctuations are not reported in the insurer's profit and loss statement (P&L). Instead, they are carried in a separate account on the liability side of the insurer's balance sheet, known as the Other Comprehensive Income account (OCI). When these assets are sold, the OCI account is reversed, and realized gains or losses are recorded in the P&L. This approach is the US GAAP default for the valuation of bond holdings.

Formally, under the simplifying assumption that assets can only be sold at the end of each period, investment gains $g_{t,t+1}$ over the period $[t, t+1]$ on an asset can be calculated according to:

$$g_{t,t+1}^{FMV} = n_t \cdot (S_{t+1} - S_t) + n_t \cdot D_{t,t+1} \tag{1}$$

when reporting at fair market value. Here, n_t represents the number of the assets held at time t, S_t refers to the assets' market price at time t, and $D_{t,t+1}$ is the cash distribution received per asset over the period $[t, t+1]$ (e.g., coupon or dividend payments). Under historic cost valuation, when assets are sold at time $t+1$ (i.e. $n_{t+1} \leq n_t$), investment gains are given by:

$$g_{t,t+1}^{HCV} = (n_t - n_{t+1}) \cdot (S_{t+1} - S_0) + n_t \cdot D_{t,t+1} \tag{2}$$

where S_0 represents the initial purchase price of the asset.

Most US life insurers do not follow US GAAP, however. Instead, they rely on the statutory accounting principles issued by the National Association of Insurance Commissioners (NAIC). These are specific accounting guidelines for insurers that permit the companies to value their bond portfolios in their annual statements using a historical cost approach.[3] This has been the preferred practice as it helps protect insurers' balance sheets and income statements against short-term capital market volatility. In the context of a participating life insurance product, this *accounting smoothing* has direct implications for the benefit stream received by the policyholders, since *surpluses* to be shared with the annuitants are conventionally computed only using *realized* gains and losses.

To illustrate the impact of accounting-based payout smoothing, we describe a stylized insurance provider offering single-premium participating life annuity contracts. The world in which this insurer operates includes capital market risk, systematic longevity risk, and idiosyncratic mortality risk. In such an environment, the insurer prices the annuity product using a specific mortality table along with an assumed interest rate for discounting benefits (also called the guaranteed interest rate). The company then generates surpluses in two ways: via investment returns and the annuitant pool actual mortality. If the company's return on the assets backing the liability is greater than the guaranteed interest rate, and/or if realized annuitant mortality exceeds what had been expected, the insurance company earns a surplus. The company can influence the expected risk and return profile of uncertain surplus payments by the choice of assets in its portfolio. The non-guaranteed or participating surplus is set each year by the insurer's Board of Trustees.

A Simple Model of a Participating Life Annuity

Our model of a realistically-calibrated company for a pool of PLA policyholders with uncertain capital markets and mortality dynamics incorporates the key institutional features outlined (more detail is provided in Maurer et al. 2014). Using this structure, we seek to examine how smoothing techniques affect benefit streams and the insurer's profitability and solvency. We assume that the insurance company sells PLA contracts paying constant guaranteed lifetime benefits *GB* per annum to a closed pool of annuitants, all of the same age. The liabilities resulting from the annuity promises are carried on the insurer's balance sheet as the Actuarial Reserve. In exchange for the promised benefit stream, the firm collects annuity premiums that are calculated based on the firm's guaranteed interest rate *GIR* and actuarial survival tables. The monies collected, which are carried on the insurer's balance sheet as the General Account, are then invested in a constant-mix portfolio of stocks and a bond fund. Furthermore, we assume that the insurer is equipped with a certain amount of equity in order to be able to cover potential losses from the annuity business. The corresponding assets are assumed to be held in a cash account. Table 3.1 summarizes the insurer's balance sheet.

TABLE 3.1. The insurer's balance sheet

Assets	Liabilities
General Account	Actuarial Reserve
► *Stocks*	
► *Bond Fund*	
	Equity
	► (*OCI*)
Cash	► *Reserves*

Note: General Account represents the PLA premiums collected. Actuarial Reserve represents the liabilities corresponding to the promised guaranteed lifelong benefit stream. OCI (Other Comprehensive Income) represents unrealized gains/losses, applicable only under OCI accounting.

Source: Authors' representation.

Every year, the insurer pays policyholders out of its asset income as well as from the sale of assets (sold at market prices). Annuitants receive the guaranteed benefit *GB* and, in addition to that, a positive participating surplus payment if the insurer's total stochastic investment return exceeds its guaranteed interest rate, and if realized mortality, which is stochastic in both mortality tables and individual mortality experience, exceeds expectation.

To assess how policyholders would value the stochastic PLA income stream *GB* depending on their risk aversion and time preferences, we use an expected utility framework. In particular we assume the consumer has a time additive constant relative risk aversion (CRRA) utility function:

$$U = E_0\left[\sum_t \beta^t \, {}_tp_x^P \frac{L_t^{1-\gamma}}{1-\gamma}\right] \tag{3}$$

where β represents the time preference factor, γ the degree of relative risk aversion, ${}_tp_x^P$ the individuals' (subjective) survival probability, and L_t the PLA benefit received at time t. We then convert the expected lifetime utility U from the PLA benefit stream into a utility-equivalent fixed life annuity *FLA* (following Maurer et al. 2013b). This can be thought of as the constant guaranteed lifetime income stream which will make the policyholder indifferent to the upside potential of a PLA with stochastic surpluses.

Calibration

We simulate 5,000 cases of the PLA sketched here for a pool of 10,000 equally aged males. The simulation starts with the annuity purchase at age

65 and continues until the last individual in the pool has died. For the illustration, we assume that the annuity pays a fixed guaranteed income stream *GB* of $10,000 for life, which, given sensible assumptions, requires the purchaser to put up a single premium of $163,400. In addition to the guaranteed annuity benefit, the insurer promises to share 90 percent of surpluses with the annuitants. The remaining 10 percent of surpluses are cashed in by the insurer and increase its equity, which we initially set to 4 percent of the Actuarial Reserve. In case the firm's equity is exhausted due to adverse capital market or mortality shocks, surplus payments to the annuitants are suspended until the equity has been replenished.

To model the stochastic returns on cash (i.e., the 1-year spot rate) and the bond fund (target duration: 10 years), we rely on a 3-factor CIR model as in Chen and Scott (1993), which we calibrate to US 3-month T-bill rates and US Treasury zero yields (with maturities 1 to 10 years) over the period 01/1988–12/2012. Excess returns on stocks over the short-term interest rate as well as dividend yields are based on S&P 500 data (12/1981–12/2012).

Annuitants are assumed to have identical time preference factors of $\beta =$ 0.96 and coefficients of relative risk aversion of $\gamma = 5$. Survival probabilities ${}_tp_x^P$ are based on US mortality data as provided by the Human Mortality Database (2014), which we develop stochastically over time using the 2-factor model of Cairns et al. (2006). Based on these rates, Bernoulli experiments are conducted for each single individual in every period to determine if said individual remains in the PLA pool for another period.

To study the implications of accounting smoothing for annuitant well-being and firm profitability, we analyze 11 constant-mix asset allocations (0–100 percent bonds in 10 percent steps) under five accounting regimes: HCV only, FMV only, OCI only, US GAAP Default (Bond valuation: OCI; Stock valuation: FMV), and NAIC Default (Bond valuation: HCV; Stock valuation: FMV).

Key Results

To explore how alternative accounting regimes influence annuitant well-being, Panel A of Figure 3.1 depicts what benefits a fixed life annuity (FLA) would need to provide, if it were to produce annuitant utility equal to that of a PLA paying a fixed annual benefit of $10,000 plus a variable surplus given different investment strategies. The three black lines (solid, dashed, and dotted) illustrate what happens when all of the assets are evaluated according to a single valuation rule (HCV, FMV, OCI). The two gray lines (solid and dashed) indicate results when stocks are valued at FMV, and bonds according either to OCI (the US GAAP Default) or HCV (the NAIC Default).

Panel A

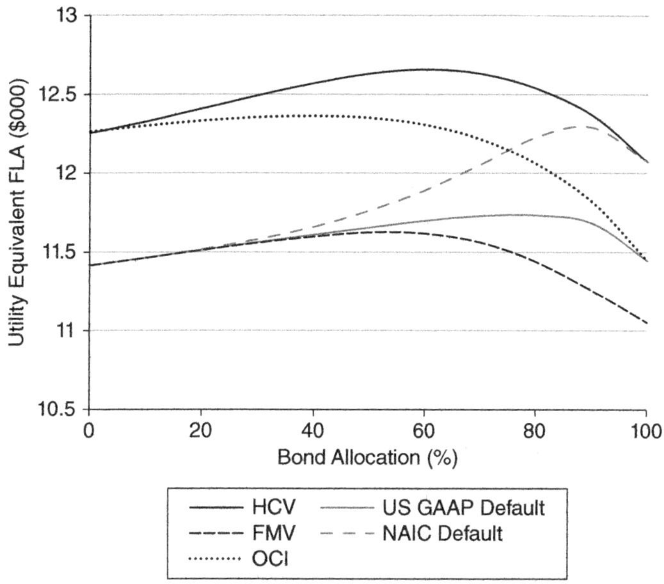

Panel B

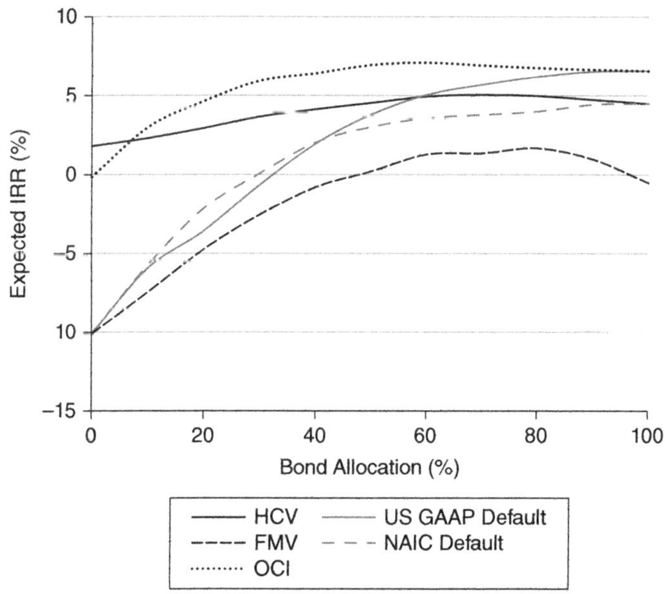

Figure 3.1 Effect of alternative valuation methods on PLA policyholder and insurer outcomes

Notes: Panel A shows the utility equivalent fixed life annuity (in $000) that generates the same utility as a Participating Lifetime Annuity (PLA) with guaranteed initial lifelong annual benefits of $10,000 based on a time-additive CRRA utility function for alternative valuation scenarios. Panel B shows the expected internal rate of return (IRR). FMV = fair market valuation, HCV = historical cost valuation, OCI refers to other comprehensive income valuation, US GAAP Default = bond valuation OCI and stock valuation FMV, NAIC Default = bond valuation HCV and stock valuation FMV. Calibration: Male age 65 in 2013; initial guaranteed PLA benefits: $10,000; time preference: $\beta = 0.96$; relative risk aversion: $\gamma = 5$; GIR: 3%; mortality table: "Annuity 2000" (PLA present value $163,400); bonds fund duration: 10 years; surplus allocation to annuitant: 90%.

Source: Authors' calculations; see text and Maurer et al. (2014).

When the insurer invests only in bonds, the FLA is worth 9 percent more under full HCV accounting (solid black line) than under the FMV method (dashed black line); $12,069 vs. $11,052). Similar utility increases are observed for other asset allocations. In other words, accounting smoothing through historical cost valuation dominates fair market valuation from the annuitant's perspective. Moreover, under both of these single valuation rules, the utility-maximizing bond fraction is about 50–60 percent—i.e., annuitants prefer a diversified portfolio allocation for the assets backing their PLA.

The fixed lifetime annuity under OCI (dotted black line) is worth more than with FMV, between 3.5 and 7.5 percent. Here, unrealized gains/losses do not directly affect the surplus under OCI, which results in lower undesired volatility in surplus payments. Despite that, unrealized losses do reduce the insurer's equity and through this channel may reduce the allocation of surplus to the annuitant. This explains why the utility-equivalent FLA is up to about 5.5 percent lower than under pure HCV (solid black line).

It is not surprising that under the two mixture approaches, the (gray) utility-equivalent value curves of the affected policyholder lie between the two extremes. As stocks are valued at FMV under US GAAP defaults, US GAAP (solid gray line) and FMV produce the same outcomes at low bond allocations. By contrast, for high bond fractions, US GAAP valuations are similar to those obtained with OCI. We observe similar results for NAIC valuation (dashed gray line): for a low bond allocation, results are similar to FMV, while at a high bond percent the pattern tracks that of the HCV approach. Moreover, the NAIC technique provides more value to the annuitant than the US GAAP methodology, because the former protects the policyholder from asset volatility with additional smoothing.

Next we take the insurer's perspective to study how alternative asset valuation methods impact the internal rate of return (IRR) on capital provided by the insurer's shareholders. Specifically, we compute the expected IRR over our 5,000 simulation paths, accounting for the initial equity investment, potential periodic dividend distributions to the shareholders over the lifetime of the annuity, and what the investors receive at the end of the product's lifespan, namely the value of equity capital and any actuarial reserves that remain when the last annuitant dies. The time horizon for each of the 5,000 simulation runs depends on the stochastic time of death of the last annuitant.

Panel B of Figure 3.1 plots the expected internal rates of return as a function of the insurer's asset allocation and the accounting regime in place. Again, the three black lines (solid, dashed, and dotted) describe the scenarios with a single valuation rule (HCV, FMV, OCI); the two gray lines refer the US GAAP (solid) and the NAIC (dashed) Default rules.

Comparing the solid and the dashed black lines, we see that insurers would prefer HCV over FMV for all portfolio compositions, due to higher expected internal rates of return. Moreover, IRRs under HCV are strictly positive, ranging from 3 to 4 percent depending on the asset allocation. By contrast, expected IRRs resulting from FMV are negative for both the all-stock and all-bond allocations (−10 and −0.5 percent, respectively), and only slightly positive for bond allocations of 50–90 percent. Under FMV, surpluses will be paid to the policyholders even if gains are unrealized. At the same time, unrealized losses will not be borne by the annuitants. This is in contrast to the HCV, where unrealized gains and losses may offset over time. The asymmetric impact of value fluctuations on payment streams also results in IRRs generally increasing with the bond share, as these generate less volatile asset returns.

Expected IRRs under OCI (dotted black line) generally exceed those under HCV (solid black line) for the majority of asset allocations, as unrealized losses can result in lower surplus payments. This increases the firm's potential to retain more returns and hence improves IRRs.

For the default valuation methods of US GAAP (solid gray line) and the NAIC (dashed gray line), expected IRRs represent weighted averages of the IRRs under FMV and OCI or under FMV and HCV. Overall, for realistic asset allocations, US GAAP Defaults will result in higher expected insurer profitability.

In summary, when looking at reasonable asset allocations, smoothing capital market return fluctuations via accounting techniques is attractive for PLA policyholders as well as for insurers. In particular, investing heavily in bonds combined with valuing assets based on historic costs produces stable returns, and, consequently, the costs for the guarantees embedded in the PLA contracts are low. Given a preference for stable PLA payouts over time, policyholders will approve of these conservative investment and valuation strategies.

Conclusion

As we have shown, policyholders seeking a guaranteed benefit plus some upside potential can benefit greatly from participating payout annuities, which help smooth some of the systematic shocks due to capital market uncertainty as well as systematic and idiosyncratic longevity risk. Our realistically-calibrated model of this product demonstrates how alternative accounting techniques influence policyholder welfare as well as insurer profitability and stability. Our findings indicate that smoothing in the case of participating life annuities is favorable to consumers and insurers. That is, it mitigates the potentially unduly large impact of short-term volatility on long-term contracts such as annuities. Therefore, smoothing is beneficial for risk-averse annuitants and profitable for insurers.

This implies that the current debate about whether to push insurance companies to undertake fair market valuation is not merely about rules—the answer to the question will have real financial impacts. As such, our work is related to the general discussion about advantages and disadvantages of HCV vs. FMV methods in the accounting literature (see, e.g., Busillo et al. 2016; Ellul et al. 2013; Laux and Leuz 2009, 2010).

Our chapter is also related to studies of household portfolio choice and annuitization which have primarily focused on fixed payout annuities, where capital market and mortality risks are solely borne by the insurer. Only a limited number of studies has examined unit-linked annuities which allow the insurer to share investment and longevity risk with the policyholder (see, e.g., Piggott et al. 2005; Denuit et al. 2011; Richter and Weber 2011; Maurer et al. 2013a). Based on those studies and our findings here, we believe that participating annuities offer retirees a favorable combination of access to the mortality credit and a smoothed payout stream for life.

Our results should be of interest to policymakers seeking to strengthen financial security in old age by optimizing the management of 401(k) plan drawdown, for example through stimulating growth in the annuity market.[4] Pushing annuity providers toward fair market valuation and away from the historic cost approach might improve information disclosure for the companies' current and future shareholders. Yet it could also reduce the attractiveness of PLA products for both policyholders and insurance companies.

Endnotes

1. This chapter draws on and simplifies our related study (Maurer et al. 2014).
2. TIAA-CREF in 2012 held 3.6 million annuity contracts and managed assets of $487B. The TIAA Traditional Annuity builds up capital during the accumulation phase, whereby contributions paid by policyholders earn a minimum guaranteed yearly interest rate (depending on the vintage when premiums are paid) plus a non-guaranteed surplus. Here we concentrate only on the liquidation phase of the product. In the European market, participating life annuity products are also on offer, comparable to the TIAA product outlined in the text; see Maurer et al. (2013b).
3. Lombardi (2009) offers additional information on valuation requirements. Also, under NAIC rules, insurers may discount the liabilities resulting from the guaranteed benefit with a fixed interest rate specified at the beginning of the contract (i.e., the guaranteed interest rate). See for instance TIAA-CREF (2011).
4. As the senior advisor to the US Secretary of the Treasury and Deputy Assistant Secretary for retirement and health policy, Mark Iwry, noted: 'One solution is to

provide for a predictable lifetime stream of income, such as an annuity provided under a retirement plan or IRA. By pooling those who live shorter and longer than average, everybody can essentially put away what's necessary to reach the average life expectancy, and those who live longer than average will be protected' (Steverman 2012).

References

Bleck, A. and X. Liu (2007). 'Market Transparency and the Accounting Regime,' *Journal of Accounting Research*, 45(2): 229–56.

Busillo, J., T. Harvey, and B. Hoffman (2016). 'Mark-to-Market Accounting for United States Corporate Pensions: Implementation and Impact,' in O. S. Mitchell, R. Maurer, and J. M. Orszag, eds, *Retirement System Risk Management: Implications of the New Regulatory Order*. Oxford: Oxford University Press, pp. 51–67.

Cairns, A., D. Blake, and K. Dowd (2006). 'A Two-Factor Model for Stochastic Mortality with Parameter Uncertainty: Theory and Calibration,' *Journal of Risk and Insurance*, 73: 687–718.

Chen, R. R. and L. Scott (1993). 'Maximum Likelihood Estimation for a Multifactor Equilibrium Model of the Term Structure of Interest Rates,' *Journal of Fixed Income*, 3: 14–31.

Denuit, M., S. Haberman, and A. Renshaw (2011). 'Longevity-Indexed Annuities,' *North American Actuarial Journal*, 15(1): 97–111.

Ellul, A., A. C. Jotikasthira, C. T. Lundblad, and Y. Wang (2013). 'Mark-to-Market Accounting and Systemic Risk: Evidence from the Insurance Industry,' *Economic Policy*, 29(78): 297–341.

Herget, R. T., M. J. Freedman, S. M. McLaughlin, and E. P. Schuering (2008). *US GAAP for Life Insurers*. 2nd edn. Schaumburg, IL: Society of Actuaries.

Human Mortality Database (2014). *US Death Rates* (Period 1x1). Last modified Nov. 16, 2012. Version MPv5, 1933–2010. <http://www.mortality.org>.

Jorgensen, P. L. (2004). 'On Accounting Standards and Fair Valuation of Life Insurance and Pension Liabilities,' *Scandinavian Actuarial Journal*, 104(5): 372–94.

Laux, C. and C. Leuz (2009). 'The Crisis of Fair-Value Accounting: Making Sense of the Recent Debate,' *Accounting, Organizations and Society*, 34: 826–34.

Laux, C. and C. Leuz (2010). 'Did Fair-Value Accounting Contribute to the Financial Crisis?' *Journal of Economic Perspectives*, 24: 93–118.

Lombardi, L. J. (2009). *Valuation of Life Insurance Liabilities*. 4th edn. Winsted, CT: ACTEX Publications.

Maurer, R., O. S. Mitchell, R. Rogalla, and V. Kartashov (2013a). 'Lifecycle Portfolio Choice with Systematic Longevity Risk and Variable Investment-linked Deferred Annuities,' *Journal of Risk and Insurance*, 80(3): 649–76.

Maurer, R., O. S. Mitchell, R. Rogalla, and I. Siegelin (2014). *Accounting and Actuarial Smoothing of Retirement Payouts in Participating Life Annuities*. Pension Research Council Working Paper No. WP2014-02. Philadelphia, PA: Pension Research Council.

Maurer, R., R. Rogalla, and I. Siegelin (2013b). 'Participating Payout Life Annuities: Lessons from Germany,' *ASTIN Bulletin*, 43: 159–87.

Ng, S. and L. Schism (2010). 'Low Interest Rates Hurt Insurers' Bottom Lines,' *Wall Street Journal*, Nov. 6. <http://online.wsj.com/news/articles/SB10001424052748704405704575596932278239578>.

Piggott, J., E. A. Valdez, and B. Detzel (2005). 'The Simple Analytics of a Pooled Annuity Fund,' *Journal of Risk and Insurance*, 72: 497–520.

Richter, A. and F. Weber (2011). 'Mortality-Indexed Annuities: Avoiding Unwanted Risk,' *North American Actuarial Journal*, 15: 212–36.

Steverman, B. (2012). 'Mark Iwry: Bringing Annuities to 401(k)s,' Bloomberg, Apr. 17. <http://www.businessweek.com/news/2012-04-17/mark-iwry-bringing-annuities-to-401-k-s>.

TIAA-CREF (2011). Audited Statutory—Basis Financial Statements as of December 31, 2011 and 2010 and for the three years ending December 31, 2011. New York: TIAA-CREF. <http://www1.tiaa-cref.org/ucm/groups/content/@ap_ucm_p_tcp/documents/document/tiaa01007823.pdf>.

4

Mark-to-Market Accounting for United States Corporate Pensions: Implementation and Impact

Joseph Busillo, Thomas Harvey, and Bryan Hoffman

Defined benefit (DB) pensions have been an ongoing management challenge for United States corporate plan sponsors. Among the many issues is how to properly account for the associated assets and liabilities, providing clarity regarding the plan itself while not diluting transparency into the underlying business performance of the corporate plan sponsors. Traditional generally accepted accounting principles (GAAP) for pensions is a somewhat Byzantine mechanism attempting to balance these two often conflicting goals. There is an alternative approach that a small segment of plan sponsors has recently implemented for their pension plans: mark-to-market (MTM) accounting. Shedding to various degrees the smoothing mechanisms provided under GAAP, this method exposes not only the balance sheet but also the income statement to the volatility of annual pension performance (cf. Maurer et al. 2016).

Most plan sponsors have been extremely reluctant to pursue this approach. Concerns over shareholder and market reactions have limited adoption of MTM to a handful of plan sponsors. Our expectation was that the accounting methodology should have a negligible effect on a plan sponsor's share value. In this chapter, we explore a number of aspects of MTM to better understand the following:

(1) the relative appeal of GAAP and MTM accounting standards to plan sponsors, and why a plan sponsor would or would not adopt MTM;
(2) the impact of MTM accounting on investors and plan sponsor share price;
(3) the reaction of MTM adoption on equity analysts, ratings agencies, and management teams; and
(4) the impact of MTM adoption on investment strategy.

Moreover, we provide alternatives to the most common pension sponsor investment strategies and an evaluation of their efficiency under MTM.

Overview of MTM Pension Accounting

The implementation of Accounting Standards Codification 715 (ASC 715) in 2006 moved pension economics out of the footnotes and directly onto the financial statements of corporate America. The goal was to incorporate the net assets and liabilities of DB plans onto corporate balance sheets so that a company's investors could gain a more transparent view of the financial impact associated with its pension plan. However, under the current GAAP, plan sponsors can use a variety of techniques to smooth out that impact.

GAAP rules allow for delayed recognition on the income statement of gains or losses on pension plans' assets and liabilities. Plan sponsors can also use an expected return figure that reflects their long-term expected returns on their current portfolios. Annual variances between expected and actual market returns are accrued in 'accumulated other comprehensive income' (AOCI) on the balance sheet. Likewise, deviations from expected liability growth are accrued in AOCI. The AOCI amounts are then amortized over time on the income statement, usually over the expected future working lifetime of plan participants. Plan sponsors are, in effect, shielded from a significant portion of the actual volatility of their DB pension assets and liabilities.

Appeal of GAAP

GAAP provides a significant cushion to a plan sponsor's income statement, generally accomplishing the goals as intended: to minimize financial statement volatility from noncore operations (i.e., the DB pension). GAAP effectively permits the plan sponsor to decrease the year-to-year volatility of pension expenses on corporate financial statements. This smoothing of real asset returns and delayed recognition spreads immediate gains and losses into the future, bleeding them in over time. Companies are thus shielded from reporting the immediate impact of significant adverse market events.

In addition, as the predominant methodology for accounting for DB plans, the use of GAAP supports comparability between corporations and across time periods. Despite its many inherent weaknesses, GAAP—as it is almost universally applied—enjoys the obvious benefit of widespread acceptance.

The current accounting framework also allows plan sponsors to favor equities over fixed-income assets in DB plan investment allocations. Increased equity allocations raise the expected returns used to determine pension expense, while any losses experienced through such an implementation are amortized over time. Plan sponsor earnings are thus shielded from the volatility inherent in an aggressive portfolio allocation, while the higher expected returns increase earnings in the near term.

Note that this feature may not always be beneficial. That is, the ultimate investors are not shielded to the extent that there is a settlement event that requires a short-term recognition of the pro-rata portion of the loss that may be outstanding.

Weaknesses of GAAP

In an effort to account for the impact of pension economics without overwhelming the underlying operating company's financial performance, GAAP conventions smooth out the actual DB pension results and amortize these results over a period of time. This approach may work if the actual performance is at variance with the predicted performance within a modest band, and these variances generally offset each other year to year. Unfortunately, a large adverse market event—such as the one experienced in 2008—has a relatively large and long-term effect. For most DB plan sponsors, the financial crisis created a large pool of unamortized losses to be recognized over time. While enjoying the significant shield GAAP provided at the time, most plan sponsors find themselves facing an extended period of amortizing large losses, creating an ongoing earnings drag.

For many with closed or frozen DB plans, these additional 'costs' are related to legacy benefits that bear little relationship to the organization's current operations and cost structure. Plan sponsors are struggling with how to account for these legacy benefits and minimize pension plan expense volatility, while providing clarity to investors regarding the financial performance of their base operations.

The United States MTM Alternative

The typical GAAP mechanisms that a DB pension plan uses in its financial statements result in a smoothing of asset values. This smoothing is such that the expected return on assets is more stable, as well as accruing gains or losses into the AOCI account that are amortized into the income statement over time. The expense can be booked on a prospective basis and any gain or loss will accrue in the AOCI at the end of the year to be amortized in future years.

Alternatively, a sponsor is able to elect to account for its plan without these smoothing mechanisms. This method is known as mark-to-market

TABLE 4.1. Annual pension cost ($)

	GAAP	MTM	Diff
Service Cost (Benefits Accrued)	10.2	10.2	0.0
Interest Cost	77.0	77.0	0.0
Expected Return on Assets	(95.6)	(95.6)	0.0
Amortization of Actuarial Losses	20.0	0.0	(20.0)
MTM (Gain)/Loss	*NA*	*(12.3)*	*(12.3)*
= Total Pension Cost	11.6	(20.7)	(32.3)

Notes: GAAP refers to Generally Accepted Accounting Principle; MTM refers to Mark-to-Market; Diff refers to the difference between GAAP and MTM costs.

Source: Authors' calculations.

(MTM) accounting, or a fair value accounting approach. In full MTM accounting, the sponsor can only book its DB plan expense retrospectively. This means that actual gains or losses from assets and liabilities for the current year will be booked as current year expenses. To accomplish this, the sponsor uses the fair market value of assets. The expected return on assets will be replaced with actual return on plan assets and the amortization period for any gains or losses is in essence changed to one year. An example of this is shown in Table 4.1.

Why MTM is Attractive to Plan Sponsors

The major benefit of implementing MTM accounting for a pension plan is that the company can restate historical financial statements to reflect actual plan losses experienced. The company can also remove 'escrowed' losses—losses incurred in the past but still awaiting future amortization—from its income statement. Through adoption of MTM, the plan sponsor can effectively eliminate the drag on earnings from future pension loss amortizations.

Furthermore, some plan sponsors feel that the move to an accounting policy without smoothing is more transparent and consistent with the direction in which accounting rules are headed. Since there is no fundamental change in the underlying cash flows or health of the company, the draw may be a cleaner, more transparent policy.

Finally, given the low interest rates experienced over the past five years, plan sponsors have implemented MTM under the belief a rate rise is inevitable. Rising interest rates would reduce the pension liability, likely creating an MTM gain. Rising liability discount rates would potentially become a tailwind to expense reductions, increasing future earnings.

Why Plan Sponsors have been Reluctant to Adopt

The risk in a transition to MTM accounting arises from the fact that the company's pension expense is likely to be more volatile going forward. Shifting to MTM accounting also carries the potential threat of a negative earnings impact, as happened when the 2012 decline in interest rates overwhelmed the rise in pension asset values and eroded funding levels in most plans.

Many US DB plan sponsors have been reluctant to give up the income-level smoothing mechanisms of traditional GAAP and adopt MTM. In dialogue with management teams, multiple issues drive this reticence, including concerns over the impact of earnings and earnings per share (EPS) volatility on investor, equity analyst, and ratings agency reactions. Management teams are also often incentivized by GAAP earnings and sensitive regarding the impact that MTM accounting could have on annual earnings.

In an effort to evaluate these concerns in the context of shifting to MTM, we analyze each in turn. Our expectation was that, as a noncash item, the accounting for DB pensions should have a negligible impact on a firm's share price, analyst review, or credit rating.

Investors

The first questions we considered were whether investors view the shift to MTM negatively, and whether companies pay a price in terms of share value for making the move. For each of the 23 companies in our analysis, SEI conducted an event study to evaluate movements in share price over a five-day period surrounding the announcement of the accounting change. In addition, the analysis included each company's Q4/2012 earnings release in order to provide insight into the MTM impact for the full calendar year. We then constructed a capital asset pricing model line for each company, based on actual performance relative to that of the appropriate subset of the S&P 1500, and we used regression analysis to predict an expected change in company return given a change in benchmark return.

Results indicated that the companies studied experienced no statistically significant changes in share price that would reflect a direct, obvious shareholder response to the implementation of MTM accounting. Moreover, the analysis showed no change in share price as a result of the 'noise' inherent in using actual asset and liability returns on financial statements, rather than including those results in the footnotes. Although a few early adopters such as Verizon experienced abnormally large but transitory changes in share price following the initial announcement, those changes did not translate into sustained effects on share value, either positively or negatively. This research confirms what we expected: with no cash implications, changes in accounting measures have no direct impact on share prices.

Analyst community

Next, we looked at whether analysts appreciate the change in accounting for pension expenses and whether they recognize the impact on earnings volatility for comparison purposes. For some time, analysts have frequently employed MTM analysis in evaluating 'core' earnings and the cash impact of DB pension plans. For large companies in which the plan is large relative to market capitalization, analysts unwind GAAP treatment of losses and focus on the projected cash impact of the plan going forward. Likewise, in comparing an MTM company's EPS with traditional GAAP comparables, analysts generally unwind the MTM adjustment, using the company's smoothed GAAP earnings across time periods to compare performance.

A careful review of the Q4/2012 earnings calls of the 23 companies in our study revealed little to no discussion of the impact of MTM accounting versus GAAP for the organizations' pensions, nor did company representatives spend time discussing the resulting volatility in their earnings. Analysts appeared to be unsurprised by the earnings drag that MTM companies felt in 2012 due to the decline in interest rates. Across all 23 calls, there were very few questions and no direct criticisms of the new accounting implementation. It is worth noting that, in many analyst reports, pension liabilities were still calculated using GAAP, meaning the MTM impact was adjusted out of the analysts' annual earnings forecasts for those companies. For an example of our analysis see Table 4.2.

Ratings agencies

We also looked at whether a plan sponsor's credit rating tended to be affected by a move to MTM accounting. Reviews of the rating practices of Standard & Poor's, Moody's, and Fitch, as well as discussions with Moody's Investor Services, indicate that a shift to MTM by a plan sponsor does not cause a significant disruption to the financial analysis practices of the major ratings agencies. Among several other non-GAAP adjustments that the ratings agencies make to corporate financial statements, applying full MTM treatment for pensions appears to be standard practice.

At the same time, pensions and pension volatility have a discrete but limited effect on overall ratings. Compared with a company's revenue and debt, pension-related factors generally have a modest impact on its credit rating. Significant changes to a plan's funded status may limit credit rating upgrades, but such changes are unlikely to lead directly to a downgrade if they are not accompanied by other changes in the company's creditworthiness. Since the major ratings agencies already are, in effect, using MTM in

TABLE 4.2. Pension descriptors

In millions (USD$)			Pension			Asset Allocation			Pension Metrics			
Company	Ticker	MTM Announcement Date	Assets	Liabilities	Funded Ratio (%)	Equity (%)	FI (%)	Other (%)	Pension Assets/ Market Cap (%)	Pension Assets/ Adj Corp Assets (%)	Pension Assets/ Book Value (%)	Unfunded PBO/ EBITDA
Albermarle	ALB	2012	553.3	762.4	74	57.8	27.6	14.6	9.6	16.4	29.1	0.3x
Ashland	ASH	2011	3,320.0	4,877.0	68	51.0	47.0	2.0	48.4	21.5	81.0	2.0x
AT&T	T	2011	45,060.0	58,910.0	76	55.0	34.0	11.0	23.0	25.0	49.0	0.4x
Babcock &Wilcox	BWC	2012	2,127.7	2,780.0	77	6.0	51.0	43.0	62.1	43.6	219.7	1.9x
ConAgra	CAG	2012	3,243.3	3,817.5	88	49.0	23.0	28.0	22.0	14.1	63.5	0.2x
Eastman Chemical	EMN	2012	2,298.0	3,133.0	73	52.0	26.0	22.0	20.0	16.6	76.0	0.6x
FirstEnergy	FE	2011	6,671.0	8,975.0	74	16.0	57.0	27.0	41.9	11.7	51.3	0.8x
Graftech	GTI	2011	163.1	231.8	70	11.8	88.2	0.0	16.1	6.6	12.1	0.3x
Honeywell	HON	2010	18,872.0	22,389.0	84	49.3	37.1	13.6	29.9	31.1	137.0	0.7x
IBM	IBM	2010	91,688.0	106,129.0	86	39.8	52.0	8.3	40.0	43.0	482.0	0.5x
HIS	IHS	2011	161.0	180.7	89	28.3	67.4	4.2	2.2	4.3	10.0	0.1x
Johnson Controls	JCI	2012	4,642.0	5,761.0	81	49.2	40.2	10.6	18.0	13.0	39.0	0.4x
Kellogg	K	2012	4,374.0	5,238.0	84	66.2	24.4	9.4	18.0	22.3	157.0	0.4x
LS Starrett	SCX	2011	107.4	145.5	74	27.0	12.0	61.0	153.6	31.3	86.3	4.5x
PerkinElmer	PKI	2012	336.3	580.5	58	55.0	39.0	6.0	8.8	8.1	18.3	0.8x
PolyOne	POL	2011	410.4	597.2	69	70.6	21.3	8.1	16.0	16.0	65.0	0.8x
Rexnord	RXN	2011	577.7	720.6	80	30.0	67.0	3.0	31.3	15.0	130.8	0.4x
Reynolds American	RAI	2011	5,422.0	6,293.0	86	29.0	59.0	12.0	20.0	25.0	100.0	0.3x
SAIC	SAI	2011	86.0	94.0	91	43.0	57.0	0.0	1.6	1.4	3.3	0.0x
Teradyne	TER	2012	302.9	376.5	80	13.0	85.8	1.2	9.6	10.8	16.2	0.2x
United Parcel Post	UPS	2012	25,742.0	32,957.0	78	44.4	33.4	22.2	31.0	40.0	637.0	2.3x
Verizon	VZ	2011	18,282.0	26,773.0	68	43.7	35.4	20.9	12.0	7.5	21.4	0.6x
Windstream	WN	2012	999.0	1,400.1	71	44.2	51.4	4.4	20.2	6.8	90.0	0.2x
Median MTM Cos					76.5	44.2	33.4	22.2	20.0	16.0	65.0	0.4x
US Public Medians					74	53.0	37.1	9.9	10.9	9.5	20.9	0.2x

Source: Authors' calculations.

their analyses, a shift to MTM accounting should have a negligible impact on a particular plan sponsor's credit rating.

Internal management

Finally, we evaluated how management incentives were affected by the change in EPS that results from the increased volatility in pension gains and losses. It is not unusual for some portion of a management team's incentive compensation to be tied to annual GAAP earnings performance. Since pension expenses average approximately 10 percent of a corporate EPS, the additional volatility associated with an MTM implementation has the potential to have a material impact on earnings. In response, based on available proxy statements, all companies adopting MTM accounting have appeared to revise their compensation plans to exclude the MTM adjustment, effectively shielding management bonuses from the volatility of actual pension performance.

Interestingly, many of the companies that SEI surveyed did not de-risk their pension plans to reduce volatility prior to implementing MTM accounting. Instead, they chose to maintain more aggressive investment portfolios. The net effect of combining the higher expected return in accounting for pension expense, eliminating the amortization associated with historical losses, and adjusting out the MTM impact, is that management ultimately gets the benefits of a more favorable EPS without the penalty of past poor performance. In many respects, this is an ideal outcome for management.

Pension Allocation Not Generally Changed by Accounting Method

Looking at the companies that have adopted MTM, we did find it surprising that those companies did not generally change their DB plan asset allocation in response to the switch. Most sponsors stick to a traditional mix of 60/40 equities/fixed-income strategies, similar to the investment strategy followed by a large majority of corporate pension plans using traditional GAAP pension accounting. Rather than address the impact of pension plan volatility through a better asset/liability match, most plans simply use non-GAAP adjustments to address those results, rather than reduce the actual economic volatility.

We continue to believe that many corporate plan sponsors' reticence to adopt MTM is based on the concerns outlined, and that annual volatility will have an undesirable impact on earnings. This concern over earnings

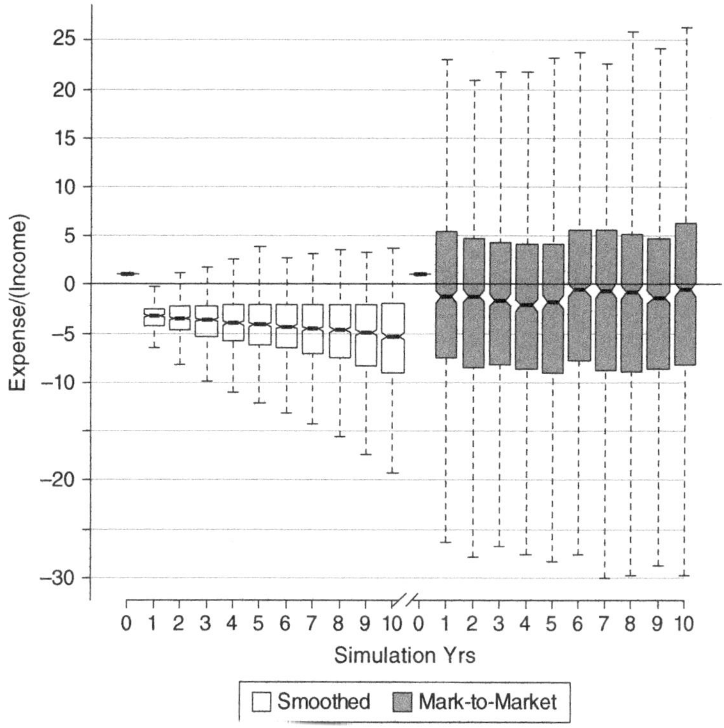

Figure 4.1 Volatility comparison 60/40

Source: Authors' calculations.

volatility is a reasonable one. We ran a simple Monte Carlo simulation using SEI's proprietary capital market assumptions to show the inherent risks to GAAP EPS of maintaining a traditional asset allocation when adopting an MTM accounting policy. We use a three-factor, short-rate model to determine the near-term interest rate. The three factors are inflation, real rates, and an option-adjusted spread. These factors are projected using an autoregressive (AR) model [AR(1) process] with drift. After the short rate is determined, we can determine the long rate on the yield curve using standard methods in stochastic calculus. The return is then determined on the long bond associated with that rate and all other asset classes are correlated to this return. The ultimate output is 1,000 simulations over 10 years for all asset classes and full-yield curves. Figure 4.1 shows the increased volatility that can be expected when an MTM policy is adopted (note that this does not show the one-time effect of switching from smoothed accounting to MTM). Clearly, switching to an MTM accounting method without some shift in asset allocation could cause undesired volatility and stress.

Perhaps more critically, the economic exposures associated with this strategy can be significant. A poorly matched asset–liability investment strategy poses several challenges to the plan sponsor, including increasing the value at risk through limiting the natural liability hedge associated with investments in long-duration fixed income; increasing potential required contributions in adverse scenarios, including poor capital markets and declining discount rates; and creating significant uncertainty around projected contribution levels.

Despite these challenges, most plan sponsors continue to pursue a heavily equity-oriented strategy within their DB pensions, in an effort to benefit from the higher expected long-term returns on equities to reduce the 'costs' associated with the pension liability. Given the increased transparency associated with MTM accounting and the immediate impact of pension portfolio returns on corporate earnings under the MTM framework, sponsors switching to MTM might also consider a change in investment strategy.

Two alternatives to the typical equity-centric allocation paradigm are of interest. The first, liability-driven investment (LDI), focuses on closely matching liability exposures and seeks to minimize funded status volatility. The second, risk parity, pursues a more balanced approach to risk without sacrificing expected return, giving management the opportunity to reduce funded status volatility without reducing expected incentive-based compensation, which typically remains based on expected return on pension assets even after the switch to MTM accounting.

Method 1: liability-driven investment

Given the nature and timing of promised benefit payments, a full liability matching strategy with high-quality fixed-income assets is a natural default position for a DB plan. Since the purpose of the plan is to provide employees with income during retirement (a form of deferred wages), it is not clear why the associated expense should be treated differently than any other corporate liability. A full LDI method (at 100 percent funded) will allow the plan to maintain the current funded ratio with the smallest possible tracking error.

Method 2: risk parity

The second approach can be thought of as a more diversified substitute for the traditional 60/40 portfolio. In this context, rather than generating optical diversification by focusing on capital allocations, risk parity seeks genuine diversification by balancing risk allocations across asset classes. Details of this strategy will now be discussed.

A primer on risk parity

Risk parity investing emphasizes risk exposure diversification, not simply dollar allocations. This distinction can be illustrated quite powerfully by considering the traditional 60/40 equity/fixed-income DB plan portfolio. While this portfolio initially appears quite balanced, with nearly equal dollar (capital) allocations to both stocks and bonds, a risk decomposition paints an entirely different picture. Because equities are so much more volatile than intermediate-term fixed income, the 60/40 dollar split derives over 90 percent of its risk from equities. Thus, when volatility is taken into consideration, the apparent diversification of the 60/40 portfolio disappears.[1] Risk parity investing seeks to restore balance to the portfolio by allocating equal amounts of risk to each asset class, seeking genuine diversification by risk instead of optical diversification by capital.

In order to achieve such balanced risk allocations, risk parity portfolios must invest higher dollar amounts into less volatile asset classes and vice versa. Naturally, the initial act of reducing the size of equity investments and allocating more to fixed income would be expected to reduce the expected return (and risk) of the resulting portfolio. Depending on the risk tolerance and return requirements of the investor, this outcome might not be desirable. In such instances, a risk parity portfolio typically employs a modest amount of leverage (generally obtained via derivative contracts) to restore the portfolio's expected return and volatility to the desired levels. Hence risk parity portfolios need not be 'conservative,' low-risk investments; they can be geared to target the same level of expected volatility as the 60/40 portfolio, the equity market as a whole, or any other level deemed appropriate. The crucial distinction is that, by achieving this level of volatility in a more diversified fashion, risk parity offers the potential for higher returns for any given level of volatility when compared to more concentrated alternatives such as the 60/40 portfolio.

The benefits of risk parity in an asset-only context have been addressed at length in the financial literature. Interestingly, these advantages become even more powerful in a liability-relative setting. As mentioned earlier, LDI constitutes an intuitive and sensible default option for pension asset portfolios as it allows for the lowest volatility of funded status. Nevertheless, it cannot be ignored that many sponsors are reluctant to adopt a full LDI strategy for a variety of reasons. While risk parity is no substitute for true LDI, it could potentially offer a significantly more efficient alternative to equity-heavy allocations, such as the 60/40 portfolio, in an asset–liability framework.

Put simply, risk parity offers a more efficient asset portfolio in a DB plan setting because the assets it holds bear at least some resemblance to a typical

DB plan's liability stream. Most liability structures closely resemble a 'short' position in long-duration fixed income; this is the default position of a DB plan prior to the formation of any asset portfolio. Plans that invest their assets in equity-heavy portfolios, such as the 60/40 portfolio, thereby do little to hedge their liabilities. Given the 60/40 portfolio's more than 90 percent concentration in equity risk, the performance of such an asset portfolio has little to do with the change in the value of the plan's liabilities. This mismatch creates extreme volatility in terms of the true economic exposures underlying the plan's surplus or deficit.

By contract, a risk parity approach allocates a meaningful amount of its risk budget to nominal, investment-grade fixed income. Consequently, it can reasonably be expected to correlate more closely with a plan's liabilities, potentially reducing the 'tracking error' of the asset portfolio relative to the liability stream, thereby reducing the volatility of a plan's surplus or deficit. Again, because the risk parity portfolio can be geared to target any desired level of risk or return, this reduction in surplus risk need not come with a decline in expected return. Rather, sponsors who are willing to accept a certain level of risk (such as those currently following a 60/40 allocation) can still accept that amount of risk, but with potentially higher returns and improved surplus efficiency, by allocating to a risk parity portfolio.

Risk parity's potentially improved efficiency can be demonstrated both historically and prospectively. First, it is useful to conduct a historical analysis comparing the performance of the 60/40 portfolio and a naive risk parity portfolio relative to the Citigroup Intermediate Pension Liability Index (CPLI), with emphasis on both return and risk relative to the liability proxy. The analysis here is based on the 20-year period, 1995–2014, with the sample limited by data availability for the CPLI. In this example, the 60/40 portfolio is constructed using the S&P 500 for equity exposure and the Barclays US Aggregate for fixed income. The static weights for the naive risk parity portfolio are calculated by balancing risk contributions from the S&P 500, Barclays US Aggregate, and Bloomberg Commodity Index over the full 20-year period. Once these weights are determined, the portfolio is levered to match the full sample volatility of the 60/40 portfolio so that each portfolio exhibits the same level of risk over the sample period.

Figure 4.2 highlights the intuitive argument that a risk parity asset portfolio should offer less tracking error than a 60/40 asset portfolio with the same level of volatility. This exhibit plots the rolling three-year annualized tracking error of each asset portfolio relative to the CPLI over the sample period. Clearly, both asset allocation paradigms produce large amounts of liability-relative risk, and risk parity is far from a perfect hedge to the CPLI. Nevertheless, it seems clear that risk parity should offer 'less' tracking error relative to liabilities. The 60/40 portfolio consistently experiences larger deviations from the liability benchmark compared to the risk parity portfolio.

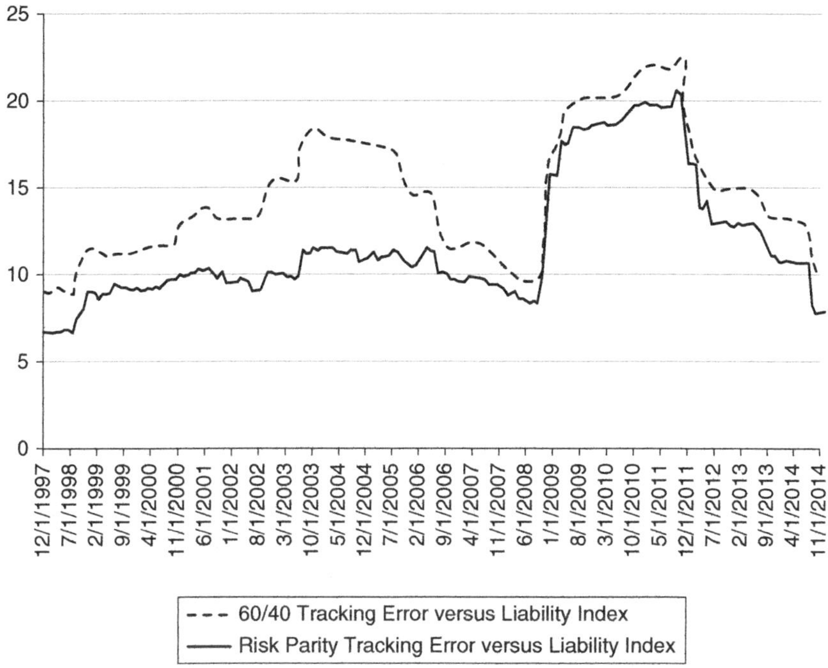

Figure 4.2 Rolling three-year tracking errors versus Citigroup Pension Liability Index (CPLI)

Source: Authors' calculations.

Even risk-averse plan sponsors need to know whether risk parity's reduction in surplus volatility comes at the cost of lower returns. Given its improved diversification profile and the ability to target any desired level of portfolio volatility, there are compelling ex ante reasons to expect that risk parity should be able to outperform its more concentrated counterparts, on average. If the asset portfolio can be constructed so that it is fully compensated for every unit of risk that it assumes (regardless of how much total risk that involves), the expected return on that portfolio ought to be higher than that on a more concentrated, and less efficient, portfolio. The 20-year sample period results in Figures 4.3 and 4.4 support this intuition and demonstrate that, over this historical sample, a volatility-matched risk parity portfolio outperformed a 60/40 implementation in both absolute and risk-adjusted terms. Given the higher historical return and the lower tracking error relative to liabilities, risk parity offered a considerable improvement in terms of surplus efficiency over this period.

It is both natural and valid to question the time-period-specific nature of these outcomes. Without question, the secular decline in bond yields has

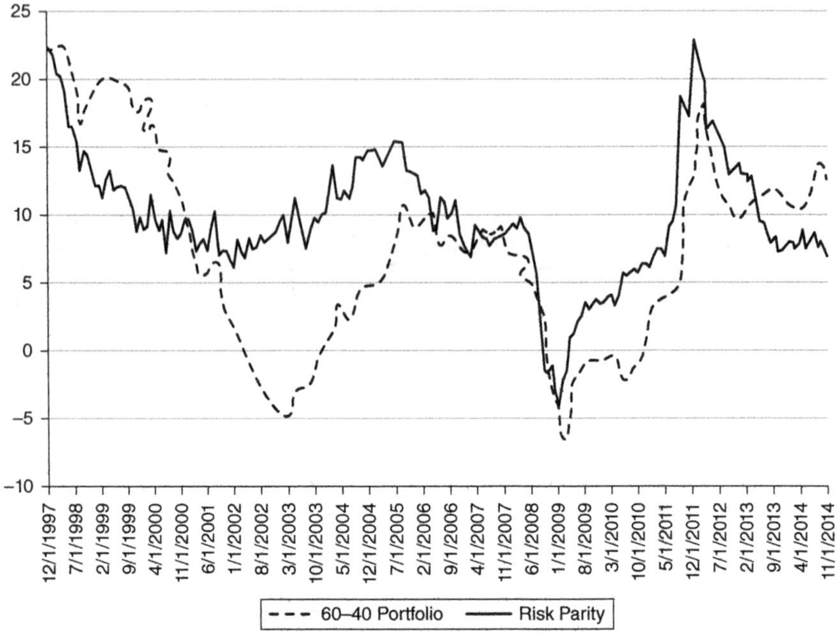

Figure 4.3 Rolling three-year returns

Source: Authors' calculations.

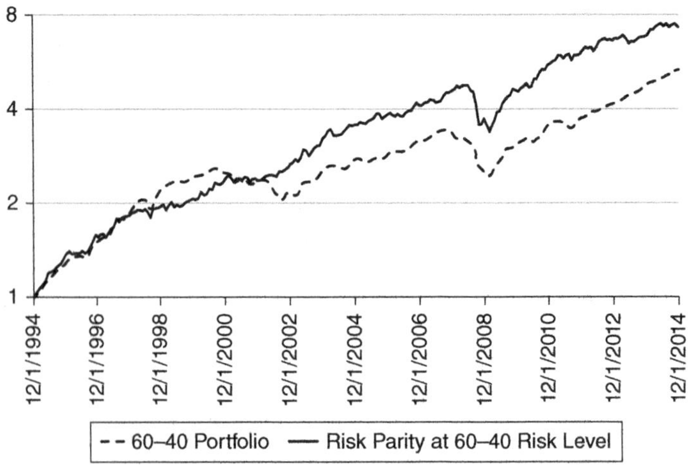

Figure 4.4 Cumulative growth of $1 investment

Source: Authors' calculations.

provided a tailwind for any strategy that allocated meaningfully to fixed income over the past 20 years compared to more equity-centric alternatives. With interest rates considerably lower now than at the beginning of the sample period, forward-looking expectations for risk parity's outperformance versus the 60/40 portfolio should be more modest. While the volatility-reducing properties of risk parity in the DB context remain equally compelling on a forward-looking basis, it is clear that this sample period is a relatively favorable one for the performance of risk parity compared to less balanced alternatives.

Fortunately, forward-looking prospects for risk parity returns remain quite strong, both absolute and relative to the 60/40. Central to this expectation is the more diversified nature of risk parity compared to its more popular and concentrated counterpart. Because the 60/40 derives over 90 percent of its risk from stocks, it is inherently betting that stocks will offer far higher risk-adjusted returns than bonds over the investment horizon. In fact, for such extreme risk concentration to be defensible from a mean-variance optimization perspective, stocks would have to offer over *three times* the Sharpe Ratio (risk-adjusted return) of bonds. With less extreme assumptions for the relative performance of stocks and bonds, the diversification offered by a risk parity allocation is rewarded with higher expected risk-adjusted returns compared to more concentrated alternatives, such as the 60/40. The introduction of liabilities and the tracking error-reducing potential of risk parity make this tradeoff even more compelling than in an asset-only context.

This advantage can be illustrated on a forward-looking basis using SEI's proprietary equilibrium capital market assumptions for expected returns, risks, and correlations among asset classes. Using our assumptions for the 60/40 portfolio, under each asset allocation paradigm, the risk parity portfolio, an LDI portfolio, and a generic liability stream, expected DB pension expenses are simulated for the next decade. The choice of asset portfolio construction mechanism produces the expected effects on both the level and volatility of pension expense. While risk parity dominates the traditional 60/40 paradigm in terms of surplus efficiency, neither methodology can match the liability-hedging properties of full LDI.

The fundamental tradeoffs of these strategies appear in Figure 4.5. The traditional 60/40 approach has far more volatility than the LDI or risk parity strategy. The LDI strategy has minimal expense over the projection period with the lowest amount of volatility. While the 60/40 and risk parity portfolios might be expected to produce positive net income on average, this expectation comes at the expense of significantly higher volatility. Given that the purpose of a DB pension plan is not to generate accounting income, LDI seems to be a much more sensible 'starting point' for plan sponsors, who can then deviate from a full hedging policy in a thoughtful and measured fashion if they view the risk/return tradeoff as favorable.

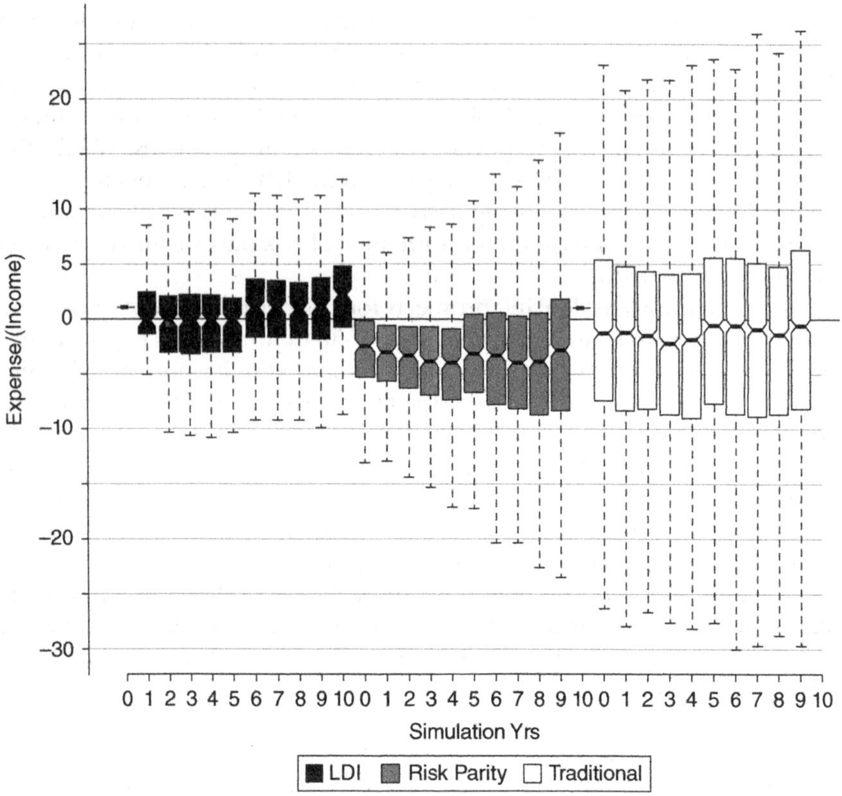

Figure 4.5 Asset allocation under mark-to-market

Note: LDI refers to liability-driven investment.

Source: Authors' calculations.

Conclusion

Despite problems with traditional GAAP for US corporate pensions, plan sponsors have been reluctant to adopt full MTM accounting. Concerns over the resulting additional earnings volatility and the reaction to this likely volatility from investors, equity analysts, and ratings agencies have played key roles. Additional concerns regarding the impact of earnings volatility on compensation plans, as well as the general level of additional earnings 'noise' from actual pension performance, has caused management teams to be wary of adopting this approach. Based on our analysis, however, we believe these concerns are overstated, and that as a noncash accounting change, none of these concerns are material enough to warrant preferring one method over the other.

To the extent that the adoption of MTM accounting has been made in conjunction with the standard investment portfolio implementation, plan sponsors will likely experience a level of expense volatility that can reduced by alternative investment strategies. When measured in relation to the plan expenses and liabilities, both an LDI strategy and a risk parity strategy reduce surplus volatility versus traditional optimized 60/40 implementations. Plan sponsors evaluating a shift to MTM and sensitized to earnings volatility may find that an alternative asset implementation better aligns both their accounting and financial goals.

Endnotes

1. S&P Capital IQ, based on monthly data from 1995 to 2004, with the S&P 500 representing equities and the Barclays US Aggregate representing fixed income.

References

Maurer, R., O. S. Mitchell, R. Rogalla, and I. Siegelin (2016). 'Accounting-based Asset Return Smoothing in Participating Life Annuities: Implications for Annuitants, Insurers, and Policymakers,' in O. S. Mitchell, R. Maurer, and J. M. Orszag, eds, *Retirement System Risk Management: The New Regulatory Order.* Oxford: Oxford University Press, pp. 40–60.

5

Risk Disclosure in the European Insurance Industry: Implications for Occupational Pension Funds

Karel Van Hulle

The original aim of insurance undertakings and occupational pension funds is to pool risks. Through various types of insurance policies, insurance undertakings allow individuals to prepare for their old age by offering them a fixed guarantee. That guarantee is delivered on the basis of an insurance premium paid by policyholders and invested by insurance entities. Similarly, occupational pension funds provided for pension entitlements on the basis of an agreement between the employer and the employees. The entitlement was delivered on the basis of premiums paid by the employer on behalf of the employees and invested by the pension fund at its own risk (often sponsored by the employer).

Because of the volatility in financial markets and increasing longevity, insurance entities and occupational pension funds in the European Union (EU) are moving away from providing fixed guarantees. Investment risk is then no longer borne by the institution, but instead transferred to policyholders (unit-linked businesses) and to the members of the pension fund (defined contribution (DC) plans), who now bear investment risk.

Risk disclosure must take account of this changing environment. It is important to first describe the regulatory changes before analyzing risk disclosure in more detail.

Solvency II: The New Risk-Based Solvency Capital Regime for the European Insurance Industry

All (re)insurance entities, or so-called undertakings, in the EU (about 5,000 in number) must comply with insurance legislation adopted by the Council of the European Union and the European Parliament. This takes the form of a directive, which is a legal instrument addressed to the 28 member states of the EU, requiring them to transpose its provisions into national law within a stated period of time. Application of European legislation by member states is supervised by the European Court of Justice. From January 1, 2016, all EAA member states, that is, all EU member states plus Iceland, Liechtenstein, and Norway, must apply the new risk-based solvency capital regime, commonly referred to as Solvency II. This new regime constitutes a complete overhaul of past insurance solvency regulations, and as such, it will have a profound impact on the activities of (re)insurance entities in the EU.

Why Solvency II?

The prior solvency regime, often referred to as Solvency I, was developed in the 1970s (Sandström 2011). It required insurers to set up technical provisions for their expected risks and to create a capital buffer, called a solvency margin, for unexpected risks. The capital buffer mainly looked at underwriting risk. The disadvantage of this limited approach to risk became apparent during the capital market crisis at the beginning of the 21st century. The capital buffer did not require insurers to hold sufficient capital for market risk, and there were no specific rules dealing with concentration risk. As a result, many insurers that were heavily invested in equity suffered major losses when the value of their investments went down.

In general, Solvency I did not contain an incentive for insurers to manage their risks properly. As a result, some insurers were operating with too much capital, while other insurers were underwriting business for which they lacked capital. Furthermore, studies have shown that, when insurers fail, it is less likely due to an insufficient amount of capital, but more likely to a lack of proper governance and poor management (Sharma 2002). This qualitative aspect of prudential supervision, already recognized in Basel II, had not yet been reflected in EU insurance regulation. Another important weakness that resulted from Solvency I is that insufficient attention was being paid to group supervision. Most supervisors in the EU were in favor of solo supervision and looked at group supervision as a form of supplementary supervision, rather than as a form of supervision in its own right.

In terms of public disclosure and supervisory reporting, Solvency I mainly provided for (limited) supervisory reporting. Public disclosure was limited to the filing of financial statements and an annual report. However, these financial statements, which also served as a basis for prudential supervision under Solvency I, were not fully harmonized (European Economic Community 1991). Moreover, comparability of financial statements between undertakings was limited. This was particularly true for the valuation of technical provisions, for which no agreement could be reached on a uniform accounting treatment.

The 1999 Financial Services Action Plan undertook a reform of the Solvency I regime (European Commission 1999). In contrast to the banking sector, which had already been the subject of a series of reforms, the insurance sector had thus far managed to remain outside the scope of the reforms. It was felt that the creation of an internal market for financial services in the EU could not really take place without a modernization of EU insurance regulation.

Development of Solvency II

The development of the new EU risk-based solvency capital regime started with the European Commission (EC) developing, together with experts from the finance departments of member states and from national supervisory authorities, a Framework for Consultation. This set out the main characteristics of the new solvency regime. On the basis of this Framework, the EC developed a series of questions addressed to the Committee of European Insurance and Occupational Pensions Supervisors (CEIOPS), set up in 2001 as part of the so-called Lamfalussy reform. This grew out of a report submitted by a Committee of Wise Men under the chairmanship of Alexandre Lamfalussy (Lamfalussy 2001). This report emphasized the important role of national supervisory authorities in the practical implementation of EU legislation on financial services. The report also advocated a principles-based approach to regulation, whereby EU regulation should only set principles that could then be implemented by the EC and by national supervisory authorities.

The EC sent out three series of Calls for Advice to CEIOPS over the period 2005–6. This resulted in about 1,000 pages of technical advice subsequently summarized into 60 pages of EU legislation that formed the basis for the new solvency regime. At the request of member states, the EC also codified the 13 existing insurance Directives into one single document, to which were added the new provisions containing the new solvency regime. These replaced the old Solvency I solvency provisions. This document was introduced in 2007 as the official proposal for a Solvency II Framework Directive (European Commission 2007).

Following the Lamfalussy approach, Solvency II was developed as a regulatory regime with different levels. Level 1 contained the basic principles of the new solvency regime. Because of its importance, this level of legislation was adopted by the Council of the European Union and the European Parliament (the co-legislators). Level 2 comprised the implementing measures developed by the EC based upon a delegation from the Council and the European Parliament and upon advice submitted by CEIOPS. Level 3 consisted of Guidelines and Recommendations from CEIOPS to ensure a common interpretation of the new rules. Finally, at Level 4, a series of measures was put in place to ensure proper enforcement.

After the adoption of the Solvency II Framework Directive by the Council and the European Parliament on November 29, 2009 (European Union 2009), the EC and CEIOPS started to prepare the Level 2 and Level 3 measures during the course of 2009–11. The new regime was supposed to start on November 1, 2012, but the financial crisis, initially believed to only influence the Level 2 implementing measures of Solvency II (CEIOPS 2009a), caused important delays in the process. In order to improve the supervisory architecture in the EU, the EC proposed to transform the existing European committees of supervisors, including CEIOPS, into authorities with more powers and resources in order to strengthen EU prudential supervision. This led to the creation of EIOPA, the successor of CEIOPS (European Union 2010a). The creation of EIOPA in turn made it necessary to amend the recently adopted Solvency II Framework Directive. This was done through a new proposal, called Omnibus II, which the Commission introduced in February 2011 (European Commission 2011). This proposal also included a number of transitional measures not provided for in the Solvency II Framework Directive, but which were felt necessary to smooth the transition from Solvency I into Solvency II.

The negotiation of Omnibus II took more time than expected (three years), for a number of political and technical reasons. On the political side, the European Parliament, whose powers had been increased as a result of the Lisbon Treaty of December 13, 2007 (European Union 2007), wanted to have more say in the development of the new solvency regime. It therefore insisted that a number of topics traditionally dealt with by the EC would now be adopted at Level 1. Furthermore, it insisted that the Solvency II Framework Directive would allow the adoption of Regulatory Technical Standards and Implementing Technical Standards, which would be developed by EIOPA and become legally binding after endorsement by the EC. The advantage of this approach was that both the Council and the European Parliament would then have the possibility to scrutinize the texts before their endorsement at the EC. On the technical side, the low interest rate environment and the volatility in financial markets made it difficult to develop a solution for the treatment of long-term guarantees. It was difficult to agree on the definition of the appropriate risk-free rate for the discounting of technical provisions, since the government bond rate, which had until the break-out of the financial crisis been considered as the reference point for a risk-free rate, could no longer be considered as risk-free. In addition, because of the existence of many different life insurance products, a one-size-fits-all solution for the treatment of long-term guarantees was not possible. Moreover, it was necessary to introduce tailor-made transitional measures for the existing book of life insurance contracts, which had been negotiated in a completely different legal and economic environment.

Omnibus II was finally adopted on April 16, 2014 (European Union 2014). Because of the delay in the finalization of the Level 1 regulation, it was impossible to proceed with the adoption of the Level 2 and Level 3 rules. As a result, the start date of Solvency II had to be postponed several times. The Level 2 legislation was adopted as a Commission Delegated Act on October 10, 2014, published in the *Official Journal of the European Union* on January 17, 2015 after a three-month scrutiny by the European Parliament and the Council (European Commission 2014a). Meanwhile, EIOPA had started the development of the Level 3 rules in the form of technical standards (Regulatory Technical Standards and Implementing Technical Standards) and guidelines. All relevant texts were finalized in June 2015. As a result of the delays in the development of Solvency II, the new regime became applicable in 2016. Member states need to transpose the Framework Directive of 2009 (amended by Omnibus II in 2014) by March 31, 2015. In total, the Solvency II package will comprise about 2,000 pages of regulation.

Essential features of Solvency II

Solvency II follows the three-pillar approach of Basel II. The first pillar contains the quantitative requirements; the second pillar the qualitative requirements; and the third pillar the supervisory reporting and disclosure requirements. The three pillars are of equal importance and are interlinked. Overarching them is group supervision, which is equally important to solo supervision (see Figure 5.1).

As the new solvency regime applies to all (re)insurance entities, the nature, size, and complexity of the businesses concerned must be taken into account. This is done through the proportionality principle, which applies to all provisions in each of the three pillars. Moreover, this principle must be respected by the EC and by EIOPA in the further development of the Level 2 and Level 3 measures, and it must also guide supervisory authorities when carrying out their task.

Pillar 1 requires the development of a solvency balance sheet in which all assets and liabilities are calculated on a market-consistent basis. Two capital requirements are introduced: a Solvency Capital Requirement (SCR) which reflects unexpected quantifiable risks (such as market risk, credit risk, underwriting risk, and operational risk) and can be calculated on the basis of a standard formula[1] or on the basis of an internal model to be approved by the supervisory authority and a Minimum Capital Requirement (MCR), which represents an absolute floor. If the SCR is breached, the supervisory

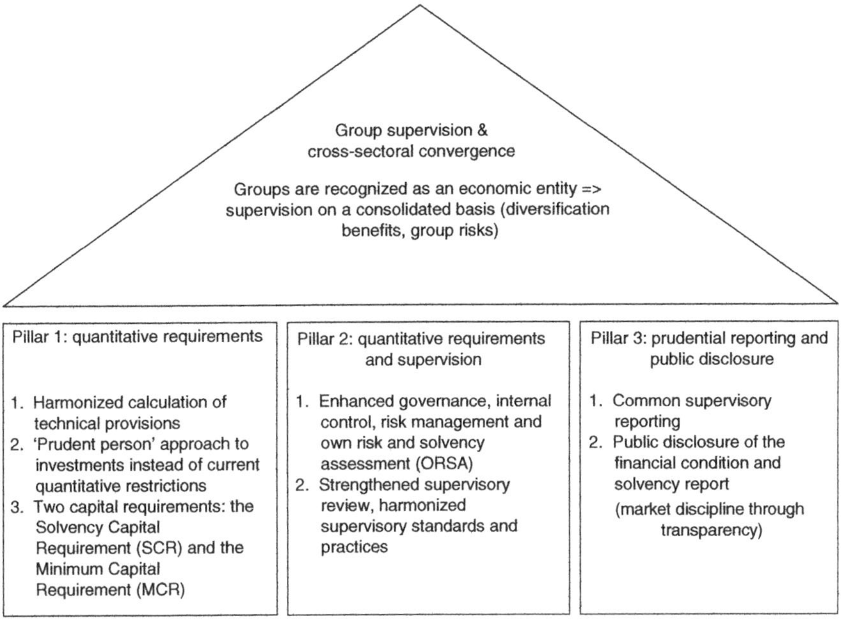

Figure 5.1 Financial regulation: three pillars and a roof

Source: Author's contribution.

authority must analyze the causes for the breach together with the insurance undertaking concerned as part of the Supervisory Review Process (SRP). This dialogue is an essential feature of Solvency II, and remedies must be taken to ensure that the SCR is restored as quickly as possible. If the Minimum Capital Requirement (MCR) is breached, the supervisory authority must place the undertaking into run-off. The SCR does not provide an absolute guarantee, since it is calculated on the basis of a confidence level of 99.5 percent VaR over a one-year time horizon. Figure 5.2 provides an overview of Pillar 1.

Pillar 2 introduces the new governance rules, which require all insurers to implement four functions: risk management, internal control, internal audit, and actuarial. The persons managing these functions as well as the members of the board must be fit and proper. Each undertaking must develop an own risk and solvency assessment (ORSA) at least annually, in which it examines its solvency position in comparison with its SCR. The ORSA, which can be regarded as the DNA of the insurance undertaking, must ensure that the undertaking does not underwrite business for which it lacks the necessary capital. Pillar 2 also introduces new (more extensive) powers for supervisory authorities, such as on-site and off-site inspection, and stress testing.

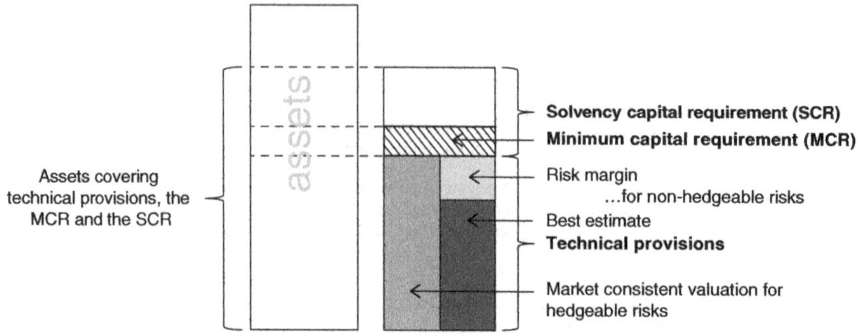

Figure 5.2 Overview of Pillar One

Source: Author's contribution.

Pillar 3 deals with public disclosure and supervisory reporting. All insurers must produce a Solvency and Financial Condition Report which must be made publicly available. In addition, they must provide supervisory authorities with the regular ORSA supervisory report, along with annual and quarterly quantitative templates specifying in greater detail and supplementing the information presented in the Solvency and Financial Condition Report. Small insurers may be relieved from some of the supervisory reporting requirements on the basis of the proportionality principle.

As group supervision has now been elevated to the same importance as solo supervision, parent undertakings will also have to calculate a group SCR and a group MCR. They must conduct a group ORSA, prepare and publish a Group Solvency and Financial Condition Report, and submit to national supervisory authorities annual and quarterly quantitative templates.

Occupational Pension Funds

Occupational pension funds became the subject of EU regulation rather late, to some extent due to the fact that pension policy had traditionally been regarded as 'national territory.' In accordance with EU law, member states retain full responsibility for the organization of their pension systems, as well as for decisions on the relative roles of each of the three retirement system pillars (social security, occupational pension funds, and private insurance/savings). Attempts by the EC to create an internal market for occupational pension funds were initially strongly resisted by member states, as they were considered a direct attack on what had been traditionally regarded as an area of exclusive competence for member states.

Today, there are about 110,000 pension funds in the EU, most of which are situated in Ireland (62,000), the UK (44,600), the Netherlands (381),

Italy (310), Belgium (199), Portugal (191), Germany (178), and Sweden (85). There are virtually no employer-based pension funds in the new member states in Central and Eastern Europe, or in the Baltic States.

The Institutions for Occupational Retirement Provision (IORP) Directive of 2003

The 1999 Financial Services Action Plan stressed the urgent need to deal at EU level with the prudential supervision of institutions for occupational retirement provision (IORPs). Two main reasons were given. First, occupational pension funds are major financial institutions with a key role in ensuring the integration, efficiency, and liquidity of financial markets. Second, making them subject to a coherent EU legislative framework would allow them to benefit fully from the advantages of the internal market.

The first step on the way to an internal market for occupational pension funds was made by the IORP Directive. An occupational pension fund is defined in Article 6(a) of this Directive as

> an institution, irrespective of its legal form, operating on a funded basis, established separately from any sponsoring undertaking or trade for the purpose of providing retirement benefits in the context of an occupational activity on the basis of an agreement or a contract agreed, individually or collectively between the employer(s) and the employee(s) or their respective representatives, or with self-employed persons, in compliance with the legislation of the home and host Member States. (European Community 2003: 5)

The Directive required occupational pension funds to be registered and to be supervised by a competent supervisory authority. It laid down some solvency rules (technical provisions, investment rules, regulatory own funds) and made it possible for undertakings located in one member state to sponsor an occupational pension fund authorized in another member state. The prudential rules for occupational pension funds that offer defined benefits are similar to those applying to life insurance undertakings. They are therefore also required to hold regulatory own funds that serve as a buffer. Occupational pension funds that only provide for DC pension schemes do not have to hold a capital buffer.

As far as technical provisions are concerned, Article 15 of the IORP Directive required IORPs to establish an adequate amount of liabilities corresponding to the financial commitments arising out of pension contracts. Where IORPs provide for defined benefit (DB) pension schemes, they are required to establish sufficient technical provisions in respect of the total range of these schemes. The minimum amount of these technical provisions is to be calculated on a forward-looking, going-concern basis, including a margin for adverse deviation. The Directive does not require a risk-free discount rate: rather, it allows the use of asset-based rates, high-quality corporate bond yields, and government bond yields. Article 14(2) of the IORP Directive provides for supervisory powers if an institution fails to establish sufficient technical provisions, but it does not include the explicit supervisory power to require the IORP to increase the amount of technical provisions.

In terms of transparency, the Directive requires an occupational pension fund to provide certain information to the competent authorities, such as its annual accounts and annual reports. Yet there are no specific rules for these annual accounts and annual reports. The authorities are particularly interested in collecting information about funding, operational, market, liquidity, and credit risks (EIOPA 2011). Members and beneficiaries must also receive, on request, a copy of the annual accounts and of the annual report, as well as of the statement of investment policy principles. Each member may also request detailed and substantial information on key elements of the pension scheme.

Revision of the IORP Directive

Though one of the main objectives of the 2003 Directive was to open up the market for cross-border pension arrangements, it must be admitted that the Directive was not a success. Indeed, the number of cross-border arrangements increased marginally from 70 in June 2008 to 76 in 2015. Compared with the total number of occupational pension funds in the EU (110,000), this can hardly be called an impressive achievement (EIOPA 2015). There are numerous reasons for this: the need for an occupational pension fund to respect the local social and labor law (and the lack of clarity about this concept), the need to ensure that the technical provisions are fully funded at all times in the case of cross-border activity, the difficulty of transferring pension assets from one member state to another, and the difficulties in dealing with different national supervisory authorities in home and host member states. Although the last topic was governed by the so-called Budapest Protocol in the context of CEIOPS (CEIOPS 2009b), the working relationships between home and host authorities were made difficult by a lack of clarity about the applicable rules. CEIOPS therefore called several times on the EC to revise the IORP Directive on this particular issue.

While the EC was preparing an overhaul of its solvency rules for insurance undertakings, the question was raised in 2006 whether occupational pension funds should be included in the scope of the new solvency regime (Solvency II). There was some logic to this, particularly for DB schemes. In fact, past reference had been made in the IORP Directive to the Solvency I rules applying to life insurance undertakings, rules that would be abolished under Solvency II. It would therefore seem logical to make the new solvency rules also applicable to occupational pension funds. Yet after reflection, the EC decided not to extend the scope of application of Solvency II to occupational pension funds because the Quantitative Impact Studies (QIS) that analyzed the potential impact of the new solvency regime on the insurance industry did not cover occupational pension funds. It was believed to be imprudent to extend the application of the new regime without prior examination of the potential impact. Yet organizing a new QIS specifically for occupational pension funds would have delayed the introduction of the new solvency regime.

During the negotiation of the Solvency II Framework Directive in the European Parliament, several amendments were tabled asking for an extension of the scope to include occupational pension funds. In the end, the Council and the European Parliament decided to keep the status quo. In the Preamble of the Solvency II Framework Directive (recital 138), the EC was asked to conduct a review of the IORP Directive as soon as possible.

On July 7, 2010, the Commission published a Green Paper for consultation on adequate, sustainable, and safe European pension systems (European Commission 2010). It drew almost 1,700 responses from across the EU, including from member states, national parliaments, business and trade union organizations, civil society, and industry representatives. The Green Paper puts much emphasis on the adequacy and sustainability of pension promises. In order to ensure sustainability, the Green Paper proposed a revision of the solvency rules in the IORP Directive. In order to ensure that occupational pensions can actually deliver what they promise, the liabilities and the assets to cover those liabilities must be properly reflected on the solvency balance sheet. In a follow-up White Paper on adequate, sustainable, and safe European pension systems of February 16, 2012, the EC confirmed its intention to revise the IORP Directive (European Commission 2012a).

On April 7, 2011, the EC asked EIOPA for advice on a revision of the IORP Directive. The EC gave three main reasons: the development of measures which would simplify the setting up of cross-border pension schemes; the introduction of a risk-based solvency regime for occupational pension funds coupled with measures that would allow pension funds to benefit from risk mitigation mechanisms; and a modernization of the prudential rules covering DC schemes. EIOPA organized two consultations on its draft advice. On February 15, 2012, EIOPA came forward with its final advice (518 pages), and it organized an exchange of views among stakeholders during a public hearing in March 2012 (EIOPA 2012).

In its advice on possible new (harmonized) solvency rules, EIOPA proposed the adoption of a holistic balance sheet to allow full comparability between the different risk-sharing mechanisms that exist in member states.

The allocation of the demographic and financial risks of occupational pension commitments differs greatly between member states. Thus, risks are sometimes borne by the pension fund itself (e.g., in the Netherlands), by the sponsoring undertaking (e.g., in the United Kingdom), by the members and beneficiaries (e.g., in the case of DC pension schemes), or any combination thereof. European pension funds also use different security mechanisms, such as solvency capital, sponsor support, and pension protection schemes, and they use different benefit adjustment mechanisms, such as conditional indexation, for-profit mechanisms, and the possibility of reducing accrued benefits as a measure of last resort.

In the holistic balance sheet proposed by EIOPA, all security and benefit adjustment mechanisms must be explicitly included. Thus, the asset side would include the value of sponsor support and pension protection schemes, while the liability side takes account of the unconditional, conditional, and discretionary nature of the benefits as well as possible benefit reductions. The holistic balance sheet follows the market-consistent approach of Solvency II: all assets and liabilities must be valued on a market-consistent basis. In the view of EIOPA, this is the only way to achieve a comparable and realistic view of an occupational pension fund's financial situation. The Solvency Capital Requirement (SCR) in the holistic balance sheet measures whether the pension fund has sufficient capital, security mechanisms, and/or benefit adjustment mechanisms to absorb demographic and financial shocks given a certain confidence level (99.5 percent VaR over a one-year time horizon).

At the request of the EC, EIOPA carried out a QIS in 2012 to collect information on the financial impact of the holistic balance sheet on occupational pension funds. Results of this QIS were published in July 2013 (EIOPA 2013), and eight member states participated in the exercise: Belgium, Denmark, Ireland, the Netherlands, Norway (member of the European Economic Area), Portugal, Sweden, and the United Kingdom. In the benchmark scenario, IORPs were requested to include all security and benefit adjustment mechanisms on their holistic balance sheet, and to value all assets and liabilities on a market-consistent basis by discounting future cash flows using the risk-free interest rate. It is important to note that IORPs providing only pure DC schemes, which do not provide any guarantees, were not included in the QIS exercise.

In its report on this QIS exercise, EIOPA pointed out that the overall impact of the holistic balance sheet differed substantially across participating countries, from substantial surpluses in some countries to large shortfalls in other countries. This is due to differences in the availability of financial assets and the relative strength of the existing security and benefit adjustment mechanisms. For instance, German 'Pensionsfonds' are able to reduce the SCR to zero through the loss-absorbing capacity of sponsor support and pension protection schemes, the latter effectively absorbing all residual risk. On the other hand, the German 'Pensionskassen' in most cases have sponsor support but are not covered by the national pension protection scheme. This results in a relatively modest shortfall relative to liabilities and the SCR. In Ireland, there was a substantial shortfall because the sponsor support on which the IORP can count is not legally mandatory, so the employer can choose not to provide support. In the UK, there is a shortfall with respect to liabilities as well as the SCR. All IORPs in the UK are covered by unlimited sponsor support, but the value of sponsor support recognized is, in most cases, not sufficient to close the gap, nor does the Pension Protection Fund guarantee the full level of benefits. EIOPA decided to continue its technical work to improve the definitions and methodologies for implementing the holistic balance sheet. In 2014, it launched a public consultation on 'Further Work on Solvency of IORPs' (EIOPA 2014), met with great reservations by the pension fund sector.[2]

The main argument against introducing a Solvency II type of regime was that the holistic balance sheet approach was conceptually wrong. It suggested that a volatile mark-to-market valuation of pension liabilities would be unsuitable for the assessment of very long-duration pension liabilities, since reflecting these liabilities at their current market value would be purely theoretical and not informative on future developments of the IORP's financial position. Other arguments referred to the unacceptable burden that such a regime would place on IORPs and their sponsors, with the consequence that employers would no longer want to provide this important social benefit and that members' benefits would be lowered as the members would have to bear additional costs. The holistic balance sheet would not be suitable as a regulatory instrument at EU level. At most it could serve as an internal risk management tool. As stated by Pensions Europe: 'Putting more money aside to cover risks that might be overcome over time would also make long-term investment financing of the economy more difficult and would have a substantial impact on further economic development, innovation and growth' (2015: 3).

The issue of volatility was also discussed at the OECD, which concluded that

> disclosure to plan stakeholders based on current market values of pension assets and liabilities may be appropriate to increase transparency, and the use of current market values could improve risk management. However, regulators should operate flexibly when reviewing a scheme's funding position or regulators should enable pension funds and plan sponsors to dampen somewhat the volatility of market prices when determining contributions. (Yermo and Severinson 2010: 4–5)

Meanwhile, after serious lobbying by the social partners at EU level,[3] and by an alliance of five governments (Belgium, Germany, Ireland, the Netherlands, and the United Kingdom), published on the website of the

Belgian Federation of Pension Funds (BVPI), the EC announced in May 2013 that it would come forward with a proposal to revise the IORP Directive without a Solvency II-type regime. The proposal was presented in March 2014 (European Commission 2014b). Although it left the solvency rules in the 2003 Directive largely untouched, the proposal led to a great deal of controversy in the EC and the business community. Within the EC, the Impact Assessment Board, whose opinion is required for every proposal made by the EC, refused to give a positive opinion on the proposal to revise the IORP Directive. In the business community, Business Europe called for 'a thorough overhaul' of the new Commission proposal. This statement led to an opposing statement in December of 2014 by a number of organizations representing civil society,[4] insisting that 'this modest proposal' should be adopted as quickly as possible. Under the Greek and Italian Presidencies, the Council made swift progress in the course of 2014 and adopted its position on the proposal on December 10, 2014. This position enabled negotiation with the European Parliament. However, because it was uncertain whether the EC would withdraw its proposal, the European Parliament only appointed a Rapporteur for the proposal in December 2014. The discussion within the European Parliament is ongoing, with a vote in the European Parliament to be followed by negotiations with the Council and with the EC. The plenary vote in the European Parliament took place in December 2015. Final approval by the Council and the European Parliament seems likely during the course of 2016.

Essential features of the Revised IORP Directive Proposal

The revised IORP proposal had four key objectives: (1) to improve governance and risk management within IORPs; (2) to remove the remaining obstacles for cross-border provision of services; (3) to ensure that supervisors have the necessary tools to effectively supervise IORPs; and (4) to provide clear and relevant information to members and beneficiaries.

While there was a great deal of disagreement about the usefulness of introducing quantitative rules similar to Solvency II, most stakeholders agreed that there was a need to improve the governance requirements for occupational pension funds (European Commission 2012b). A number of examples of failures or difficulties resulting from a lack of risk management in pension funds were provided in the EC's Impact Assessment Report accompanying the Revised IORP Directive Proposal (2014c). There also was a large degree of support for improved information for pension scheme members and beneficiaries, particularly in the case of DC pensions.

The governance provisions (Articles 21 to 30) were largely borrowed from Solvency II, (Articles 40 to 50 of the Solvency II Framework Directive) although they are less detailed. IORPs will have to put in place key governance functions: risk management, internal audit, and actuarial (only required for IORPs that run DB pension schemes). Internal control is not established as a separate function. The persons occupying these functions must be fit and proper. Great importance is attached to proper risk management. Similar to the ORSA for insurance undertakings under Solvency II, IORPs will need to carry out their own risk assessment by producing a risk evaluation for pensions in order to document that assessment (Article 29). If conducted properly, this risk evaluation should clearly show any funding gaps and force IORPs to think about ways and means to close that gap. In the proposal, the EC can further develop the principles in the Directive concerning risk evaluation in a Delegated Act. However, the Delegated Act 'shall not impose additional funding requirements beyond those foreseen in the Directive' (Article 30).

As under Solvency II (Article 29 of the Solvency II Framework Directive), supervision of IORPs will have to be based on a prospective and risk-based approach (Article 61). The proposal (Article 63) also introduces the Supervisory Review Process, which is a key element of Solvency II (Article 36 of the Solvency II Framework Directive). Although Article 63 of the proposal is more modest than Article 36 of the Solvency II Framework Directive, it still upgrades the role of the supervisory authorities by requiring them to carry out an assessment of the qualitative requirements relating to the system of governance, of the risks the institution faces, and of the ability of the institution to assess those risks. It also introduces stress-testing as a monitoring tool. IORPs must also make available to the competent authorities a copy of their risk evaluations for pensions (Article 64). New provisions (Articles 66 to 71) deal with professional secrecy; the transmission of information to central banks, monetary authorities, European Supervisory Authorities—EIOPA, European Securities and Markets Authority (ESMA), and European Banking Authority (EBA)—and the European Systemic Risk Board (ESRB); the disclosure of information to government administrations responsible for financial legislation; and conditions for the exchange of information.

A crucial feature of the proposal concerns the information to members and beneficiaries. It introduces a Pension Benefit Statement standardized at EU level (Articles 40 to 54) that provides pension scheme members with simple and clear information about their individual pension entitlements. It aims to support informed decision-making about pension adequacy (answering the question 'do I need to save more to maintain my standard of living after retirement?') and investment strategy (answering the question 'is my investment approach right?'). The Pension Benefit Statement was inspired by the Key Investor Document (KID) required under the legislation on open investment funds (European Union 2010b). It is particularly important in the case of DC pension schemes where members bear investment risk. In order to have a standardized document, the proposal provides for the EC to further specify the form and the contents of the Pension Benefit Statement in a Delegated Act (Article 54). The proposal also provides for information to be given to prospective members (Article 55), to members during the pre-retirement phase (Article 56), and to beneficiaries during the pay-out phase.

The Council adopted its position on the EC proposal in December of 2014 (the so-called 'general approach'). Any disagreements between the Council and the European Parliament will be dealt with during a Trilogue, in which both co-legislators and the EC will participate. The Council's position departs to some extent from the proposal introduced by the EC. The most important departures include the fact that the Council does not accept any Delegated Act, which means that the provisions in the Directive on subjects such as the Risk Evaluation for Pensions and the Pension Benefit Statement will have to be self-sufficient. Moreover, the Council introduces internal control as the fourth key function. The Council also considers that persons running the IORP should have adequate professional qualifications collectively, rather than individually. The Council further details the contents of the Risk Evaluation for Pensions. And the Council removed some of the form requirements for the Pension Benefit Statement and made a clearer distinction between the information to be given in the case of a DC pension scheme and a DB pension scheme.

Comparison between Insurance Undertakings and Occupational Pension Funds

The discussions about applying Solvency II measures to occupational pensions clearly show that there often is a lack of understanding about the differences between insurance entities and pension funds. Identifying who bears the ultimate risk and what types of risk disclosures are relevant is thus in order.

Are occupational pension funds financial institutions?

It is often argued that occupational pension funds are financial institutions like banks or insurance undertakings. Accordingly, the same risk-based solvency approach should apply to all such categories of financial institutions, and doing otherwise would destroy the level playing field in the market.

Nevertheless, this view overlooks the fact that occupational pension funds are institutions created by the social partners, employers, and employees. It is for them to decide what pension entitlements will be available and under which conditions. Under this latter perspective, several consequences flow. First, in terms of the definitive character of the pension promise: a pension promise agreed between the social partners can more easily be changed than an insurance contract. Second, in terms of the party that bears the ultimate risk: occupational pension funds are linked to a sponsoring employer, while insurance undertakings are ultimately liable for the risks which they underwrite. Third, in terms of transparency: because of their close linkage to a sponsoring employer, there may be less need for occupational pension funds to provide information (such as financial statements) to the public at large than is the case for insurance undertakings. Fourth, in terms of the supply of capital: the suppliers of capital to an occupational pension fund (employers and members) have more extensive commitments than providers of equity to insurance undertakings. They may be required to provide additional capital in the case of a shortfall, they might have to accept a reduction in the benefits, or they may have to spread the cost between generations for schemes of a collective nature. Fifth, in terms of the governance of the institution: occupational pension funds are not-for-profit entities and the members or their representatives are often closely involved in the governance of the institution. Sixth, in terms of supervision: the average duration of pension fund liabilities is longer than in the case of insurance undertakings, which means that more time can be given to occupational pension funds to recover a funding deficit. Seventh, in terms of the competent authority for supervision: as occupational pension funds can be seen as part of the broader social policy of the country, the competent authority for the supervision of occupational pension funds is not necessarily the same as the competent authority for the supervision of insurance undertakings.

Despite these differences, occupational pension funds manage assets worth €2.6 trillion and are important players in the financial market. They are important institutional investors and can compete with insurance entities. This is particularly true in a number of European countries (for instance, Sweden), where insurance entities carry the pension liabilities on their balance sheet. Less stringent investment rules and the use of a discount rate that is not risk-free (for instance, determined by reference to the expected rate of return on assets) can distort a pension fund's true financial situation. It can therefore rightly be argued that the overall supervisory regime for occupational pension funds should broadly follow that which applies to banks and insurance entities. This is also valid from a financial stability point of view, considering the overall importance of occupational pension funds and the size of DB pensions. In terms of transparency, it is difficult to argue that members should not be informed about the funding position of their DB pension scheme. In the end, it is all about risk. Information based upon a mark-to-market valuation, properly applied and taking into account the long duration of pension liabilities, is still the best reflection of risk.

The movement from DB to DC

Initially, the workplace-based pension schemes offered in Europe were DB schemes. The employer committed to pay to the employee a lifetime monthly benefit on retirement for each year of service. The risks during the accumulation phase (e.g., investment and operational risk) and the biometric risk during the pay-out phase (mortality) are fully borne either by the employer, the pension fund, or both. By contrast, in DC schemes, the employer commits to contributing on behalf of the employees a certain cash amount per month of service. At retirement, the employee can access the savings accumulated in the pension fund to finance the pay-out phase, and risks during the accumulation phase are fully borne by the employee. The employee also fully bears the biometric risk during the pay-out phase, unless national law mandates the purchase of an annuity (as was the case in the UK until recently). Between the two ends of the spectrum, there are a number of hybrid schemes such as average-salary DB schemes, DC schemes with guarantees, part DB/DC schemes, etc. Hybrid schemes also share the risks between employers and employees.

DC schemes are comparable to investment funds because the outcome depends entirely on investment returns. DB schemes are comparable to life insurance products because they offer protection against risk. DB schemes are not necessarily risk-free for members and beneficiaries: they may reduce accrued pension rights if their funding position deteriorates. This happened, for instance, in the Netherlands, where since the outbreak of the financial crisis, 68 IORPs were compelled to curtail accrued pension rights, affecting 300,000 individuals. In the UK, pension funds that fail may be taken over by the Pension Protection Fund, but in that case, pension rights are cut by 10 percent (European Commission 2014c).

For a number of reasons such as the low interest rate environment and the increase of longevity, many occupational pension funds have discontinued DB pension schemes and are now operating DC pension schemes. In the EU, the predominant pension scheme is DC in Bulgaria, Denmark, Ireland, Greece, Spain, France, Italy, Cyprus, Latvia, Lithuania, Luxembourg, Hungary, Austria, Poland, Romania, Slovenia, and Slovakia; while it is DB in Belgium, Germany, the Netherlands, Portugal, Finland, Sweden, and the United Kingdom (European Commission 2014c). Those who oppose the introduction of risk-based solvency requirements for occupational pension funds argue that the introduction of such a regime could further fuel the movement towards DC pensions. The solvency debate is largely limited to those occupational pension funds that offer DB pension schemes. Already today, the IORP Directive provides for a different treatment between IORPs that operate a DB pension scheme and IORPs that operate a DC pension scheme. It is only in the first case that IORPs must hold a capital buffer. If a risk-based solvency regime were to be broadly introduced, that distinction would remain. But IORPs that only operate DC pension schemes would need to introduce a capital buffer for operational risk.

The movement from DB to DC can also be seen in the insurance industry. Low interest rates and rising longevity have led many insurers to avoid long-term guarantees and instead introduce various forms of unit-linked products whereby the policyholder bears the ultimate investment risk. By doing so, insurance undertakings will need to hold less capital.

Looked at from a Solvency II perspective, occupational pension funds and insurance undertakings find themselves in a similar situation: as both move away from offering some form of hard guarantee, they must hold less capital. This is not so much the result of the new risk-based solvency regime, but the logical consequence of a policy change responding to the new socio-economic environment. For both sectors, the question that remains is how to deal with existing contracts that offer long-term guarantees. Under Solvency II, this matter has been dealt with in the context of the amendment of the Solvency II Framework Directive by Omnibus II. A similar solution (including a long transition period) could also be introduced for occupational pension funds. Key in this respect is an agreement on the applicable risk-free discount rate for the calculation of pension liabilities.

Risk Disclosure

The transparency requirements under Solvency II (Pillar 3) distinguish between supervisory reporting and public disclosure. At present, the EU requirements (which are minimum requirements) on supervisory reporting and public disclosure for insurance entities and pension funds are relatively modest. This will fundamentally change for insurers under Solvency II. For the first time, harmonized information will be available at the EU level, both to national competent authorities (and to EIOPA), and to the public at large. This will be done through a supervisory reporting package which includes quarterly and annual reporting templates, through the Solvency and Financial Conditions Report, and through the annual accounts and annual report. Both in the supervisory reporting package and in the Solvency and Financial Conditions Report, risk disclosure plays an important role. Risk disclosure under Solvency II relates to the risks incurred by the insurance entity and it will be available to the public at large.

For occupational pension funds, the proposal to revise the 2003 Directive will introduce more elaborate supervisory reporting requirements. Because of the absence of harmonized Pillar 1 requirements (on capital and on valuation of assets and liabilities), the information collected by national competent authorities and transmitted to EIOPA or to the ESRB will remain difficult to compare. In terms of public disclosure, occupational pension funds are not required to provide any specific information about the risks incurred to the public at large. The information requirements are limited to the prospective members, members, and beneficiaries. A key element in the disclosure to the members is the new proposed Pension Benefit Statement. Risk disclosure in the case of occupational pension funds is directed to the members and beneficiaries and covers the risks related to their pension scheme. This information is not available to the public at large.

Solvency and Financial Conditions Report (SFCR)

The SFCR is a new document introduced under Solvency II, which seeks to further market discipline. Article 51 of the Solvency II Framework Directive lists the main elements, which must be disclosed in the SFCR:

(1) a description of the business and the performance of the undertaking;
(2) a description of the system of governance and an assessment of its adequacy for the risk profile of the undertaking;
(3) a description by risk category of the risk exposure, concentration, mitigation, and sensitivity;
(4) a description—separately for assets, technical provisions, and other liabilities—of the bases and methods used for their valuation, together with an explanation of any major differences in the bases and methods used for their valuation in financial statements; and
(5) a description of the capital management process.

These requirements are further elaborated upon in Articles 290–303 of the Delegated Act of November 2014. Article 295 of the Delegated Act deals specifically with disclosures related to the risk profile of the undertaking. These include:

(1) quantitative and qualitative information regarding the risk profile, separately for underwriting risk, market risk, credit risk, liquidity risk, operational risk, and other material risks;
(2) information regarding the risk exposure (including from off-balance sheet positions and the transfer of risk to special purpose vehicles), such as a description of the measures used to assess risks within the undertaking, a description of the material risks that the undertaking is exposed to, and a description about the investment of assets in accordance with the prudent person principle;

(3) a description of the material risk concentration to which the undertaking is exposed;
(4) a description of the techniques used for mitigating risks and the processes for monitoring the continued effectiveness of these techniques;
(5) with regard to liquidity risk: the total amount of the expected profit included in future premiums;
(6) with regard to risk sensitivity: a description of the methods used, the assumptions made, and the outcome of stress-testing and sensitivity analysis for material risks and events; and
(7) other information regarding the risk profile of the insurance undertaking.

In case of major developments significantly affecting the relevance of the SFCR, the information must be updated frequently.

Insurers are not required to disclose any specific information about specific risks incurred by policyholders. The presumption is that, if all relevant risks are properly managed by the undertaking, the solvency position resulting from this will most likely (subject to the agreed confidence level) allow the insurer to deliver its promises to policyholders. In terms of specific product-related disclosures to policyholders, the Solvency II Framework Directive (Articles 183–6) includes the provisions of the earlier Directives which deal particularly with the pre-contractual information to be delivered to policyholders. These provisions were not updated during the negotiation of Solvency II. Most member states have, however, extended the information requirements in their national insurance legislation, as part of their insurance contract law.

Risk disclosure by occupational pension funds

As indicated before, present EU legislation does not impose any public disclosure on occupational pension funds. Pension scheme arrangements agreed between an employer and its employees are regarded as private arrangements. Moreover, the beneficiaries of the pension scheme arrangements are at the same time members of the pension fund, so the disclosure provisions in the 2003 Directive are limited to information requirements directed to the members and beneficiaries. The information to be given to the members and beneficiaries in accordance with Article 11 of the 2003 Directive comprises the annual accounts and annual reports, the statement of investment principles, and some information concerning the pension benefits. Members bearing investment risk must receive information concerning investment options, along with information on risk exposure and costs related to the investments.

The proposal to revise the 2003 Directive does not fundamentally change this approach. Contrary to Solvency II, the proposal does not introduce any requirement for occupational pension funds to disclose their overall risk position to the outside world. However, following the advice of EIOPA, the proposal attaches a great deal of importance to more in-depth information of the members through the new Pension Benefit Statement. This Statement must be sent to each member at least once every 12 months free of charge with an explanation of any material change to the information contained in the pension statement compared to the previous year in an accompanying letter. The statement should be easily understandable and should not be more than two pages. It should clearly state whether there is a full guarantee (by the institution or the sponsoring undertaking), no guarantee at all (where the member bears the investment risk), or a partial guarantee. Where a guarantee is provided, the statement must briefly explain the nature of the guarantee, the current level of financing of the member's accrued individual entitlements, the mechanisms protecting accrued individual entitlements, and any benefit reduction mechanisms. The statement must further include information about the balance after calculation of the contributions and the costs and show the projected benefits under various hypotheses as well as give information about past performance.

For pension schemes where members bear investment risk, the pension benefit statement must contain information about the risk and return profile showing a graphical indicator of the risk and return profile of the pension scheme or, where applicable, of each investment option. For pension schemes where members bear investment risk and where they have a choice between different investment options, the statement must indicate the investment profiles providing a list of the investment options available and a short description of each option. For pension schemes where members bear investment risk and where an investment option is imposed on the member by a specific rule specified in the pension scheme (default option), additional information must be provided concerning the rules based on actual age, the rules based on the member's targeted retirement age, and other rules. The EC will further elaborate the details both in terms of form and substance by way of a Delegated Act.

In addition to the Pension Benefit Statement, the proposal includes information requirements for prospective members, for members during the pre-retirement phase, and for beneficiaries during the pay-out phase. On request, members or beneficiaries should receive a copy of the annual accounts and annual reports and of the statement of investment policy principles.

In the 'general approach' agreed by the Council on December 10, 2014, a clearer distinction is made between the information to be provided in the Pension Benefit Statement where the pension scheme provides for a given level of benefits and where the pension scheme does not provide for a given level of benefits. For pension schemes where members bear investment risk, the Pension Benefit Statement should provide an explanation of investment risks which are materially relevant, a brief explanation of the actual return, and very importantly, a statement that the lowest risk profile does not mean a risk-free investment.

Since in most member states pension scheme arrangements move away from providing specific guarantees, a proper disclosure of the risks associated with DC pension schemes is particularly important, as the members of the pension scheme bear the ultimate risk of the investment. The proposed revision of the 2003 Directive responds to this concern. It was the intention of the EC to produce a uniform Pension Benefit Statement, similar to the Key Investor Document for open investment funds (UCITS). The Council does not seem to want that and has removed the possibility for the EC to introduce such a statement by way of a Delegated Act.

One should not, however, forget that there are still many DB pension schemes in the EU. For the members of those schemes, the situation does not fundamentally change. There is no way for them to find out to what extent the occupational pension fund is 'at risk.' The risk evaluation for pensions, which should allow occupational pension funds to have a better insight into their risk position, remains an internal document that is only available to the management of the pension fund and to the competent authority. Yet risk evaluation does not mean much if it is not based on agreed valuation standards. These valuation standards should reflect proper risk management. This means that it will be difficult to move away from a market-consistent valuation. There are various ways in which a market-consistent valuation can be calculated, particularly for pension liabilities (Actuarial Association of Europe 2015). Problems concerning the back book can be dealt with through long transition periods and through an appropriate definition of the risk-free discount rate.

Conclusion

The development of an EU risk-based solvency capital regime will seriously enhance the quality of risk management by insurance entities. Through the Solvency and Financial Condition Report, it will be possible to get a better insight into how insurers manage their risks and their related capital positions. Public disclosure of these documents will further stimulate insurance undertakings to do it right.

It is regrettable that the reforms recently proposed for pension funds do not go all the way. Although it can be argued that occupational pension funds should not make their solvency positions public just as insurance undertakings do, it would nevertheless be beneficial to them if they were required to follow clear rules in terms of how to draw up a solvency balance sheet. This chapter has shown that the development of a risk-based solvency balance sheet in the case of occupational pension funds is more complex than in the case of insurance undertakings. Yet it could be possible to develop such a risk-based solvency balance sheet in stages, for instance by starting the process with a requirement for occupational pension funds to draw up a market-consistent balance sheet and impose risk-based capital requirements in a second stage. Members of DB pension schemes should have the right to know whether their pension fund is at risk, whether there is a funding gap, and how the pension fund intends to address this. Existing problems relating to the back book can be dealt with through long transition periods and through an appropriate definition of the risk-free discount rate.

In terms of risk disclosure, the introduction of a Pension Benefit Statement is a positive development. It allows members of occupational pension funds who bear the risk of their investment to gain a better insight into the risks that they incur and the final entitlement that they could expect based upon their investment choice or the choice made on their behalf by the employer (as a default option).

The absence of a proper solvency regime for pension funds in the EU creates an unfair treatment between policyholders of insurance undertakings and DB pension scheme members. This cannot be justified by the differences between a pension promise and an insurance contract. Members of DB pension schemes should have the right to know whether their pension fund is at risk, whether there is a funding gap, and how the pension fund will seek to address this. This is in the end a question of consumer protection. Through the absence of proper disclosure, DB pension scheme members are not currently in a position to protect themselves in the EU. The pension funds stress test launched by EIOPA in May 2015 coupled with the quantitative assessment of a potential use of the holistic balance sheet may provide some further insight into the possible consequences of introducing a risk-based solvency regime for pension funds in the EU.

Glossary of Terms

CEIOPS	Committee of European Insurance and Occupational Pensions Supervisors
EAA	European Economic Area
EBA	European Banking Authority
EC	European Commission
ECON	Economic and Monetary Affairs Committee of the European Parliament

EIOPA	European Insurance and Occupational Pensions Authority
ESMA	European Securities and Markets Authority
EMPL	Employment and Social Affairs Committee of the European Parliament
ESRB	European Systemic Risk Board
FEMM	Women's Rights and Gender Equality Committee of the European Parliament
IORP	Institutions for Occupational Retirement Provision
JURI	Legal Affairs Committee of the European Parliament
MCR	Minimum Capital Requirement
Omnibus II	Directive 2014/51/EU of Apr. 16, 2014 amending the Solvency II Framework Directive
QIS	Quantitative Impact Study
SCR	Solvency Capital Requirement
SFCR	Solvency and Financial Conditions Report
Solvency II Framework Directive	Directive 2009/138/EC of Nov. 25, 2009 establishing a new risk-based solvency regime for insurance and reinsurance undertakings in the EU

Endnotes

1. This is attached as an annex to the Framework Directive of 2009 and further specified in the Delegated Act of Oct. 10, 2014.
2. See, e.g., the comment letters from the UK National Association of Pension Funds (www.napf.co.uk), the Dutch Pensioenfederatie (www.pensioenfederatie.nl), and the European organization representing occupational pension funds, Pensions Europe (www.pensionseurope.eu).
3. See the joint letter of the European Trade Union Confederation (ETUC) and Business Europe of Feb. 14, 2012.
4. See <www.concordeurope.org>.

References

Actuarial Association of Europe (2015). *Clarity Before Solvency: A Discussion Paper on the Application of Market Consistency to Pension Funds in Europe.* Brussels: Actuarial Association of Europe. <http://actuary.eu/documents/AAE-Clarity-before-Solvency-19-05-2015-FINAL.pdf>.

CEIOPS (2009a). *Lessons Learned from the Crisis.* CEIOPS-SEC-107/08. Frankfurt: CEIOPS. <https://eiopa.europa.eu/CEIOPS-Archive/Documents/Reports/CEIOPS-SEC-107-08-Lessons-learned-from-the-crisis-SII-and-beyond.pdf#search=filename%3ACEIOPS-SEC-107-08-Lessons-learned-from-the-crisis-SII-and-beyond.pdf>.

CEIOPS (2009b). *Protocol Relating to the Collaboration of the Relevant Competent Authorities of the Member States of the European Union in Particular in the Application of the Directive 2003/41/EC of the European Parliament and of the Council of 3 June 2003 on the Activities and Supervision of Institutions for Occupational Retirement Provision (IORPs) Operating Cross-Border Activity.* CEIOPS-DOC-08-06 Rev1. Frankfurt: CEIOPS. <https://eiopa.europa.eu/CEIOPS-Archive/Documents/Protocols/CEIOPS-Revised-Budapest-protocol.pdf>.

EIOPA (2011). *Report on Reporting Requirements to Supervisory Authorities.* CEIOPS-OP-68-10 Rev5. Frankfurt: EIOPA. <https://eiopa.europa.eu/Publications/Reports/OP-68-Reporting-Requirements-final.pdf>.

EIOPA (2012). *EIOPA's Advice to the European Commission on the Review of the IORP Directive 2003/41/EC.* EIOPA-BOS-12/015. Frankfurt: EIOPA. <https://eiopa.europa.eu/Publications/Consultations/EIOPA-BOS-12-015_EIOPA_s_Advice_to_the_European_Commission_on_the_review_of_the_IORP_Directive.pdf>.

EIOPA (2013). *Report on QIS on IORPs.* EIOPA-BoS-13/124. Frankfurt: EIOPA. <https://eiopa.europa.eu/Publications/Quantitative%20impact%20studies/EIOPA-BoS-13-124_-_Report_on_QIS_on_IORPs-20130704.pdf>.

EIOPA (2014). *Consultation Paper on Further Work on Solvency of IORPs.* CP-14-040. Frankfurt: EIOPA. <https://eiopa.europa.eu/Pages/Consultations/Consultation-Paper-on-Further-Work-on-Solvency-of-IORPs-%28CP-14040%29.aspx>.

EIOPA (2015). *2015 Market Development Report on Occupational Pensions and Cross-Border IORPs.* EIOPA-BoS-15/144. Frankfurt: EIOPA. <https://eiopa.europa.eu/Publications/Reports/15.2_EIOPA_BoS_15-144_Market%20development%20report%202015.pdf>.

European Commission (1999). *Implementing the Framework for Financial Markets: Action Plan.* COM(1999)232, May 11, 1999. Brussels: European Commission. <http://ec.europa.eu/internal_market/finances/docs/actionplan/index/action_en.pdf>.

European Commission (2007). *Proposal for a Directive of the European Parliament and of the Council on the Taking-up and Pursuit of the Business of Insurance and Reinsurance (Solvency II).* <http://ec.europa.eu/finance/insurance/solvency/solvency2index_en.htm>.

European Commission (2010). *Green Paper: Towards Adequate, Sustainable and Safe European Pension Systems.* Brussels: European Commission. <http://ec.europa.eu/finance/pensions/iorp/index_en.htm>.

European Commission (2011). *Proposal for a Directive of the European Parliament and of the Council Amending Directives 2003/71/EC and 2009/138/EC and Regulations (EC) N° 1060/2009, (EU) N° 1094/2010 and (EU) N° 1095/2010 in Respect of the Powers of the European Supervisory Authority (European Insurance and Occupational Pensions Authority) and the European Supervisory Authority (European Securities and Markets Authority).* <http://ec.europa.eu/finance/insurance/index_en.html>.

European Commission (2012a). *White Paper: An Agenda for Adequate, Safe and Sustainable Pensions.* Brussels: European Commission. <http://ec.europa.eu/finance/pensions/iorp/index_en.htm>.

European Commission (2012b). *Public Hearing on the Revision of the Directive on Institutions for Occupational Retirement Provision (IORP II Proposal)*. Brussels: European Commission. <http://ec.europa.eu/finance/pensions/iorp/index_en.htm>.

European Commission (2014a). *Commission Delegated Regulation (EU) 2015/35 of 10 October 2014 Supplementing Directive 2009/138/EC of the European Parliament and of the Council on the Taking-up and Pursuit of the Business of Insurance and Reinsurance (Solvency II)*. <http://ec.europa.eu/finance/insurance/solvency/solvency2/index_en.htm>.

European Commission (2014b). *Proposal for a Directive of the European Parliament and of the Council on the Activities and Supervision of Institutions for Occupational Retirement Provision (Recast)*. COM/2014/0167 final of March 27, 2014. <http://ec.europa.eu/finance/pensions/iorp/index_en.htm>.

European Commission (2014c). *Commission Staff Working Document: Executive Summary of the Impact Assessment Accompanying the Document 'Proposal for a Directive of the European Parliament and of the Council Amending Directive 2003/41/EC on the Activities and Supervision of Institutions for Occupational Retirement Provision,' IORP II*. SWD (2014) 102 final. <http://eur-lex.europa.eu/legal-content/EN/TXT/PDF/?uri=CELEX:52014SC0102&from=EN>.

European Community (2003). *Directive 2003/41/EC of the European Parliament and of the Council of 3 June 2003 on the Activities and Supervision of Institutions for Occupational Retirement Provision*. <http://ec.europa.eu/finance/pensions/index_en.htm>.

European Economic Community (1991). *Council Directive (91674/EEC) of 19 December 1991 on the Annual Accounts and Consolidated Accounts of Insurance Undertakings*. <http://ec.europa.eu/finance/accounting/legal_framework/insurance_accounts/index_en.htm>.

European Union (2007). *Treaty of Lisbon Amending the Treaty on European Union and the Treaty Establishing the European Community, Signed at Lisbon, 13 December 2007*. <http://eur-lex.europa.eu/legal_content/EN/TXT/?uri=CELEX:12007L/TXT>.

European Union (2009). *Directive 2009/138/EC of the European Parliament and of the Council of 25 November 2009 on the Taking-up and Pursuit of the Business of Insurance and Reinsurance (Solvency II)*. <http://ec.europa.eu/finance/insurance/solvency/solvency2/index_en.htm>.

European Union (2010a). *Regulation (EU) N° 1094/2010 of the European Parliament and of the Council of 24 November 2010 Establishing a European Supervisory Authority (European Insurance and Occupational Pensions Authority), amending Decision N° 716/2009/EC and Repealing Commission Decision 2009/79/EC*. <http://ec.europa.eu/finance/insurance/index_en.htm>.

European Union (2010b). *Commission Regulation (EU) No. 583/2010 of 1 July 2010 Implementing Directive 2009/65/EC of the European Parliament and of the Council as Regards Key Investor Information and Conditions to be Met When Providing Key Investor Information and or the Prospectus in a Durable Medium Other than Paper or by Means of a Website*. <http://eur.lex.europa.eu/legal-content/EN/TXT/?uri=CELEX>.

European Union (2014). *Directive 2014/51/EU of the European Parliament and of the Council of 16 April 2014 Amending Directives 2003/71/EC and 2009/138/EC and Regulations (EC) N° 1060/2009, (EU) N° 1094/2010 and (EU) N° 1095/2010 in Respect of the Powers of the European Supervisory Authority (European Insurance and Occupational Pensions*

Authority) and the European Supervisory Authority (European Securities and Markets Authority). <http://ec.europa.eu/finance/insurance/solvency/solvency2/index_en.htm>.

Lamfalussy (2001). *Final Report of the Committee of Wise Men on the Regulation of European Securities Markets.* Brussels: Committee of Wise Men. <http://ec.europa.eu/internal_market/securities/docs/lamfalussy/wisemen/final-report-wise-men_en.pdf>.

Pensions Europe (2015). *Position Paper on EIOPA Consultation Paper on Further Work on Solvency of IORPs of 17 February 2015.* Brussels: PensionsEurope. <http://www.pensionseurope.eu/system/files/PensionsEurope%20Position%20paper%20solvency%20on%20IORPs%20-17-02-2015.pdf>.

Sandström, A. (2011). *Handbook of Solvency for Actuaries and Risk Managers: Theory and Practice.* London and New York: Chapman & Hall.

Sharma, P., ed. (2002). *Prudential Supervision of Insurance Undertakings.* Report by the Conference of Insurance Supervisory Authorities of the member states of the European Union. <http://ec.europa.eu/internal-market/insurance/docs/solvency/impactassess/annex-c02_en.pdf>.

Yermo, J. and C. Severinson (2010). *The Impact of the Financial Crisis on Defined Benefit Pension Plans and the Need for Countercyclical Funding Regulations,* OECD Working Papers on Finance, Insurance and Private Pensions No. 3. Paris, France: Organisation for Economic Co-operation and Development. <http://www.oecd-ilibrary.org/finance-and-investment/the-impact-of-the-financial-crisis-on-defined-benefit-plans-and-the-need-for-counter-cyclical-funding-regulations_5km91p3jszxw-en>.

6

Pensions, Risk, and Global Systemically Important Financial Institutions

Brian Reid and Dan Waters

Following the 2008–10 financial crisis, global policymakers enacted some of the most sweeping financial regulatory reforms in the past 70 years. In a fundamental policy shift, regulators explicitly incorporated monitoring, mitigating, and managing systemic risk into their regulatory missions or mandates. Policymakers initially focused on addressing systemic risk in the banking sector, but in recent years they have broadened their focus to include nonbank financial intermediaries, such as insurance companies, asset managers, and pension funds.

This chapter summarizes the global discussion surrounding systemic risk. Specifically, it focuses on whether pension funds and asset managers that provide investment products and services to pension plans are sources of systemic risk. The first section briefly describes systemic risk and the institutions policymakers put in place to identify and monitor sources of that risk. Given that regulators have tended to focus on banks and the prominent role they played in the 2008 financial crisis, the second section discusses the banking model, explains why banks are vulnerable to severe financial shocks, and how the banking model has influenced regulators' thinking on systemic risk in other sectors, specifically pensions and asset management. The final sections examine several theories about how pensions, and the funds in which they invest, could pose risks to the financial system.

Defining Systemic Risk

Financial institutions are risk-management organizations. They not only manage the risks from the assets that they hold or oversee, but also obligations to shareholders, depositors, pensioners, and others who hold claims on them or their products. If asset prices decline, a financial institution may not be able to meet those obligations in full. The impact of a financial institution not having sufficient assets to meet its obligations can be idiosyncratic, affecting only those individuals or entities that have direct claims on a failed financial institution, or systemic, affecting the broader financial system if a financial institution's failure creates wider damage to the economy.

For example, a defined benefit (DB) pension fund may have insufficient assets to meet its future obligations to retirees. This shortfall can arise if the sponsor of the pension plan made insufficient contributions to the plan, or if asset returns were inadequate. If the pension plan's sponsor is unwilling or unable to offset the shortfall, then the plan's participants and pensioners will not receive the promised levels of retirement income, causing them economic harm.

The OECD (2015) highlighted the risk that DB pension funds may not be able to meet their obligations following a period of prolonged low interest rates. It noted that because central banks have maintained low interest rates to spur slow economic growth following the economic downturn in the United States and Europe, pension funds may face a low interest rate environment for the foreseeable future. With the current levels of contributions, low interest rates, and fixed contribution periods, many DB pension funds will likely not meet their obligations if they are fixed as a ratio of workers' earnings. Lower payouts could reduce the well-being of current and future pensioners. If pension sponsors choose to increase contributions to shore up these funds, the costs of doing so may impair the profits of the firms sponsoring the funds and impose greater burdens on current workers or taxpayers making contributions to support the funds.

An underfunded DB pension fund may present certain risks for workers, pensioners, and plan sponsors, but such a fund is unlikely to cause the financial system itself to cease functioning. In assessing risks of systemically important institutions, regulators have focused on how the collapse of a single firm or group of financial institutions could create a cascading effect that encompasses an even larger set of financial and nonfinancial firms. This concept of systemic risk adheres most closely to the definition that Acharya et al. (2012) and Tarullo (2009) have set forth. They define systemic risk as the risk that a firm or group of firms will fail and disrupt the financial system's ability to funnel capital from investors to borrowers, thus causing damage to the broader economy.

An example of this definition of systemic risk and the economic breakdown it can cause occurred in the summer of 2007 during the beginning of the financial crisis. It started in the asset-backed commercial paper (ABCP) market. Issuers of ABCP use this short-term debt to finance credit card receivables, auto loans, and other medium-term credit. Leading up to the crisis, some ABCP programs pooled together mortgages and mortgage-backed securities and used commercial paper to finance them. As US housing prices began to fall and default rates rose, some of the funding programs suffered losses. Banks that had provided credit support to some of these programs absorbed the losses on their balance sheets (Acharya and

Schnabl 2010), but other programs did not have bank credit support and defaulted on their ABCP. After several ABCP issuers collapsed, lenders quickly pulled back from similar issuers (Covitz et al. 2013).

This rapid contraction in ABCP led to a pullback in the supply of capital that helped finance consumption and investment, and the contraction of credit caused the broader US economy to tip into a recession. A year later, following Lehman Brothers' collapse in September 2008, the commercial paper market suffered another sharp decline. Investors thought there was a higher probability that issuers of financial paper would default after Lehman Brothers collapsed (Kacperczyk and Schnabl 2009), and in response, they reduced their supply of short-term credit to banks and finance companies. The contraction of credit to these financial intermediaries threatened the collapse of more financial institutions and further damage to the broader economy. These events prompted the Federal Reserve to provide several emergency credit facilities, including two for the commercial paper market, to support the flow of short-term credit to financial and nonfinancial institutions (Duygan-Bump et al. 2013).

This definition of systemic risk, as illustrated by the preceding example, is quite broad and has no clear set of boundaries for monitoring and regulating systemic risks. Historically, central banks have monitored and mitigated risks in the banking system, but as nonbank financial intermediation has grown, governments have given regulators broad authority to scan the financial landscape for emerging risks and tools to address them.

In the United States, the Dodd–Frank Act, among other things, established the Financial Stability Oversight Council (FSOC) to identify risks to US financial stability, promote market discipline, and respond to emerging threats to financial stability. The FSOC has 10 voting members comprised of representatives of financial regulators and is chaired by the Secretary of the Treasury. As one of its tools for monitoring and maintaining financial stability, the FSOC can designate nonbank institutions as systemically important financial institutions (SIFIs). The standard for designation is whether an institution could pose a threat to US financial stability because of its material financial distress, or because of the nature, scope, scale, concentration, interconnectedness, or mix of its activities. Once an institution is designated, it is subject to enhanced prudential regulation and consolidated supervision by the Federal Reserve, even if the primary regulator is another federal financial regulator. In addition, as specified by the Dodd–Frank Act, a SIFI is subject to risk-based capital requirements and susceptible to paying into a resolution fund in the event of its failure.

In Europe, the Parliament created the European Systemic Risk Board (ESRB) to coordinate and oversee risks within the European Union.[1] The Parliament also extended monitoring and overseeing systemic risk to the European Securities and Markets Authority (ESMA), which assesses financial risks and works to safeguard the stability of the European Union's financial system.[2]

In 2009, the Group of 20 created the Financial Stability Board (FSB) as a successor to the Financial Stability Forum (FSF), which was founded in the 1990s to improve coordination and cooperation among national and international financial regulators. Shortly thereafter, the International Organization of Securities Commissions published revised objectives and principles of securities regulation, which included a new principle, advising securities regulators to have—or contribute to—a process to monitor, mitigate, and manage systemic risk (IOSCO 2010). Internationally, the Financial Stability Board has taken on the role of identifying sources of global systemic risk.

Systemic Risk: Expanding the Scope beyond Banks to Nonbank Financial Institutions

As policymakers broadened their monitoring of systemic risk to include nonbank financial institutions, they drew heavily from their understanding of how banks contribute to systemic risk. Some of the first studies that examined the connections between banks and nonbank financial institutions drew parallels between bank and nonbank intermediated credit, and thus started referring to nonbanks as 'shadow banks' and their activities as 'shadow banking'. For example, Pozsar et al. (2010) set forth a detailed description of shadow banking, explaining how nonbank financial institutions intermediate credit between borrowers and lenders and how they are interconnected with banks and the broader financial system. Shortly thereafter, the FSB (2011a) released a consultative report on possible systemic risks in nonbank financial institutions and markets, in which it drew parallels to bank sources of systemic risk and referred to such institutions as shadow banks.

Shadow banking is a broad term, with various policymakers defining it differently. As a result, some pension funds and their activities have been captured under the umbrella of shadow banking, and thus could be analyzed as sources of systemic risk. For example, while DB pension funds typically have been excluded from narrow definitions of shadow banking, they often are identified as engaging in shadow banking activities, such as securities lending or investing in asset-backed securities issued by shadow banks. Moreover, the FSB (2012) and the IMF (2014) have used even broader definitions of shadow banking, which capture DB plans, their investment activities, and the funds in which they invest.

Products used in defined contribution (DC) plans, such as mutual funds and other pooled investment products that provide investors daily liquidity by allowing plan participants to move assets among these funds, have also been caught under the shadow banking umbrella. Indeed, some policymakers, including the IMF (2015), have included such funds in their broad definition of shadow banks. Of particular concern have been pooled products that invest in fixed-income securities or emerging markets. Regulators and even some market participants have highlighted the risk of investors quickly shifting from one asset class to another, which could force the managers of those funds to rapidly sell securities. If those securities trade in illiquid markets, asset flows could cause sharp declines in prices, leaving many financial firms temporarily unable to meet their obligations until asset prices return to their fundamental values. These scenarios paint a picture in which pensions or the products that they invest in present risks to the overall economy, which could cause the financial system to no longer function.

These concerns about one-sided trades are similar in their nature to bank runs, once again indicating that financial regulators continue to rest heavily on banking models when examining systemic risk. Yet capital market financial intermediation and the financial institutions that operate in them, such as pension funds and asset managers, are fundamentally different from bank-based financing. Next we explain why.

The banking model

Banks are susceptible to collapse and are sources of systemic risk because of the interplay between their assets and liabilities. Banks hold portfolios of loans and marketable securities, and these assets rise and fall in value. They finance these assets by issuing short- and medium-term debt and deposits. These borrowings or liabilities have stated nominal values, which create a fixed set of claims on the banks. Given that the value of banks' assets can vary but their liabilities cannot, banks hold capital to help absorb changes in asset values and to help protect bank depositors and creditors from losses. Yet if a bank does not have enough capital to absorb a large drop in asset values, debt holders and uninsured depositors can suffer losses. The interplay between these risks, banks' limited ability to absorb losses, and the nature of banks' liabilities makes them particularly vulnerable to financial and economic shocks.

When asset prices change, banks' heavy reliance on debt to finance their balance sheets also magnifies the effects on their capital. One measure of the degree to which asset returns are magnified is the balance sheet leverage ratio. The ratio is calculated by dividing a bank's balance sheet assets by its capital. A leverage ratio of 10:1 means a 1 percent decline in the value of a bank's assets will cause its capital to fall by 10 percent. Among the largest banks in the United States, the average balance sheet leverage ratio is 9:1.

Because banks have limited amounts of capital to absorb losses, uninsured depositors and other lenders are apt to pull back their funding to banks during periods of financial market stress when asset prices fall sharply. This was particularly acute during 2008, when investors lending to banks on a short-term basis were unsure of the solvency of large European and US banks and reduced their lending to them. The tightened supply of credit to banks was evident in both higher interest rates that the banks had to pay for unsecured debt and an overall contraction in the amount of commercial paper outstanding. For example, interest rates on dollar-denominated commercial paper rose sharply on September 15, 2008, the day that Lehman Brothers failed, and remained at elevated levels until the Federal Reserve created two funding facilities that supplied nearly $350 billion in financing to the commercial paper market.

Rapidly rising interest rates can cause several problems for a bank. First, because many bank assets earn fixed rates of interest, sharply rising short-term interest rates can cause a bank's cost of funding to rise faster than its portfolio income. If its interest costs exceed its interest income, the bank will suffer losses, which impairs its capital. Second, rising interest rates also cause assets with fixed interest rates to fall in value, which could result in potential losses for the bank. Finally, rising interest rates can impair a bank's ability to borrow on a secured basis. Banks frequently use bonds and other assets to collateralize certain types of borrowing, and lenders often require that the assets used to secure a loan be repriced or marked-to-market, usually on a daily basis. If interest rates rise and bond prices fall, a bank must post additional collateral to secure the borrowing. If bond prices fall significantly, the bank may no longer have sufficient collateral at current market prices to secure the financing necessary to fund its portfolio.

Investment and interest rate risks are further compounded for banks because large portions of bank balance sheets are illiquid, meaning some of their securities are difficult to sell without incurring losses in value. If a bank's borrowers or depositors pull back quickly, the bank may not be able to sell loans or securities rapidly enough, and at a high enough price, to cover the fixed value of its liabilities. When a bank has to sell assets for less than it has valued them, those realized losses are absorbed by its capital, which erodes the buffer the bank has to protect its uninsured lenders and depositors. The short-term nature of much of a bank's borrowings is also compounded by the problem that a bank's depositors and other funders can rapidly pull back their money whenever they choose, leaving the bank unable to finance itself in times of financial stress. Thus, a downward spiral of selling assets at fire-sale prices ensues, forcing the bank to realize losses, which further erodes its capital and leads lenders to pull back even more before the bank becomes insolvent. This experience, often referred to as a run, can cause a bank to quickly collapse.

The interaction between a bank's investment, interest, and liquidity risks creates a key link between investment and systemic risk, and it helps explain why the subprime crisis threatened to bring down large numbers of US and European banks during the 2008–10 financial crisis. While the amount of outstanding subprime loans was relatively modest, they were held in off-balance sheet entities that were affiliated with banks but had too little capital to absorb the losses (Acharya and Richardson 2009). As Lehman Brothers and other financial institutions collapsed, prices on certain mortgage-backed securities fell sharply and threatened the collapse of other banks and financial institutions.

Since 2008, regulators have put a variety of measures in place to shore up bank balance sheets. While banks are better capitalized than before the financial crisis, they still have a limited ability to withstand a loss in value of their assets because of their inherent structure and the interest, investment, and liquidity risks that they have to take on in the course of business. Moreover, bank balance sheets cannot be isolated from fluctuations in other sectors of the financial market. Thus, regulators have been analyzing other sectors for systemic risk, including pension funds, asset managers, and other nonbank financial intermediaries (Haldane 2014; Carney 2014; Tarullo 2015).

Structural differences between pension funds and banks

The structure of DB pension funds differs from banks in two important respects. DB pension funds typically do not use significant amounts of borrowed money to fund themselves, so portfolio losses do not become magnified and leave the fund unable to repay its debts. More important, DB pension fund obligations to pensioners are not redeemable upon demand. Thus, a DB pension fund does not face a risk of plan participants quickly pulling their money out of the fund.

Like DB plans, DC plans do not employ leverage. They do, however, provide plan participants with the ability to move assets between investment options or even out of the plan. To accommodate this redeemable feature of DC plans, the investment funds in a plan are typically valued on a daily basis. Plan participant claims on the funds move dollar for dollar with fund assets. So while DC plans have immediate claims that are payable on demand, the claims are always payable in full.

Although DB and DC pension plans are structurally different from banks, they do rely heavily on other types of financial institutions and products that policymakers have examined for systemic risks. DB or DC plans use either pooled investment vehicles or separate accounts to invest on behalf of their beneficiaries. DB plans predominantly use separate accounts or collective investment funds. DC plans typically use mutual funds or collective investment funds, although some large plans may also invest their plans' assets in separate accounts. A plan sponsor typically will either provide a mandate to the asset manager to guide the asset allocation strategy and risk profile of the account, or will select a mutual fund or collective investment fund with a mandate in accordance with the plan documents. In either case, however, the failure of an asset manager overseeing a fund's assets does not have any impact on the pension fund.

Fundamental differences between asset management and banks

When policymakers began to look at asset management for sources of systemic risk, they applied their knowledge of banks to asset managers and their products. Yet asset managers and the products and services they provide differ from what banks do. Asset managers do intermediate capital between investors and borrowers, but unlike banks, asset managers typically take on little or no investment risk. Rather, investors hire asset managers to construct portfolios of securities on their behalf with the understanding that they—not the manager—will absorb the portfolio's gains and losses.[3] This agency relationship limits the effect of a fund's performance on an asset manager's balance sheet to fluctuations in its management fees. It also insulates the asset manager's clients from the manager's own financial position. For example, if an asset manager cannot continue to operate, there are strict custody rules in place that protect the customer's assets and allow them to be moved to another manager.[4]

The products that asset managers oversee fall into two main groups: pooled investment vehicles (funds), and separate accounts. These two products are similar in that asset managers oversee the portfolio construction and make investment decisions according to client mandates. There is a key distinction between the two types of products though: in a fund (or pooled investment vehicle), a fund owns the securities and the investor owns a pro rata interest in a fund, while in a separate account, the investor owns the securities directly. In neither case, however, does the asset manager own or hold the assets, unlike a bank, which holds assets and takes on investment risk. Instead, with asset management, all the investment risk, including the gains and losses, passes directly to the investor.

Another distinction between asset management products and banks is the types of claims that investors have on funds or separate accounts. For example, as discussed earlier, a DC plan participant's claims on a pension fund are not fixed, as they are with a bank account. Asset managers value investors' holdings in a fund or a separate account based on current securities prices, and they set the price at the end of the day based on the market close. When asset prices fall, investor claims on a fund or a separate account decline by an equal amount.

Systemic Risk Concerns about Asset Managers and Funds

Although regulators acknowledge that asset management products and services are structured differently from banks, and thus have different risk profiles, they nonetheless have raised concerns about systemic risk in asset management (FSOC 2014). These concerns can be divided into two broad categories. The first category involves risks presented by an asset management firm. Under this entity-based approach, a regulator could designate an individual fund or asset manager as systemically important and subject it to increased supervision or regulation. The second category encompasses risks presented by asset management products or activities. Under this approach, a regulator could deem a collection of financial products or activities as systemically risky and subject them to greater regulation or ban them.

Regulators' concerns about asset managers

Regulators' concerns about asset managers mainly focus on a firm's solvency and its ability to maintain its services and fund operations. In particular, regulators are concerned that, if an asset manager fails, it could lead to disruptions in the financial markets either because investors pull back from the manager's products, or because the transitioning of a client's assets and management to another firm does not happen smoothly. These concerns have led the FSB to propose a set of criteria to identify possible investment funds and asset managers for designation as global nonbank non-insurance Systemically Important Financial Institutions (FSB 2015). Asset managers owned by banks and insurance companies would also be considered for designation, even if the parent firm was already deemed to be a global SIFI.

The FSB has proposed two threshold tests for asset managers: $100 billion in balance sheet total assets, or $1 trillion in assets under management. If an asset manager has assets above these levels, the FSB would consider it for global SIFI designation based on the FSB's assessment as to whether the asset manager could disrupt global financial markets if it faced distress or failure. Factors that the FSB proposes to consider include the firm's exposure to counterparties, the indirect impact the asset manager would have on the financial system if it was forced to liquidate its assets under management, and the critical nature of the services that it provides and the ability to find substitutes.

Regulator concerns about funds

In addition to possibly designating asset managers as systemically important, the FSB has proposed two thresholds for initially considering whether certain funds operated by asset managers should be designated as systemically important. The first threshold is any fund with $100 billion or more in assets; the second, less inclusive, threshold would be $200 billion in conjunction with a fund's overall size and trading relative to the market in which it is invested. Regulators have proposed designating funds as SIFIs because of their concerns about potential systemic risks that funds may pose to the financial system. Regulators' concerns about products and activities have largely fallen into three areas: credit/default risk, leverage risk, and liquidity risk. The nature of the concerns has shifted over time, but elements of the original models remain part of the public discourse (IMF 2014).

Credit/default risk

Credit/default risk is the area that has evolved the most. Initially, bank regulators were concerned about asset managers creating investment products that 'transformed credit risk,' meaning that the actual credit risk is not borne by investors or that investors perceive that the asset they invest in is less risky than it actually is (FSB 2011b). These concerns were largely driven by sponsor support of money market funds. Yet regulators have also recognized that fund and separate account investors (such as pension funds and 401(k) participants) bear the credit risk of their funds, and thus they have concluded that transformation of credit risk in bond and stock funds is not a significant source of risk in the asset management industry.

Leverage risk

The second concern is the extent to which asset managers provide products or services that engage in leverage. Mutual funds, Exchange Traded Funds (ETF), and Undertakings for the Collective Investment of Transferable Securities (UCITS) funds have strict limits on their use of leverage. For example, US mutual funds and ETFs must hold three dollars of assets for every dollar they borrow, and DC plans using such products also have limited leverage.

Asset management products can engage in leverage in a variety of ways. For example, a fund could borrow from a bank and invest the loan in fund assets, which magnifies the gains and losses to the nondebt holders. Alternatively, a fund could borrow through securities lending. For example, a DB plan may lend out securities and reinvest the proceeds from the lending in similar securities, amplifying the returns on that fund. Another form of leverage can arise through the use of derivatives, whereby the fund engages in a derivative transaction that increases the portfolio's risk rather than hedging it. This is particularly true if the collateral held against the portfolio is of a similar risk profile as the derivative position itself. These forms of borrowing, however, are restricted under Securities and Exchange Commission (SEC) rules for mutual funds and other regulated investment pools. Other types of asset management products, such as hedge funds, may use greater amounts of leverage, and DB plans are eligible to invest in such funds.

In practice, most regulated funds and even other types of investment products have relatively modest levels of leverage relative to banks. For example, the average balance sheet leverage ratio for the largest US mutual funds and ETFs is 1.04:1. In contrast, banks rely heavily on debt to finance their balance sheets, with 9:1 being the average balance sheet leverage ratio for the largest US banks. The implication is that, for regulated funds, and even for hedge funds, asset management products can experience large fluctuations in price without causing a fund's or separate account's assets to be less than its borrowings.

Liquidity risk

Liquidity risk is the third concern regulators have regarding the potential systemic risk that asset managers might pose to financial stability (FSB 2011b; FSOC 2014). One of the distinguishing features of many types of funds is that they will buy back an investor's shares on a daily basis; this is also known as offering daily redemptions. Regulators are concerned that this activity—coupled with some of the securities that certain funds hold—could present a liquidity risk. Specifically, regulators have hypothesized that if investors sell their interest in bond funds during a period of financial market stress, the funds may not be able to sell their assets to meet these orders, or their actions may cause prices in the bond markets to fall sharply (OFR 2013).

Feroli et al. (2014) have argued that such 'herding behavior' can distort markets, and lead securities prices to over- or undershoot their fundamental value. Because of the possibility that forced sales of securities could cause prices to fall below their previous day's value, a fund may not be able to sell its holdings for what it priced them the previous day. Hence shareholders leaving a fund may get a better price than what the portfolio manager could achieve when selling the assets, causing the remaining shareholders to absorb the difference. In this event, investors may have an advantage in leaving a fund before other investors, particularly during periods of market stress. This advantage is often referred to as a 'first-mover advantage,' and some regulators theorize that it could cause sharp investor movements out of funds and thus amplify a market downturn.

Collins and Plantier (2014) have noted that this is not a new concern, as it has resurfaced numerous times since the 1920s, particularly after periods of rapid fund growth. They argue that there is no evidence that fund sales of securities materially affect market prices. While flows and fund returns are positively correlated, the direction of causation is sensitive to the identifying assumptions used to structure empirical tests. In addition, they note that investors who own securities directly could also cause prices to fall if a large number sought to sell their holdings at once.

Regulators such as the IMF (2015) and FSOC (2014) have countered that fund investors are more likely to sell during a period of market stress than if fund investors held the securities directly. Accordingly they have sought to better understand how investing through collective vehicles may lead to greater systemic risks than investing in securities through direct ownership. For example, FSOC (2014) has theorized that there are two other potential sources of cost transfers: the trading costs and liquidity costs that a fund incurs by selling securities to meet an investor's redemptions. Accordingly, regulators have explored two hypotheses about how these cost transfers could be sources of systemic risk.

Theories about investor runs and liquidity costs

First-mover advantage and trading costs

The first theory about investor runs and liquidity costs is that the actual trading costs are borne by investors staying in a fund with outflows. Fund costs, as well as investment gains and losses, are shared on a pro rata basis among investors. But if a fund investor leaves a fund and the fund manager must sell securities to accommodate the redemption, investors who stay with the fund may bear a larger share of the trading costs. Thus if an investor leaves early from a fund that subsequently experiences more redemptions and portfolio sales, that early or first investor could be exposed to lower fund costs than those investors who remain behind and could therefore have a first-mover advantage.

US fund managers, however, have the ability to manage these costs so as to not disadvantage their remaining shareholders. First, fund managers are required to mark-to-market their fund portfolios on a daily basis using forward pricing and fair valuation methods to avoid predictable price movements. Many managers are required to either use the price that they could sell the security for, known as the bid price, or the price that is at the mid-point between the bid and ask price. The ask price is the price at which the manager could buy the security. Using a bid- or mid-price passes some of the trading costs along to investors leaving a fund, because this pricing method values the shares near to what the fund would receive if it needed to sell assets to accommodate the redemption. Another way that funds manage costs is by imposing redemption fees on investors who leave a fund within a certain window of time after investing in the fund. In addition, most funds also reserve the right to redeem shares in kind if investors with particularly large trades want to redeem quickly, so that rather than receiving cash, the investor is paid with a slice of securities. Pooled products such as mutual funds or collective investment funds often have the option to redeem in-kind if the retirement plan sponsor has not given sufficient warning that it is removing its plan from the fund.

European fund managers have other techniques for limiting the effect of shareholder flows on remaining investors. UCITS funds are allowed to use swing pricing, whereby they set a price based on market prices and whether the fund received net inflows or outflows for the day. The difference between the two prices can fluctuate and will reflect the cost of accommodating the shareholder flows on a given day. UCITS also can use dilution levies, which are charges that investors entering or exiting a fund pay to compensate other shareholders. Finally, UCITS can use gates on their funds to limit the redemptions in any given time period.

These and other techniques help minimize the costs of meeting shareholder redemptions. One measure of these techniques' efficacy is the tracking error on index funds: this is the difference between an index fund's return and the total return of the index it tracks. If shareholder flows cause funds to trade and incur transaction or liquidity costs, as regulators have hypothesized, then index funds with outflows should have larger tracking errors.

Figure 6.1 plots tracking errors for US bond index funds against the monthly net new cash flows to such funds, where the target index is the Barclays US Aggregate Bond index. The chart examines monthly data from January 2010 to December 2014, during which there was a large increase in the demand for bond funds. If the regulators' hypothesis is correct, then the figure should show a tight correlation between fund flows and tracking error. As seen, there is no such relationship, either visually or statistically. Indeed, there are many observations in the upper left quadrant that represent cases where bond index funds had outflows and investors in the fund saw their returns *rise* relative to its benchmark index, which is precisely the reverse of what the hypothesized scenario would suggest. Even considering only those months where these bond index funds had outflows and there was a negative tracking error (the lower left quadrant), there is no relationship between fund flows and fund tracking error.

The absence of any meaningful correlation between fund flows and tracking error on a monthly basis suggests that fund managers can and do employ tools to manage the impact of these flows. This therefore undercuts the regulators' theory that investors who stay in a fund with outflows bear the actual trading costs. This does not mean that all fund managers use these

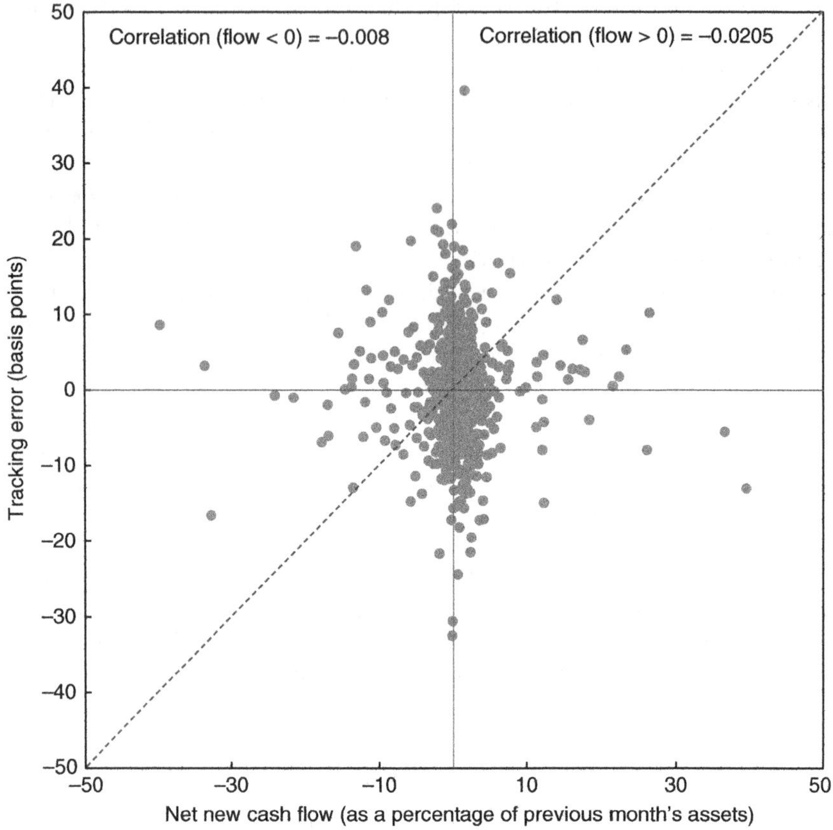

Figure 6.1 Bond index funds' flows are unrelated to their tracking errors (January 2010–December 2014)

Note: Tracking error is the difference between a fund's gross return and the total return on the fund's benchmark index. The bond index funds in this chart track either the Barclays Aggregate Bond Total Return index or the Barclays Aggregate Bond Float Adjusted Total Return index.

Source: Initially appeared in ICI (2015).

tools to the same degree or efficacy, but it does indicate that more research needs to be done to explore whether current trading techniques available to fund managers are sufficient to limit the impact of trading costs on fund performance.

First-mover advantage and liquidity asset management

The second theory is that a fund manager may try to initially avoid incurring trading costs by selling a fund's most liquid assets first, leaving the portfolio with less liquid, harder-to-value securities. Investors who remain in the fund would then be exposed to higher future liquidation and trading costs if additional investors left the fund. This theory of using the most liquid assets to meet investor outflows is sometimes referred to as a 'waterfall' theory of asset management.

Alternatively, if an asset manager does not want to alter the basic construct of the portfolio, it can sell both liquid and illiquid securities to accommodate outflows. As noted, both mutual funds and collective investment funds have investment mandates which they must adhere to. Thus, the hypothesis that asset managers would accommodate flows by selling their most liquid assets first would quickly cause the fund to deviate from its investment mandate.

One test of this hypothesis is to examine changes in cash positions of funds that may have more difficulty in selling securities, such as high-yield bond funds. For these funds, asset managers may be more inclined to use cash and other liquid assets to accommodate investor flows, leaving remaining investors at greater risk. One way to measure how asset managers adjust their funds' portfolios is to compare funds' cash ratio (the portion of the portfolio allocated to cash) over periods of time, including during periods of market stress.

Figure 6.2 plots the industry average cash ratio of high-yield bond funds over the 15-year period from 2000 to 2014. In aggregate, cash balances for high yield bond funds averaged 6.26 percent of those funds' assets. The cash ratio varied somewhat during the 15 years, but it never dropped

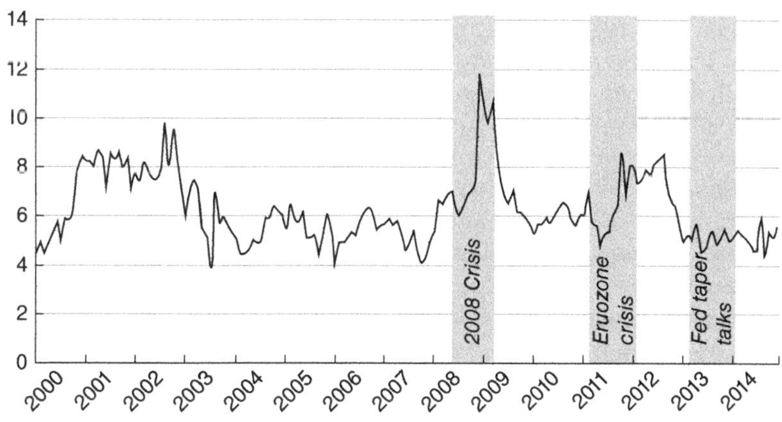

Figure 6.2 'Cash' ratio of high-yield bond funds: percentage of fund assets (monthly, January 2000–December 2014)

Note: Data exclude high-yield bond funds designated as floating-rate funds.

Source: Initially appeared in ICI (2015).

below 3.8 percent of fund total assets. Most notably, the cash ratio did not fall perceptibly during recent periods of net cash outflows from high-yield bond funds. For example, during the financial crisis, the cash ratio for high-yield bond funds *rose*, from 6.29 percent in August 2008 to 11.89 percent in December 2008, exactly the opposite of the result of the hypothetical 'waterfall' scenario.

As another example, long-term interest rates rose sharply in the United States in May and June 2013, reflecting anticipated changes in monetary policy. In June 2013, net outflows from high-yield bond funds totaled 4.4 percent of funds' total assets, which was modest as a percentage of funds' assets but large by historical standards. The cash ratio for high-yield bond funds, however, rose slightly from 4.44 percent in May 2013 to 4.53 percent in June 2013, a development also contrary to the waterfall theory of portfolio management.

Table 6.1 provides a statistical analysis of these concepts for high-yield bond funds. Using monthly fund-by-fund data, the table shows results of regressions of changes in the cash ratio for high-yield funds against their net new cash flows. If the waterfall theory is correct (i.e., that shareholder outflows tend to deplete funds' cash holdings), the 'slope' coefficients (labeled as Beta in the table) should be positive and substantially greater than zero. Also, the regressions should fit the data 'well' in the sense that the R^2 should be sizeable. The table shows results for a number of different time periods. For each period, the figure provides three regressions that use: (1) all observations in a given period (all net new cash flow); (2) observations with positive net new cash flow (net new cash flow ≥ 0); and (3) observations with negative net new cash flow (net new cash flow < 0).

As seen, the regressions provide little if any support for the waterfall theory. The slope coefficients (Beta) are considerably less than 1.0 and generally less than 0.20. Taken at face value, that suggests that individual fund cash ratios do rise and fall modestly as the funds experience net cash inflows or outflows. For example, for the period 2000–14, the Beta for net new cash flow < 0 is 0.18, which indicates that a fund that begins the month with a cash ratio of 4 percent and experiences net cash outflows of 7 percent of its assets would have a cash ratio of 2.75 percent by month-end, still well above zero.[5]

The lack of a meaningful relationship between a fund's net new cash flows and its cash ratio is underscored by examining crisis periods. For example, during the height of the financial crisis from September to November 2008, there is no evidence of any relationship between net new cash flows to high-yield bond funds and their cash ratios. The same is true of June 2013, the Taper Tantrum period; during that month, high-yield bond funds had significant total outflows, but those outflows had no apparent effect on the funds' cash positions.

TABLE 6.1. Net new cash flows have small effect on cash ratios of high-yield bond funds

		Regression Results		
Period		Alpha (Std error)	Beta (Std error)	R^2
2000–2006	All net new cash flow	−0.06 (0.07)	**0.13 (0.01)**	0.015
	Net new cash flow ≥ 0	0.23 (0.13)	**0.09 (0.02)**	0.007
	Net new cash flow < 0	−0.05 (0.10)	**0.18 (0.02)**	0.015
2007–2009	All net new cash flow	−0.07 (0.12)	**0.14 (0.01)**	0.029
	Net new cash flow ≥ 0	−0.10 (0.21)	**0.14 (0.02)**	0.035
	Net new cash flow < 0	0.16 (0.17)	**0.22 (0.05)**	0.013
2010–2014	All net new cash flow	−0.11 (0.08)	**0.20 (0.01)**	0.067
	Net new cash flow ≥ 0	−0.20 (0.13)	**0.22 (0.01)**	0.071
	Net new cash flow < 0	−0.16 (0.10)	**0.16 (0.02)**	0.031
2000–2014	All net new cash flow	−0.08 (0.05)	**0.17 (0.01)**	0.036
	Net new cash flow ≥ 0	−0.05 (0.09)	**0.16 (0.01)**	0.035
	Net new cash flow < 0	−0.05 (0.07)	**0.18 (0.01)**	0.019
Sep.–Nov. 2008	All net new cash flow	−0.07 (0.39)	**0.17 (0.06)**	0.005
	Net new cash flow ≥ 0	0.45 (1.06)	0.13 (0.09)	0.032
	Net new cash flow < 0	−0.14 (0.57)	0.19 (0.16)	0.007
June 2013	All net new cash flow	0.15 (0.42)	0.01 (0.05)	0.000
	Net new cash flow ≥ 0	−0.08 (1.54)	0.13 (0.19)	0.029
	Net new cash flow < 0	−0.21 (0.50)	−0.04 (0.06)	0.006

Note: Change in cash as percent of fund asset = $\alpha + \beta$ net new cash flow; selected periods. Data exclude mutual funds that invest in other mutual funds, variable annuities, any fund with less than $10 million in total net assets, funds specifically designed for frequent trading, funds designated as floating rate funds, and any fund-month where a merger or liquidation takes place for a fund. Bolded coefficients denote statistical significance at the 5 percent level.

Source: Initially appeared in ICI (2015).

To provide a visual example of the lack of a relationship between net cash flow and cash ratios, Figure 6.3 plots net new cash flows to individual high-yield bond funds against the change in each fund's cash ratio in June 2013. If the waterfall theory is accurate, the observations in the chart should line predominantly along the dashed 45-degree line. In other words, according to the waterfall narrative, outflows should deplete funds' cash balances while inflows should increase them. In fact, the observations in the chart are distributed essentially randomly around the vertical and horizontal axes, suggesting that there is no statistical relationship between net new cash flows and changes in funds' cash positions. Even if one focuses only on those high-yield bond funds that had outflows in June 2013 (a number of high-yield bond funds did have inflows), the posited relationship is absent.

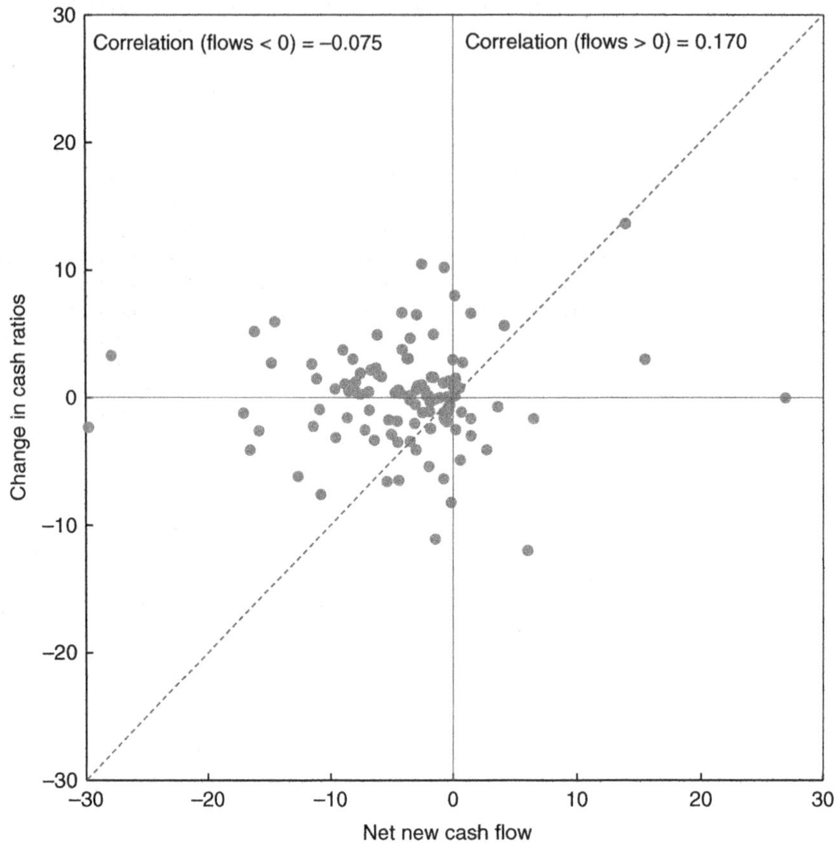

Figure 6.3 High-yield bond funds' change in cash ratio are unrelated to their flows: percentage of previous period total net assets (June 2013)

Note: Data exclude mutual funds that invest in other mutual funds, variable annuities, funds with less than $10 million in total net assets in June 2013, funds designed for frequent trading, funds designated as floating rate funds, and any fund-month where a merger or liquidation takes place for a fund.

Source: Initially appeared in ICI (2015).

In short, even during periods of market stress, the data do not support the notion that outflows cause funds to deplete their cash balances to the detriment of remaining fund shareholders. This theory is key to some of the policy prescriptions that regulators are recommending, so it is important for them to better understand how asset managers operate their funds, particularly during periods of market stress.

Fund Flows during Down Markets: Historical Experience

Although regulators have raised theoretical concerns about why investors might rapidly sell their fund shares and thus create risks to the financial system, historical experience provides little support for the theories that outflows from stock and bond funds would be so large as to pose systemic risk. Even though there have been periods of outflows from both types of funds, they have been modest when measured as a share of the existing fund assets or as a percentage of market transactions. For example, during the fall of 2008, outflows from stock and bond funds were a modest share of the existing fund assets in total. As Collins and Plantier (2014) explain, a reason for this is that a large portion of the assets held in stock and bond funds are held by retail investors, and these investors tend to move slowly.

The absence of large outflows from stock and bond funds suggests that either the economic value of the first-mover advantage is modest, or that the costs of doing so are greater than the benefits. The hypothesis assumes that the market impact from sales of fund securities in succeeding days is large enough to create a meaningful incentive for investors to try to time the markets. For a number of reasons, this is highly uncertain. For example, an investor might decide on the basis of a declining market today to redeem out of a fund, only to find the market rebounding tomorrow. Thus the redeeming investor is, in effect, trying to time the markets, a behavior against which academics and financial advisors have long cautioned fund investors. Certain investors must also consider taxes; for instance, an investor who redeems may incur a current tax liability because of capital gains. Also, the number of times an investor could seek to gain from this behavior (redeeming in an attempt to avoid market impact or other fund trading costs) is limited by frequent-trading costs or restrictions imposed by funds or 401(k) plans.

For instance, each of the 100 largest mutual funds has prospectus language indicating that it monitors for frequent trading and either imposes explicit controls to limit that activity or has the ability to bar frequent traders. Additionally, if fund investors can correctly anticipate a market impact tomorrow from fund redemptions today, so too can hedge funds and other institutional traders. But institutional traders have the distinct advantage of being able to execute a trade at any point during the trading day (or even before the trading day through derivatives markets). As a result, institutional traders may be able to arbitrage away any market impact effect well before investors in a mutual fund held inside a 401(k) plan or an individual retirement account (IRA) could execute an order, which is at the market closing price.

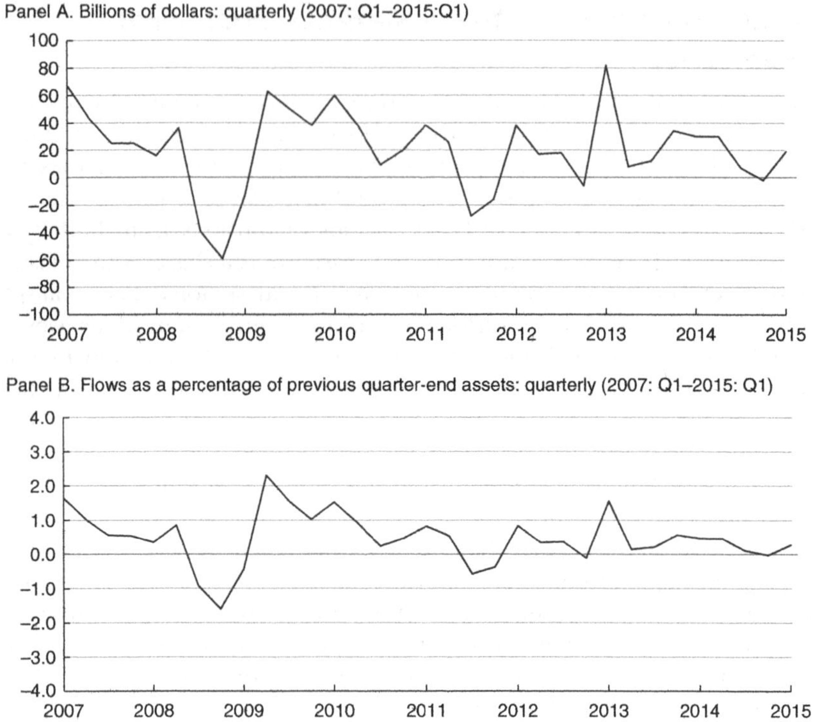

Figure 6.4 Defined contribution (DC) plan and IRA flows to long-term mutual funds
Source: Authors' calculations.

Another reason that destabilizing outflows have not been observed is that investors in retirement accounts have long investment horizons and tend not to trade heavily, even during periods of market stress. Surveys of record-keeper data undertaken by the Investment Company Institute since the fall of 2008 indicate that 401(k) investors are unlikely to make large shifts in their asset allocations or stop contributing to their plans, even during the height of the financial crisis (Holden and Schrass 2015). As Figure 6.4 shows, DC plans and IRAs had modest outflows in the fourth quarter of 2008, amounting to slightly more than $50 billion; these outflows were only about 1.5 percent of DC and IRA assets.

A final reason that fund flows tend to be muted, even during periods of market stress, is that most investors use financial advisors and brokers when investing outside of a DC plan. During periods of stress, these advisors likely discourage their clients from timing the markets and moving into and out of funds. In the past few years, though, a number of firms have begun to experiment with automated, online advisory services known as robo-advisors. These services provide asset allocation and automatic rebalancing of investments for clients inside DC plans, IRAs, and taxable accounts. Since these services are new and have not yet been tested during periods of market stress, it is unclear how they will perform and whether they could lead to herding as the programs rebalance portfolios away from asset classes that have recently fallen in price or if they could help stabilize markets as the programs rebalance investors' portfolios into asset classes with falling prices.

One of the few times when funds experienced sizeable outflows globally was in October 2008, when outflows from European-based bond funds totaled nearly 10 percent of fund assets. The outflows occurred when various government regulators sought to stem a potential run on European banks and provided new guarantees to bank deposits. These guarantees were unlimited, rather than being capped at a certain deposit amount, and they covered new money that was placed in the banks. This prompted investors in European funds to sell their shares in funds and deposit their proceeds in banks. But rather than being evidence of a structural weakness of funds, this experience indicates that policy responses during periods of market stress can potentially be destabilizing if they are not well formulated.

Conclusion

Policymakers and regulators are in the early stages of understanding sources of systemic risk and its transmission outside the banking sector. As they have turned their attention to the pension and asset management industries, they have relied heavily on an understanding of how banks contribute to systemic risk. Yet pension funds and asset managers are fundamentally different from banking in terms of their structure and risk profile. Despite these differences, some regulators have raised concerns about activities that pension funds engage in and about asset managers and their products and services. Policymakers have posed theories about how asset managers and their funds could be sources of systemic risk. Historical and empirical evidence about funds and investor behavior provide little support for these theories. Yet despite this evidence, global bodies such as the FSB have moved much closer to designating asset managers and their funds—possibly even large pension funds—as global SIFIs. The implications for plan participants and the regulatory consequences outside the United States are uncertain. In the United States, however, the implications are much clearer. If the FSOC chose to designate some funds or asset managers as SIFIs, this could cause a small group of funds and their investors, including pension plan participants, to bear significant costs upon designation (or in the event of a future collapse of another SIFI). Such costs could create large disincentives for pension funds to use any fund or asset manager designated as a SIFI.

Endnotes

1. More information on the ESRB's mission and activities is available at https://www.esrb.europa.eu.
2. More information on ESMA's mission and activities is available at http://www.esma.europa.eu/.
3. The definition of a 'security' under US federal securities laws is broad. Under the Investment Company Act of 1940 and the Securities Act of 1933, a security includes, among other instruments, any note, stock, bond, debenture, evidence of indebtedness, or certificate of interest or participation in any profit-sharing agreement.
4. For a general description of custody principles in the context of funds, see IOSCO (2014).
5. Formally speaking, the results also indicate that the link between net new cash flow and changes in a fund's cash ratio is statistically significant. That, however, is likely somewhat of an artifact due to the very large samples in the cases where the regressions span periods of several years. For instance, the regression for 2000–14 based on 'net new cash flow < 0' is highly statistically significant (a very small standard error, just 0.01), no doubt in part because the regression uses 9,527 observations. Consequently, the statistical significance of the regression coefficients is not the best indicator of the value of the strength or weakness of the relationship between a fund's cash ratio and its net new cash flows. More important however, the relationship does not fit the data well at all (the R^2 averages about 0.03—i.e., 3%—for the multi-year periods). In fact, there is nearly a complete lack of any relationship, which is contrary to the 'waterfall' theory of portfolio management, but consistent with the reality of funds' carefully managing their portfolios (including cash balances) to accommodate investor inflows and outflows while adhering to the fund's investment objectives.

References

Acharya, V. V. and M. Richardson (2009). 'Causes of the Financial Crisis,' *Critical Review*, 21(2–3): 195–210.

Acharya, V. and P. Schnabl (2010). 'Do Global Banks Spread Global Imbalances? The Case of Asset-Backed Commercial Paper during the Financial Crisis of 2007–09,' *IMF Economic Review*, 58: 37–73.

Acharya, V., R. Engle, and M. Richardson (2012). 'Capital Shortfall: A New Approach to Ranking and Regulating Systemic Risks,' *American Economic Review: Papers and Proceedings*, 102(3): 59–64. <http://dx.doi.org/10.1257/aer.102.3.59>.

Carney, M. (2014). 'The Future of Financial Reform,' speech presented at the 2014 Monetary Authority of Singapore Lecture, Singapore. <http://www.financialstabilityboard.org/wp-content/uploads/The-future-of-financial-reform.pdf>.

Collins, S. and C. L. Plantier (2014). *Are Bond Mutual Fund Flows Destabilizing? Examining the Evidence from the 'Taper Tantrum'.* Working Paper. Washington, DC: Investment Company Institute. <http://dx.doi.org/10.2139/ssrn.2510666>.

Covitz, D., N. Liang, and G. A. Suarez (2013). 'The Evolution of a Financial Crisis: Collapse of the Asset-Backed Commercial Paper Market,' *Journal of Finance*, 68: 815–48.

Duygan-Bump, B., P. Parkinson, E. Rosengren, G. A. Suarez, and P. Willen (2013). 'How Effective were the Federal Reserve Emergency Liquidity Facilities? Evidence from the Asset-Backed Commercial Paper Money Market Mutual Fund Liquidity Facility,' *Journal of Finance*, 68(2): 715–37.

Feroli, M., A. Kashyap, K. Schoenholtz, and H. S. Shin (2014). 'Market Tantrums and Monetary Policy,' paper presented at the 2014 Monetary Policy Forum, New York.

Financial Stability Board (FSB) (2011a). *Shadow Banking: Scoping the Issues.* Basel: FSB. <http://www.financialstabilityboard.org/wp-content/uploads/r_110412a.pdf>.

Financial Stability Board (FSB) (2011b). *Shadow Banking: Strengthening Oversight and Regulation: Recommendations of the Financial Stability Board.* Basel: FSB. <http://www.financialstabilityboard.org/wp-content/uploads/r_111027a.pdf?page_moved=1>.

Financial Stability Board (FSB) (2012). *Global Shadow Banking Monitoring Report 2012.* Basel: FSB. <http://www.financialstabilityboard.org/wp-content/uploads/r_121118c.pdf>.

Financial Stability Board (FSB) (2015). *Consultative Document (2nd) Assessment Methodologies for Identifying Non-Bank, Non-Insurer Global Systemically Important Financial Institutions.* Basel: FSB. <http://www.financialstabilityboard.org/wp-content/uploads/2nd-Con-Doc-on-NBNI-G-SIFI-methodologies.pdf>.

Financial Stability Oversight Council (FSOC) (2014). *Notice Seeking Comment on Asset Management Products and Activities.* FSOC-2014-0001. Washington, DC: FSOC.

Haldane, A. (2014). 'The Age of Asset Management,' speech presented at the London Business School, London. <http://www.bankofengland.co.uk/publications/Documents/speeches/2014/speech723.pdf>.

Holden, S. and D. Schrass (2015). *Defined Contribution Plan Participants' Activities, 2014.* ICI Research Report. Washington, DC: Investment Company Institute. <http://www.ici.org/pdf/ppr_14_rec_survey.pdf>.

International Monetary Fund (IMF) (2014). *Global Financial Stability Report—Risk Taking, Liquidity, and Shadow Banking: Curbing Excess While Promoting Growth.* Washington, DC: IMF.

International Monetary Fund (IMF) (2015). *Navigating Monetary Policy Challenges and Managing Risks.* Washington, DC: IMF. <http://www.imf.org/external/pubs/ft/gfsr/2015/01/pdf/text.pdf>.

International Organization of Securities Commissions (IOSCO) (2010). *Global Securities Regulators Adopt New Principles and Increase Focus on Systemic Risk.* Madrid: IOSCO. <https://www.iosco.org/news/pdf/IOSCONEWS188.pdf>.

International Organization of Securities Commissions (IOSCO) (2014). *Consultation Report: Principles Regarding the Custody of Collective Investment Scheme Assets.* Madrid: IOSCO. <http://www.iosco.org/library/pubdocs/pdf/IOSCOPD454.pdf>.

Investment Company Institute (ICI) (2015). Comment letter from Paul Schott Stevens to the Financial Stability Oversight Council. Washington, DC: ICI. <https://www.ici.org/pdf/15_ici_fsoc_ltr.pdf>.

Kacperczyk, M. and P. Schnabl (2009). 'When Safe Proved Risky: Commercial Paper during the Financial Crisis of 2007–2009,' *Journal of Economic Perspectives*, 24(1): 29–50.

Office of Financial Research (OFR) (2013). *Asset Management and Financial Stability*. Washington, DC: OFR. <http://financialresearch.gov/reports/files/ofr_asset_management_and_financial_stability.pdf>.

Organisation for Economic Co-operation and Development (2015). *OECD Business and Finance Outlook 2015*. Paris: OECD Publishing. <http://dx.doi.org/10.1787/9789264234291-en>.

Pozsar, Z, T. Adrian, A. Ashcraft, and H. Boesky (2010). *Shadow Banking*. Federal Reserve Bank of New York Staff Reports, 458. New York: Federal Reserve. <http://www.newyorkfed.org/research/staff_reports/sr458.pdf>.

Tarullo, D. K. (2009). 'Regulatory Restructuring,' Testimony before the Committee on Banking, Housing, and Urban Affairs, US Senate, Washington, DC, July 23.

Tarullo, D. K. (2015). 'Advancing Macroprudential Policy Objectives,' speech presented at 'Evaluating Macroprudential Tools: Complementarities and Conflicts,' Washington, DC.

Part II

Developments in Retirement Saving and Retirement Products

7

Determinants of Saving for Old Age around the World

Asli Demirgüç-Kunt, Leora Klapper, and Georgios A. Panos

Programs catering to the financial well-being of the elderly are experiencing strains around the world. The depletion of public coffers during the financial crisis has left governments struggling to cope with rising retirement costs triggered by aging populations, low birthrates, and weakened informal safety nets (Ellis et al. 2014). That this crisis threatens both the elderly and the young is well-established; it also endangers future generations, who will shoulder a disproportionate share of the costs of caring for older generations directly or indirectly (Gratton 1996; Fridson 2015).

Despite rising interest in the safety net for elderly people, there is limited information on the determinants of both formal and informal voluntary saving for old age. Drawing on new microeconomic data, this chapter offers a detailed descriptive analysis of old age saving around the world and across geographic regions. It also features an empirical analysis of the determinants of old age saving, using detailed individual characteristics, country macroeconomic characteristics, and country pension system characteristics. To our knowledge, this is the first study examining old age saving around the world using detailed global micro-data.

The 2014 Global Findex data reveal how and why adults save and borrow, and it also sheds light on their financial resilience to unexpected shocks (Demirgüç-Kunt et al. 2015). In 2014, 56 percent of adults around the world reported having saved money in the past 12 months. Adults in high-income OECD economies, as well as in East Asia and the Pacific, were the most likely to have done so, with 71 percent reporting that they had saved, followed by 60 percent of adults in Sub-Saharan Africa. In other regions, the figure stood at between 30 and 40 percent. The 2014 Global Findex survey also asked about three specific reasons for saving. While marked differences emerge across regions, almost 25 percent of adults worldwide reported having saved for old age in the past year. A similar share reported saving for education expenses, while 14 percent reported saving to start, expand, or operate a business. The percentage of adults saving for old age also varies considerably across economies: 39.7 percent in high-income OECD countries (hereafter

OECD^{HI}); 36.6 percent in East Asia and the Pacific (hereafter EAP); 11.8 percent in Europe and Central Asia (hereafter ECA); 10.6 percent in Latin America and the Caribbean (hereafter LAC); 9.8 percent in Sub-Saharan Africa; 9.1 percent in South Asia; and 7.0 percent in the Middle East and North Africa (hereafter MENA).

Our findings show a small gender gap in saving for old age, though it is larger in developing countries, as well as large differences based on education and employment status. All regions other than EAP exhibit patterns of higher old age saving among those with higher education. In every region, employed adults are far more likely to save for old age than unemployed adults, with the exception of South Asia. In terms of the age distribution, saving for old age rises sharply in the 36–45 age group, with delayed occurrence taking place in LAC, MENA, South Asia, and Sub-Saharan Africa. Large income disparities are also evident, with the richest centile being much more likely to save for old age, and the bottom centile far less likely.

Adults who have accounts at a financial institution or a mobile money account are about 40 to 50 percent more likely to save for old age than adults lacking such an account. Furthermore, our empirical estimates find a strong significant relationship between the probability of saving for old age and financial inclusion, a country's generic saving propensity, legal origin, and education. Residents of countries with English legal origin are more likely to save for old age, with an effect equal to 15 to 20 percent, versus countries with French legal origin. Residents of countries with higher generic saving rates are much more likely to save for old age, echoing Chen (2013), who proposed a strong cultural component shaping the propensity to save. Moreover, there is a positive relationship with GDP per capita, while interest rates and deposit insurance have insignificant effects. In addition, we find evidence that institutional arrangements enabling greater trust in the financial system, in terms of the safety net/moral hazard index based on deposit insurance, are conducive to increasing rates of old age saving (Demirgüç-Kunt et al. 2014).

Finally, the results of our empirical analysis show a moderate negative association with the size of pension benefits, a positive relationship with pension coverage, and a positive link to contributions and contribution ratios. It is also the case that a higher housing affordability index is positively related to old age saving in the majority of regions, with the exception of Sub-Saharan Africa, where the impact is insignificant. We interpret the latter findings to be in line with Poterba et al. (1995), who suggested little substitution between pension system provisions and contribution rates (and other forms of financial saving in the case of housing affordability) and saving for old age.

The next section reviews the existing literature, and the following one describes the data and presents the descriptive statistics for saving for old age around the world. Then we present the empirical analysis of old age saving, in terms of empirical strategy and estimation results with sets of individual, macroeconomic, and pension-system characteristics.

Review of Existing Literature

Research has long shown that retirees suffer from a variety of economic hardships even in developed economies with relatively strong pension systems. In their study of the United States, Bernheim et al. (2001) show that consumption dropped rapidly at the time of retirement and decreased even more post-retirement. Using UK data, Bardasi et al. (2000) reported that, on average, economic wellbeing declined sharply in the years preceding retirement, and continued to do so through retirement,[1] with women facing a swifter decline than men. Among adults in Germany, satisfaction with current household income decreased substantially on retirement, while satisfaction with free time increased, according to Bonsang and Klein (2011). Retirement had an overall negative effect on life satisfaction, with larger effects for involuntary retirement, and insignificant effects for voluntary retirement.

High levels of poverty among the elderly compound the negative economic consequences of retirement. In the US, Clark and Quinn (1999) reported that the elderly remain disproportionally represented among the near poor. Also, certain older Americans still face substantial risk of economic deprivation, even though their average economic wellbeing has significantly improved compared to older generations (Sabelhaus and Manchester 1995). Crystal and Shea (1990) also showed that elderly resources were distributed even more unequally than the rest of the population.

A number of studies has examined post-recession policy responses to these challenges. Galasso (2008) ran simulations based on the political determinants of social security contribution rates and retirement ages, and he concluded that the retirement age is likely to increase in each country, regardless of political constraints. However, according to Andersen (2008), indexing benefits and retirement ages to longevity did not ensure financial viability of the social security system. Recognizing this, Poterba (2014) suggested that individuals bear a larger share of the responsibility for determining their retirement security.[2]

According to Papke (2004), allowing participants a choice of investment options may increase their retirement savings. However, Lusardi (2003) reported that little is known about how households make saving plans and how they collect information to make savings decisions. A survey of households by the Board of Governors of the Federal Reserve System (2014) found that almost half of respondents had given little or no thought to retirement savings. Among those who had, many either did not plan to retire, expected to keep working into retirement to pay for expenses, or did not know how they would pay for their retirement.[3] Nearly a third had no retirement savings or pension. These retirement planning challenges had been exacerbated by the recession, which resulted in many respondents delaying their planned retirement.[4]

Firms have also shifted from defined benefit (DB) pensions to defined contribution (DC) pensions, where employees have to decide how much money to put into their retirement funds and how to allocate their pension wealth. But DC plans have their critics, who draw on the behavioral economics and finance literature.[5] For instance, Banks and Oldfield (2007) reported that the elderly suffer from greater cognitive, gender, and education gaps than other groups. As a result, they are less likely to have savings accounts, own shares in a company, or have private pensions. Lusardi and Mitchell (2011, 2014) reported that financial literacy is a significant determinant of retirement planning for all age groups, with elderly people suffering from the highest levels of financial illiteracy.

Recent research by Chen (2013) identified a cultural component in saving and retirement planning behavior, such that speakers of languages that grammatically associate the future and the present save more and retire with more wealth. In addition, Duflo and Saez (2002) reported that peer effects drive retirement plan participation decisions. Duflo and Saez (2003) presented quasi-experimental evidence that an individual's decision about how much to save for retirement was affected by small changes in his environment and that network effects influence participation decisions. Instead of education, Benartzi and Thaler (2007) proposed a method of influencing decisions about retirement saving plans based on the principles of 'automatic enrollment.' This involved implementing acute auto-enrollment, sensible default options, and opportunities to increase savings rates and rebalance portfolios automatically. Such design features help less sophisticated investors while maintaining flexibility for more knowledgeable participants.

Financial security for the elderly and economic growth are best served when governments adopt three pillars of old age security:[6] (1) a publicly managed pension system with mandatory participation and the limited goal of reducing poverty among the elderly; (2) a privately managed mandatory savings system; and (3) voluntary savings. The first pillar caters to redistribution, the second and third cover savings, and all three co-insure against the many risks of old age.[7] Spreading the insurance function across all three pillars creates greater income security for the old and provides greater insurance than any single pillar system. Valdés-Prieto (2002a, 2002b) reviewed the potential costs and benefits of 'three-pillar' programs, defined as those that use incentives to promote voluntary old age saving. Among the benefits of voluntary saving are the relative ease of accessing and mobilizing funds, and the prevention of potential labor market distortions. Yet voluntary savings programs may produce social costs, particularly when they involve fiscal incentives.[8]

To develop measures to improve the financial well-being of the elderly and incorporate an element of self-control in retirement planning, policy-makers must first understand worldwide retirement savings patterns. In the next sections, we evaluate these patterns using a binary measure of saving for old age, which captures whether an individual has saved for old age during the last year. Data limitations prevent us from measuring the volume of savings for old age. Nonetheless, examining savings behavior reveals a rich picture of results to inform policy design.

Who Saves for Old Age?

The data

We use data from the Global Findex database, which illustrates how people save, borrow, make payments, and manage risk.[9] It is the world's most comprehensive dataset providing consistent measures of financial service usage across economies and over time. The data were collected in partnership with Gallup, Inc. and the Bill and Melinda Gates Foundation. The survey was carried out over the 2014 calendar year as part of the Gallup World Poll, which since 2005 has continually conducted surveys of approximately 1,000 people in each of more than 160 economies and in over 140 languages, using randomly selected, nationally representative samples.[10]

Descriptive statistics

Our analysis employs a representative sample of 143 economies and 147,692 individuals, age 18 and older.[11] We use a binary variable (0/1) of the response to the question: 'In the past 12 months, have you saved for old age?' Figure 7.1 presents a global map,[12] and Figure 7.2 shows the percentage of adults who saved any money for old age during the last year by regional classification. The weighted global figure for saving for old age around the world is 24.8 percent. The top performers are Thailand, where 59.2 percent of the population saves for old age, Germany (55.1 percent), Malaysia (54.0 percent), Canada (51.7 percent), and New Zealand (51.5 percent). The bottom performers in terms of saving for old age are Niger (0.9 percent), Georgia (0.9 percent), the Republic of Yemen (1.4 percent), Jordan (1.9 percent), and Armenia (2.1 percent). The top performing

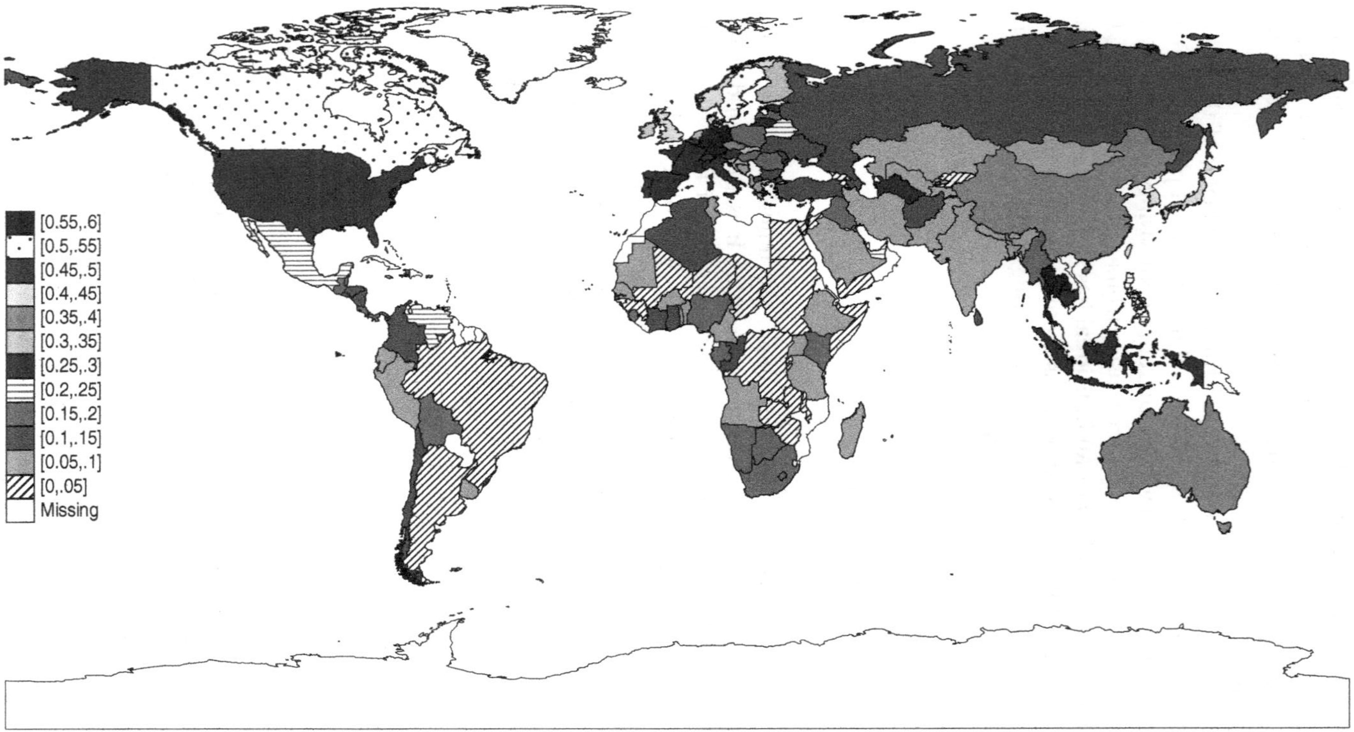

Figure 7.1 Saving for old age around the world

Note: Global FINDEX data 2015 – Weighted averages.

Source: Derived from Demirgüç-Kunt et al. (2015).

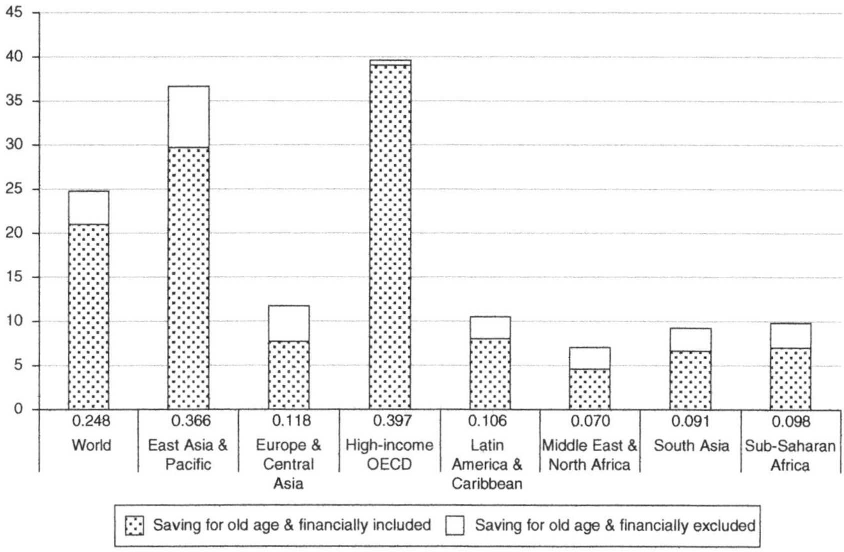

Figure 7.2 Saving rates (%) for old age around the world by financial inclusion status and region

Source: Adapted from Demirgüç-Kunt et al. (2015).

region is OECD^{HI}, though an interesting outlier is Greece amidst the debt-crisis, with 9.3 percent of the population saving for old age.

The bars in Figure 7.2 further distinguish between saving for old age and financial inclusion status, in terms of having an account at a bank or formal financial institution. It can be seen that 84.7 percent of the individuals who save for old age around the world are financially included, with the remaining 15.3 percent being financially excluded. The low figures in certain regions such as ECA and MENA could be indicative of the usage of alternative means of old age saving, such as livestock, gold, and stuffing money under the mattress. It could also be indicative of less liquid means of saving for old age, like home ownership.

Figure 7.3 presents the gender distribution of old age saving around the world and by region. The global gender gap in terms of saving for old age is in the magnitude of 2.5 percentage points (10.5 percent), with 26 percent of men saving versus 23.5 percent of women, globally. Notably, this is lower than the 9 percentage point gap in account ownership around the world. The gap is largest in South Asia and smallest in EAP, which also has the highest absolute old age saving rates.

Figure 7.4 presents educational gaps in terms of saving for old age. The global education gap is wider between tertiary and secondary education, compared to the respective gap between secondary and primary education

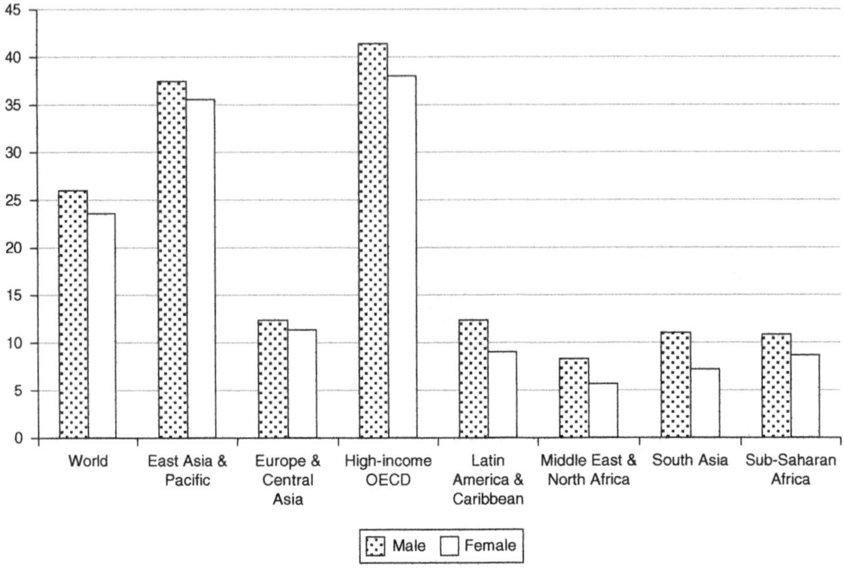

Figure 7.3 Saving rates (%) for old age around the world by gender and region
Source: Adapted from Demirgüç-Kunt et al. (2015).

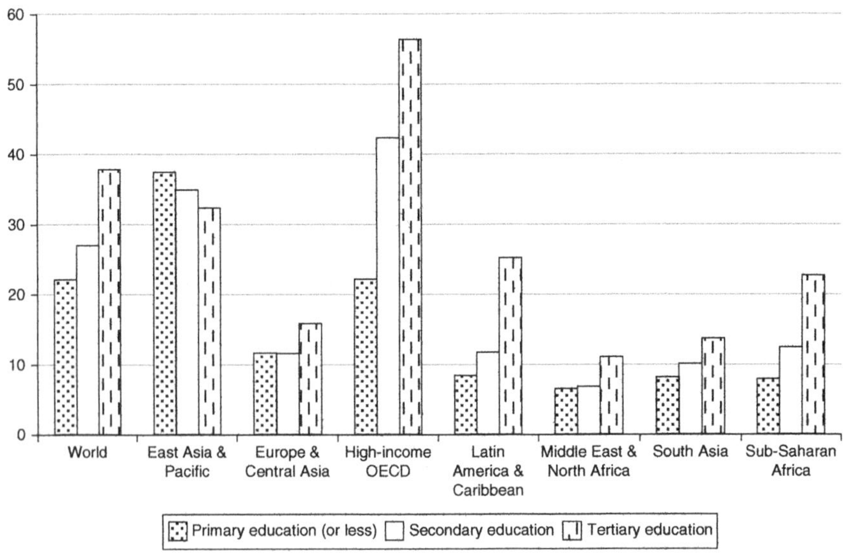

Figure 7.4 Saving rates (%) for old age around the world by educational attainment and region
Source: Demirgüç-Kunt et al. (2015); http://www.worldbank.org/globalfindex.

(or less). Specifically, 37.9 percent of individuals with tertiary education save for retirement, compared to 27 percent of individuals with secondary education and 22.2 percent of individuals with primary education or less. The old age saving gap seems to be much wider between the tertiary and secondary education groups, compared to the gap between secondary and primary education or less. The pattern is remarkably strong in LAC, in which 25.3 percent of individuals with tertiary education save for old age, compared to 11.9 percent and 8.6 percent of individuals with secondary and primary education or less, respectively.

Figure 7.5 presents the age distribution of old age saving around the world. We distinguish between six groups, age 18–25, 26–35, 36–45, 46–55, 56–65, and 65+. The 2014 Global Findex data indicate that 10.1 percent of individuals aged 18–25 save for old age, a figure that rises to 21 percent for those aged 26–35 and to 31 percent for those aged 36–45. Of the group aged 46–55, 33.3 percent save for old age and so do another 36.9 percent of the 56–65 group. The figure for those aged 65+ is close to that for the 56–65 group, at 36.5 percent. In EAP, the proportion of people saving for old age at age 26–35 is 31.9 percent, compared to half that, 16.3 percent, at age 18–25. In comparison, in ECA, the tiny figure of 3.6 percent at age 18–25 rises to 6.2 percent at age 26–35 and 8.2 percent at 36–45. A jump to 14.2 percent of the population occurs at age 45–55, with a further 20.8 percent of

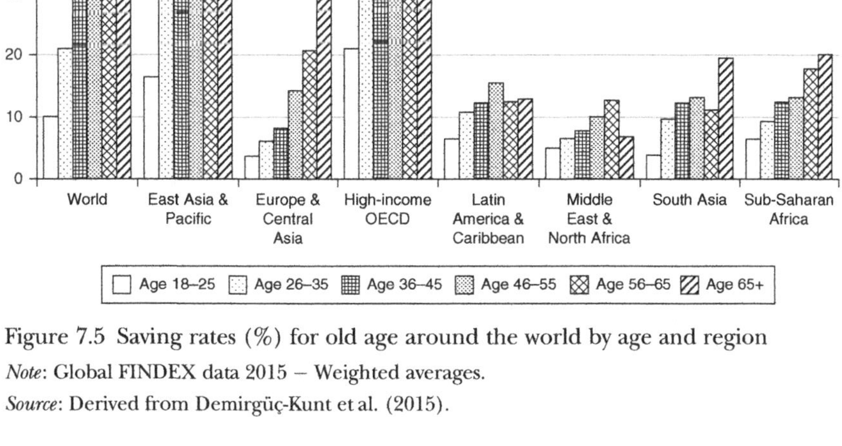

Figure 7.5 Saving rates (%) for old age around the world by age and region

Note: Global FINDEX data 2015 – Weighted averages.

Source: Derived from Demirgüç-Kunt et al. (2015).

the age group 56–65 saving for old age. The ECA figure is the highest for the 65+ group, at 29.6 percent, indicating that saving for old age peaks late.

In OECD^{HI}, the proportion of the population saving for old age rises sharply to 39.6 percent at age 26–35 and to 48.2 percent at age 36–45. The figures remain at 45.6 percent and 48 percent for ages 46–55 and 56–65, respectively. The figure for the 65+ age group is 40 percent. Notably, figures for the other four groups of countries—LAC, MENA, South Asia, and Sub-Saharan Africa—are strikingly low and remain so across the early age groups.

Aside from age patterns, we also have data by marital and family status around the world and for the regions of interest. Figure 7.6 shows that 12.6 percent of singles save for old age, compared to 29.3 percent of married people and 25.9 percent of those who are widowed/divorced/separated. Concerning family status, 21.2 percent of individuals with children younger than 15 save for old age, compared to 29.7 percent of individuals with no children younger than 15. Across all regions, married groups are more likely to save for old age.

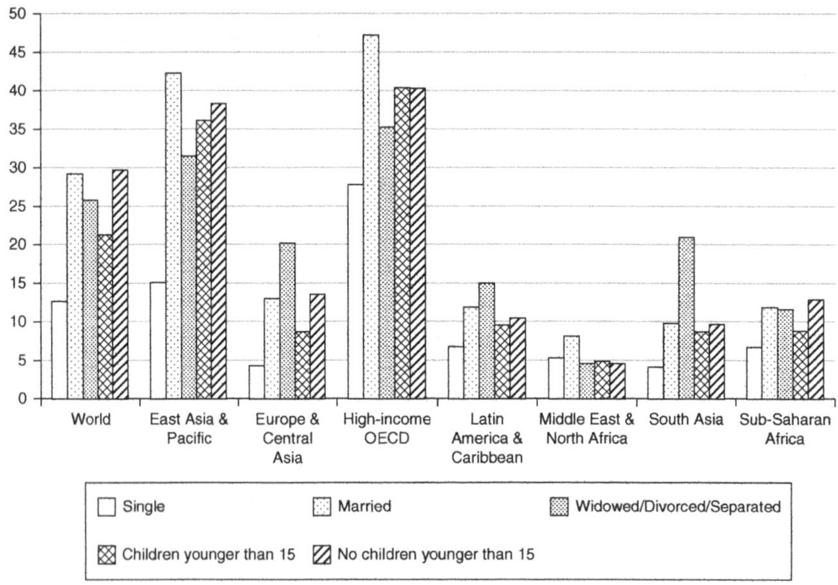

Figure 7.6 Saving rates (%) for old age around the world by family status and region

Note: Weighted averages. The figures at the top of the bars report the magnitude of the difference between: (a) single and married individuals in red (in both percentage points and as a percentage in the parenthesis), and (b) individuals with children younger than 15 and those with no children younger than 15.

Source: Adapted from Demirgüç-Kunt et al. (2015).

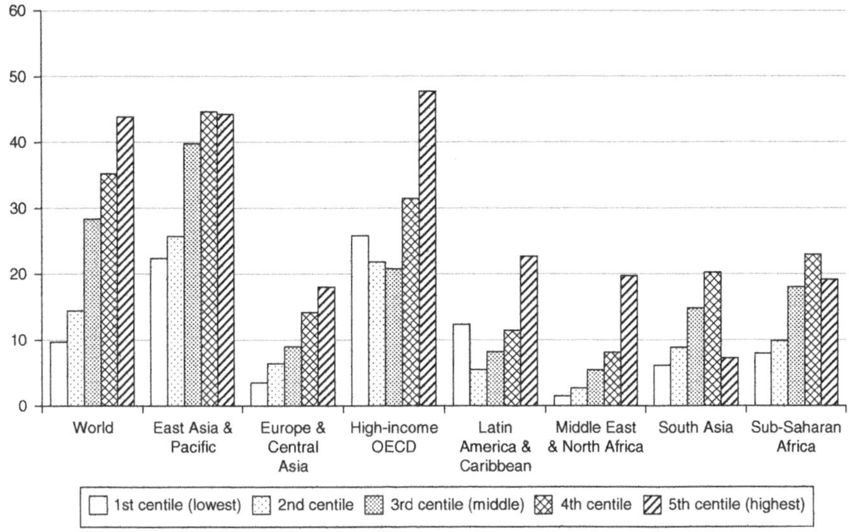

Figure 7.7 Saving rates (%) for old age around the world by household income per capita (global ranking) and region

Note: Global FINDEX data 2015 – Weighted averages.

Source: Adapted from Demirgüç-Kunt et al. (2015).

Next we examine the distribution of saving for old age by real (PPP-divided) household income per capita centile. The centiles presented in Figure 7.7 are for the global distribution of household-income-per-capita (not by country). As expected, the results show considerable inequality in the degree of financial preparedness for old age. Globally, 9.7 percent of individuals in the bottom income centile save for old age, compared to 14.4 percent in the second centile, 28.3 percent in the third income centile, 35.3 percent in the fourth centile, and 43.9 percent in the top income centile. In OECD^{HI} countries, old age saving rates are very high for the fourth and fifth income centiles. The figures for EAP and ECA also show considerably higher saving rates for old age, after the third income centile. Income inequality appears to have the most significant impact on saving for old age in LAC and MENA, with low rates of old age saving in the first four income centiles, and large measures for the top income centile.

Figure 7.8 depicts fitted lines from a fifth order local polynomial regression of old age saving on log GDP per capita in Panel A,[13] and household income per capita percentile (by country) in Panel B. Panel A indicates a positive and mildly concave relationship between real GDP-per-capita levels of US$400 and $3,000, corresponding to rates of old age saving of between 8 and 17 percent, respectively. The relationship then becomes steeply

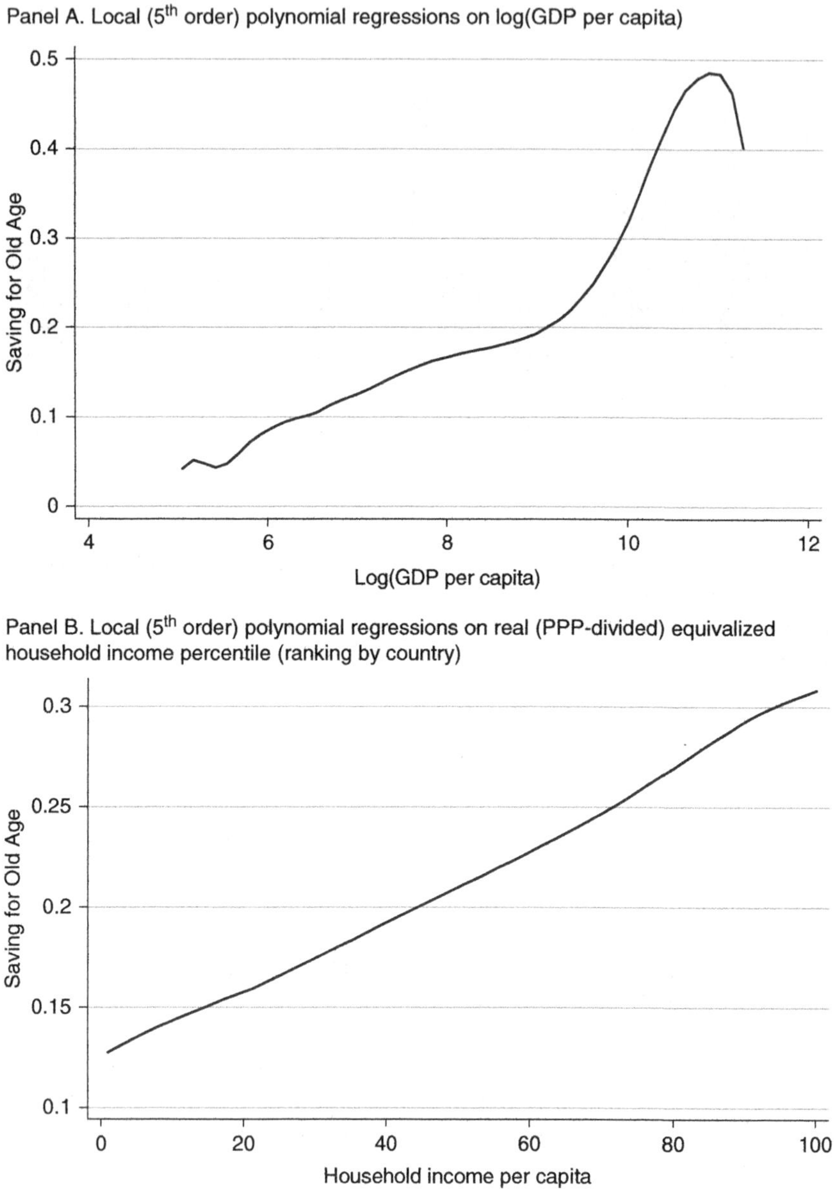

Figure 7.8 Probability of saving for old age by income

Source: Authors' calculations using Global FINDEX data 2015.

convex, with the maximum occurring at real GDP per capita levels of around $50,000, and rates of old age saving just under 50 percent. The rates of saving for old age then drop for GDP per capita above $50,000, to between 40 and 48 percent. By comparison, Panel B depicts a more or less linear relationship between old age saving and household income per capita percentile across countries. The rates of saving for old age are around 13 percent at the bottom household-income-per-capita percentile, to around 30 percent at the 97th percentile.

Finally, we differentiate saving patterns for old age across different labor market groups—self-employed, wage employed, unemployed, and out of the workforce—in Figure 7.9. There are striking differences between employed adults versus adults out of the workforce. The weighted global figures for old age saving by labor market status are 33 percent for those in paid employment, 27.4 percent for the self-employed, 17.1 percent for those out of workforce, and 11.2 percent for the unemployed.

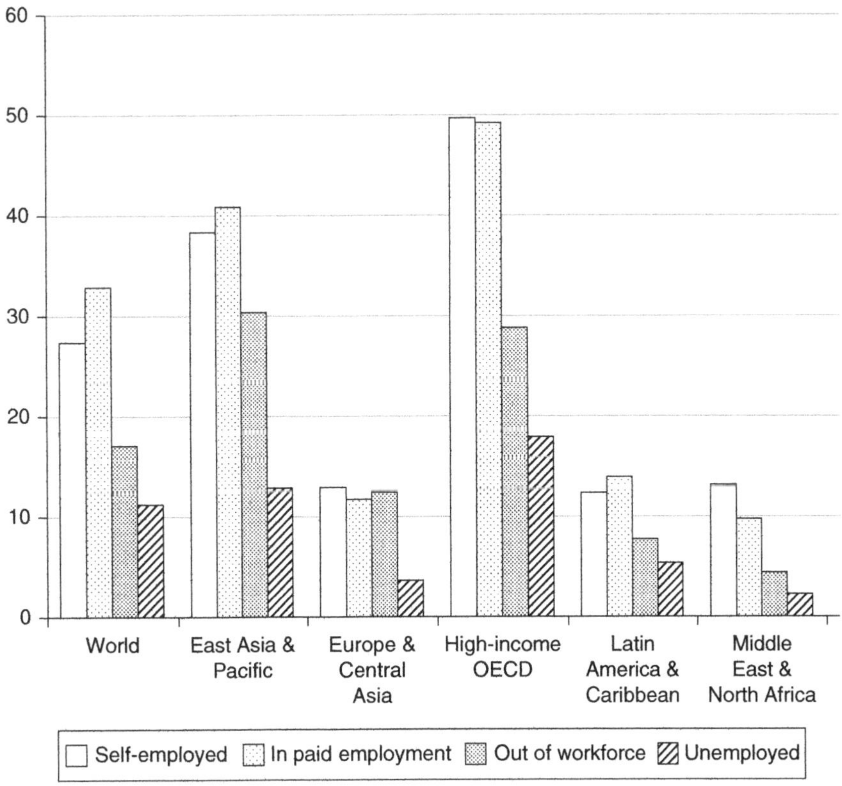

Figure 7.9 Saving for old age around the world by labor market status and region
Source: Authors' calculations using Global FINDEX data 2015 – weighted averages.

Empirical Analysis

Our empirical analysis entails several stages. First we regress the probability of saving for old age on a rich set of individual characteristics. These include gender, urban/rural region of residence, age (five groups), education (three groups), marital status (three groups), having financially dependent children, household-income-per-capita-centile (by country), and labor market status (four groups). In the primary specifications we incorporate region-fixed effects (eight groups), while we also estimate specifications with country-fixed effects for robustness (143 groups).[14]

Second, in extended models, we also include control variables for financial inclusion (owning an account at a bank or formal financial institution), having an outstanding housing loan (as a proxy for home ownership), and generic savings by country (having any savings during the last year, as a proxy for cultural factors shaping the propensity to save). We also estimate multinomial models of old age saving by financial inclusion status, and type of savings (formal versus informal/semi-formal).[15]

Third, we expand the models to incorporate country-level macroeconomic characteristics. From the World Development Indicators (WDI), we gather measures for the logarithm of life expectancy, the logarithm of per capita GDP (2011 PPP-constant levels), GDP per capita growth, the real interest rate (e.g., James and Song 2001), and the WDI legal rights index. In additional specifications, we also include control variables for legal origin (La Porta et al. 2008), the housing-affordability index (as a proxy for potential home ownership),[16] and indicators for explicit deposit insurance and the safety net/moral hazard index (Demirgüç-Kunt et al. 2014).

Fourth, we incorporate variables accounting for country pension-system characteristics, in addition to the individual and macroeconomic variables. We utilize two sources of data to capture features of pension systems. Several are derived from the Pension Watch/HelpAge's Social Pensions Database:[17] the logarithm of the benefit (in PPP international dollars), the benefit as a percentage of GDP per capita, the benefit as a percentage of the $1.25 per day poverty line, the percentage of the population over 60 covered by pension schemes, the cost of pension spending as a percentage of the country's GDP, and the logarithm of the age of eligibility. Others come from the World Bank Pensions database,[18] including the percentage contribution rate and the ratio of employer/employee contributions.

Results and analysis

Our comparison of individuals who save for old age versus those who do not[19] suggests that individuals who do save for old age are more likely to be males, reside in an urban region, have tertiary or secondary education, and to be in the older age groups. They are less likely to be in the age range 18–35, to be single or never married, to have children aged under 15, and to have primary education or less. Savers are also higher income and employed, and less likely to be self-employed, unemployed, or inactive. Old age savers are also more likely to be financially included and to have an outstanding mortgage. They tend to reside in countries with higher generic savings rates and in countries with higher GDP per capita. They reside in countries with lower GDP growth rates, higher legal rights index, and lower real interest rates. Savers for old age are less likely to be found in countries with French legal origin and more likely to be found in countries with English or German legal origin. Residents of countries that offer some form of explicit deposit insurance scheme are more likely to save for old age, as are individuals in countries with a higher safety net/moral hazard index. Old age savers are also found in countries with higher life expectancy, higher age of benefit eligibility, higher benefits, higher coverage, and higher pension costs. Finally, they are more likely to be residents of countries with higher contribution rates and lower employer/employee contribution ratios.

Table 7.1 presents estimates for the determinants of the probability of saving for old age around the world. The list of explanatory variables incorporates individual characteristics. All regressions show marginal effects from probit regressions, with robust standard errors in brackets, clustered at the country level. Estimates are weighted using country level weights. The results reveal a gender gap in savings for old age of 3.7 percent, based on the predicted probability of the model and the specification with the full set of control variables (column 4). The magnitude of the gap remains similar when incorporating country-fixed effects in column 5. The difference between urban and rural regions in saving for old age is insignificant in all specifications. The results also reveal a significant education gap in saving for old age. Individuals with tertiary education are 18.5 percent more likely to save for old age, compared to individuals with primary education or less. Moreover, individuals with secondary education are roughly 11.1 percent more likely to save for old age, compared to those with primary education or less.

Table 7.1 also shows large age differentials. For example, in column 4, individuals older than 65 are 85.1 percent more likely to save for old age, compared to the reference group age 18–25. The relative magnitudes are 77.2 percent for those age 56–65, 53.4 percent for those age 46–55, 41.8 percent for those age 36–45, and 21.8 percent for individuals aged 26–35. Married individuals are roughly 13.7 percent more likely to save for old age, while those having children under the age of 15 are somewhat more likely to save for old age (4.8 percent). Moreover, individuals in the top income centile (fifth) by country are 20.1 percent more likely to save for old age,

TABLE 7.1. Saving for old age and financial inclusion, probit regressions

	(1)	(2)	(3)	(4)	(5)
Male	0.009***	0.007**	0.006*	0.007**	0.007**
	[0.003]	[0.003]	[0.003]	[0.003]	[0.003]
Urban region	0.001	−0.004	−0.004	−0.003	−0.005
	[0.007]	[0.006]	[0.006]	[0.005]	[0.004]
Education: Tertiary	0.046***	0.037***	0.035***	0.035***	0.039***
	[0.006]	[0.006]	[0.006]	[0.005]	[0.005]
Education: Secondary	0.054***	0.032***	0.030***	0.021***	0.026***
	[0.008]	[0.006]	[0.006]	[0.005]	[0.005]
Education: Primary or less	[Ref.]	[Ref.]	[Ref.]	[Ref.]	[Ref.]
Age: 65 or more	0.179***	0.160***	0.162***	0.161***	0.159***
	[0.013]	[0.013]	[0.013]	[0.012]	[0.012]
Age: 56 to 65	0.164***	0.149***	0.147***	0.146***	0.141***
	[0.011]	[0.011]	[0.011]	[0.011]	[0.011]
Age: 46 to 55	0.118***	0.105***	0.101***	0.101***	0.097***
	[0.010]	[0.010]	[0.010]	[0.009]	[0.009]
Age: 36 to 45	0.098***	0.084***	0.079***	0.079***	0.075***
	[0.010]	[0.010]	[0.010]	[0.009]	[0.009]
Age: 26 to 35	0.052***	0.040***	0.037***	0.038***	0.036***
	[0.007]	[0.007]	[0.007]	[0.007]	[0.007]
Age: 18 to 25	[Ref.]	[Ref.]	[Ref.]	[Ref.]	[Ref.]
Married	0.031***	0.028***	0.023***	0.026***	0.029***
	[0.006]	[0.005]	[0.005]	[0.005]	[0.004]
Widowed/divorced/separated	0.004	0.004	0.002	0.01	0.016***
	[0.008]	[0.007]	[0.007]	[0.006]	[0.006]
Single	[Ref.]	[Ref.]	[Ref.]	[Ref.]	[Ref.]
Has children under 15	−0.001	0.006	0.003	0.009*	0.009**
	[0.006]	[0.006]	[0.006]	[0.005]	[0.005]
Household income per capita	0.040***	0.034***	0.033***	0.038***	0.036***
centile by country:	[0.006]	[0.006]	[0.005]	[0.005]	[0.005]
4th centile	0.019***	0.016***	0.016***	0.018***	0.017***
	[0.005]	[0.005]	[0.005]	[0.005]	[0.005]
3rd centile	[Ref.]	[Ref.]	[Ref.]	[Ref.]	[Ref.]
2nd centile	−0.030***	−0.028***	−0.027***	−0.028***	−0.027***
	[0.005]	[0.005]	[0.005]	[0.005]	[0.005]
bottom centile	−0.051***	−0.048***	−0.046***	−0.049***	−0.046***
	[0.007]	[0.007]	[0.007]	[0.007]	[0.007]
Self-employed	0.053***	0.048***	0.046***	0.046***	0.050***
	[0.007]	[0.007]	[0.007]	[0.006]	[0.005]
Wage employed	0.079***	0.061***	0.057***	0.058***	0.059***
	[0.010]	[0.010]	[0.009]	[0.007]	[0.006]
Unemployed	−0.024**	−0.026**	−0.025**	−0.017*	−0.016**
	[0.011]	[0.011]	[0.011]	[0.009]	[0.008]
Out of workforce	[Ref.]	[Ref.]	[Ref.]	[Ref.]	[Ref.]
Has any account	–	0.120***	0.115***	0.101***	0.108***
		[0.009]	[0.009]	[0.007]	[0.006]
Outstanding mortgage	–	–	0.052***	0.043***	0.045***
			[0.007]	[0.006]	[0.005]

Saved any money last year	–	–	–	0.463***	–
[country average]				[0.040]	
Country FE	–	–	–	–	+
Predicted probability	0.1891	0.1892	0.1892	0.1891	0.1891
No. of observations	147,690	147,690	147,690	147,690	147,690
Pseudo R^2	0.150	0.168	0.171	0.195	0.214
Log-likelihood	−61,069.5	−59,769.9	−59,562.2	−57,870.6	−56,473.4
LR χ^2	1,922.4***	1,948.3***	2,116.5***	3,593.3***	5,195.2***

Note: * $p < 0.10$, ** $p < 0.05$, *** $p < 0.01$.
Source: Authors' calculations from Global FINDEX data 2015—weighted averages.

compared to those in the third income centile. Individuals in the fourth income centile are 9.5 percent more likely to save for old age, compared to individuals in the third. Individuals in the second and bottom (first) income centile are 14.8 percent and 25.9 percent less likely to save for old age, compared to those in the third income centile.[20]

With respect to occupational groups, self-employed individuals are 24.3 percent more likely to be old age savers compared to the inactive group. Individuals in paid employment are about 30.7 percent more likely, while the unemployed are roughly 9 percent less likely to save for old age compared to the inactive. Financially included individuals around the world are about 53.4 percent more likely to be old age savers, while individuals who have an outstanding mortgage are roughly 22.9 percent more likely. Hence, having a mortgage for home ownership, as an alternative means of old age security, does not appear to reduce the probability of saving for old age, in our global sample.[21]

Country-specific generic savings rates have very large effects on the probability of an individual saving for old age. This supports other researchers' suggestions that cultural factors affect the individuals' attention to future events (Chen 2013). The magnitudes of the estimates do not differ substantially when excluding the group older than 65 years old in column 5, or when incorporating country-specific fixed effects (excluding the country-specific generic savings variable).

Table 7.2 presents estimates from multinomial probit models for old age savings, distinguishing by the individual state of financial inclusion, and the type of saving: formal versus informal. Results in columns A1–A3 report marginal effects for individuals who: (1) save for old age and have an account at a bank or another financial institution; (2) save for old age but do not have an account at a formal financial institution (i.e., save in some other way, such as gold, other assets, or in the home); and (3) do not save for old age. Results confirm that men are more likely to save for old age in general, by 4.4 percent (6.6) more among the financially included (excluded). Educated and urban residents are both more likely to be

TABLE 7.2. Saving for old age (OA) and financial inclusion, multinomial probit regressions

	(A) SavingOA & financial inclusion			(B) SavingOA & type of savings		
	(1) FIncl	(2) FExcl	(3) NoSavingOA	(1) FormalS	(2) InformalS	(3) NoSavingOA
Male	0.007***	0.002*	−0.009***	0.005***	−0.001	−0.004**
	[0.002]	[0.001]	[0.002]	[0.002]	[0.001]	[0.002]
Urban region	0.007***	−0.005***	−0.001	0.004**	0.002**	−0.006***
	[0.002]	[0.001]	[0.002]	[0.002]	[0.001]	[0.002]
Education: Tertiary	0.045***	−0.009***	−0.037***	0.040***	0.003**	−0.043***
	[0.003]	[0.002]	[0.003]	[0.002]	[0.001]	[0.003]
Education: Secondary	0.070***	−0.010***	−0.060***	0.052***	0.008***	−0.060***
	[0.003]	[0.001]	[0.003]	[0.003]	[0.001]	[0.003]
Age: 65 or more	0.155***	0.028***	−0.182***	0.111***	0.018***	−0.129***
	[0.005]	[0.002]	[0.005]	[0.004]	[0.002]	[0.005]
Age: 56 to 65	0.149***	0.018***	−0.166***	0.112***	0.014***	−0.127***
	[0.004]	[0.002]	[0.005]	[0.004]	[0.002]	[0.004]
age: 46 to 55	0.111***	0.008***	−0.119***	0.087***	0.011***	−0.098***
	[0.004]	[0.002]	[0.005]	[0.004]	[0.002]	[0.004]
Age: 36 to 45	0.099***	0.001	−0.101***	0.077***	0.009***	−0.087***
	[0.004]	[0.002]	[0.004]	[0.004]	[0.002]	[0.004]
Age: 26 to 35	0.057***	−0.002	−0.055***	0.043***	0.006***	−0.048***
	[0.004]	[0.002]	[0.004]	[0.004]	[0.002]	[0.004]
Married	0.028***	0.003	−0.031***	0.022***	0.004***	−0.026***
	[0.003]	[0.002]	[0.003]	[0.003]	[0.001]	[0.003]
Widowed/divorced/ separated	−0.001	0.005**	−0.003	−0.007**	0.004**	0.003
	[0.004]	[0.002]	[0.005]	[0.004]	[0.002]	[0.004]
Has children under 15	−0.007***	0.004***	0.003	0.001	0.003***	−0.004*
	[0.003]	[0.001]	[0.003]	[0.002]	[0.001]	[0.003]
Household income per capita	0.035***	0.003	−0.038***	0.026***	0.009***	−0.034***
centile by county:	[0.003]	[0.002]	[0.004]	[0.003]	[0.001]	[0.003]
4th centile	0.014***	0.004**	−0.018***	0.012***	0.006***	−0.017***
	[0.003]	[0.002]	[0.004]	[0.003]	[0.001]	[0.003]
2nd centile	−0.029***	−0.001	0.030***	−0.024***	−0.005***	0.029***
	[0.003]	[0.002]	[0.004]	[0.003]	[0.002]	[0.003]
bottom centile	−0.048***	−0.004**	0.051***	−0.045***	−0.009***	0.054***
	[0.004]	[0.002]	[0.004]	[0.003]	[0.002]	[0.004]
Self-employed	0.043***	0.009***	−0.052***	0.031***	0.013***	−0.044***
	[0.003]	[0.001]	[0.003]	[0.003]	[0.001]	[0.003]
In paid employment	0.077***	−0.001	−0.076***	0.053***	0.017***	−0.069***
	[0.003]	[0.001]	[0.003]	[0.002]	[0.001]	[0.003]
Unemployed	−0.024***	−0.001	0.025***	−0.031***	−0.001	0.032***
	[0.006]	[0.003]	[0.006]	[0.005]	[0.002]	[0.005]
Predicted probability	0.1587	0.0303	0.8110	0.1042	0.0942	0.8016
No. of observations	147,690			137,511		
F-statistic	−70,074.8			−49,240.6		
LR χ^2	17,431.1***			14,947.7***		

Note: Marginal effects from multinomial probit regressions are presented, along with robust standard errors in brackets. Standard errors are clustered at the country level. Asterisks denote the following levels of significance: * $p < 0.10$, ** $p < 0.05$, *** $p < 0.01$

Source: Authors' calculations from Global FINDEX data 2015—weighted averages.

financially included and save for old age. Older persons and married individuals are also more likely to save for old age and be financially included, while the financially excluded do so only after their mid-40s. Columns B1–B3 report estimates for individuals who respectively: (1) save for old age and have saved in the past 12 months using an account at a formal financial institution; (2) save for old age and have saved in the past 12 months informally or semi-formally, using an informal savings club or person outside the family (without saving at a formal financial institution); and (3) do not save for old age. Results show that men are 4.8 percent more likely to save for old age formally. The widowed/divorced/separated and those with children aged under 15 are more likely to save for old age informally and semi-formally, with the magnitude of the effects being 4.2 and 3.2 percent respectively. Individuals with missing income information are the income group most likely to save for old age informally, and they are less likely to do so using an account at a formal financial institution.

Table 7.3 reports estimates from models that incorporate macroeconomic country-level variables. Here we see that people living in countries having English legal origins are between 18.5 and 29.6 percent more likely to save for old age, compared to regions having French legal origin. Those from countries with other legal origin (Scandinavian or socialist) are more likely to save for old age, compared to regions with French or German legal origin, and the effects are of similar magnitude to the English legal origin effect. GDP per capita is positively associated with the probability of saving for old age, with a one standard deviation increase raising the probability by about 20 percent. All remaining macroeconomic variables have insignificant impacts on saving for old age for the pooled group of countries, with the notable exception of the safety net/moral hazard index, which is positively associated with the probability of saving for old age: a one standard deviation increase raises the probability by 4.6 percent. We interpret this last result as supportive of the view that an institutional environment enabling greater trust in the financial system also encourages old age saving.

When we incorporated country pension-system characteristics to the model (Table 7.4), we found that more generous pension schemes are generally insignificantly (and negatively) correlated with old age saving. Yet higher contribution rates and employer/employee ratios are both significantly positively related to the probability of saving for old age. The latter result is intuitive, but we interpret the former as consistent with Poterba et al. (1995) who suggest little substitution between regular retirement savings and other forms of conventional financial saving.

Since effects by region of the main variables may vary across country groups, Table 7.5 presents estimates by region for the determinants of saving for old age around the world. Here we see that greater life expectancy is positively associated with the probability of saving for old age in OECD^{HI},

TABLE 7.3. Saving for old age and country macroeconomic characteristics, probit regressions

	(1)	(2)	(3)	(4)	(5)	(6)	(7)	(8)
Log of life expectancy	–0.002	–0.071	–0.004	–0.015	0.003	0.009	0.011	0.040
German legal origin	0.004	0.003	0.003	0.001	–0.001	–0.002	–0.001	–0.003
	[0.019]	[0.018]	[0.018]	[0.018]	[0.018]	[0.019]	[0.020]	[0.018]
Other legal origin	0.041**	0.051***	0.049***	0.046***	0.045***	0.045***	0.045***	0.046***
	[0.020]	[0.017]	[0.017]	[0.017]	[0.017]	[0.017]	[0.017]	[0.016]
Log(GDP per capita)	–	0.039***	0.039***	0.041***	0.043***	0.041***	0.041***	0.040***
- PPP constant 2011		[0.010]	[0.009]	[0.009]	[0.010]	[0.011]	[0.011]	[0.010]
GDP per capita growth	–	–	0.005	0.005	0.004	0.004	0.004	0.005
			[0.003]	[0.003]	[0.003]	[0.003]	[0.003]	[0.003]
WDI Legal Rights Index	–	–	–	0.002	0.002	0.002	0.002	0.001
				[0.002]	[0.002]	[0.002]	[0.002]	[0.002]
Housing affordability index	–	–	–	–	–0.002	–0.002	–0.002	–0.004
					[0.009]	[0.009]	[0.009]	[0.009]
Missing affordability index	–	–	–	–	0.014	0.015	0.015	0.01
					[0.027]	[0.026]	[0.028]	[0.026]
Real interest rate	–	–	–	–	–	–0.001	–0.001	–0.001
						[0.001]	[0.001]	[0.001]
Deposit insurance dummy	–	–	–	–	–	–	0.003	–
							[0.018]	
Moral hazard index	–	–	–	–	–	–	–	0.008**
								[0.004]
Has any account	0.110***	0.099***	0.101***	0.101***	0.102***	0.102***	0.102***	0.100***
	[0.009]	[0.009]	[0.008]	[0.008]	[0.009]	[0.009]	[0.009]	[0.009]
Outstanding mortgage	0.049***	0.046***	0.046***	0.045***	0.045***	0.046***	0.046***	0.046***
	[0.007]	[0.007]	[0.007]	[0.007]	[0.007]	[0.007]	[0.007]	[0.007]
Individual characteristics	+	+	+	+	+	+	+	+
Predicted probability	0.1892	0.1896	0.1895	0.1895	0.1895	0.1895	0.1895	0.1732
No. of observations	147,690	141,655	141,655	141,655	141,655	141,655	141,655	85,817
Pseudo R^2	0.175	0.180	0.180	0.181	0.181	0.181	0.181	0.192
Log-likelihood	–59,296.8	–56,621.9	–56,558.2	–56,547.0	–56,534.5	–56,530.1	–56,529.5	–39,463.8

Note: * $p < 0.10$, ** $p < 0.05$, *** $p < 0.01$.

Source: Authors' calculations from Global FINDEX data 2015—weighted averages.

TABLE 7.4. Saving for old age and country pension-system characteristics: probit regressions

	(1)	(2)	(3)	(4)	(5)	(6)	(7)	(8)
Log benefit in PPP US$	−0.004	–	–	−0.046***	−0.005	−0.009	−0.002	−0.009**
	[0.003]			[0.017]	[0.004]	[0.011]	[0.003]	[0.004]
Benefit as % of GDP per capita	–	−0.095	–	–	–	–	–	–
		[0.086]						
Benefit as % of the $1.25/day poverty line	–	–	−0.001	–	–	–	–	–
			[0.001]					
Cost of pension spending as % GDP	–	–	–	−0.003	–	–	–	–
				[0.006]				
% population over 60 covered	–	–	–	–	0.029	0.027	0.043*	0.052**
					[0.023]	[0.023]	[0.025]	[0.024]
Log age of eligibility	–	–	–	–	–	0.004	–	–
						[0.011]		
Contribution rate %	–	–	–	–	–	–	0.172**	–
							[0.067]	
Employer/employee contribution ratio	–	–	–	–	–	–	–	0.006***
								[0.002]
Has any account	0.102***	0.107***	0.102***	0.130***	0.102***	0.102***	0.111***	0.116***
	[0.009]	[0.009]	[0.009]	[0.011]	[0.009]	[0.009]	[0.009]	[0.008]
Outstanding mortgage	0.048***	0.049***	0.049***	0.061***	0.048***	0.048***	0.050***	0.045***
	[0.007]	[0.006]	[0.007]	[0.009]	[0.007]	[0.007]	[0.007]	[0.006]
Predicted probability	0.1873	0.1874	0.1873	0.2501	0.1874	0.1874	0.1898	0.1879
No. of observations	133,146	133,146	133,146	57,345	133,146	133,146	106,929	133,146
Pseudo R^2	0.187	0.185	0.187	0.173	0.188	0.188	0.192	0.186
Log-likelihood	−52,368.4	−52,533.6	−52,381.0	−26,895.4	−52,348.3	−52,345.7	−41,992.8	−54,728.1

Note: * $p < 0.10$, ** $p < 0.05$, *** $p < 0.01$.
Source: Authors' calculations from Global FINDEX data 2015—weighted averages.

TABLE 7.5. Saving for old age and regional differences, probit regressions

	EAP	ECA	OECD^{HI}	LAC	MENA	South Asia	Sub-Saharan Africa
	(1)	(2)	(4)	(5)	(6)	(7)	(8)
Log of life expectancy	−3.724***	−1.739***	1.987***	0.862***	−2.489***	0.268**	0.038
	[0.208]	[0.359]	[0.750]	[0.328]	[0.112]	[0.118]	[0.061]
English legal origin	−0.127***	–	−0.076	−0.153***	–	−0.128***	0.015
	[0.021]		[0.057]	[0.047]		[0.011]	[0.013]
German legal origin	0.621***	−0.088***	0.066	–	–	–	–
	[0.034]	[0.021]	[0.043]				
Other legal origin	–	−0.052	0.016	–	−0.062***	–	0.007
		[0.045]	[0.038]		[0.013]		[0.011]
Log(GDP per capita)	−0.277***	0.046**	0.042	−0.038*	1.142***	−0.001	0.027***
- PPP constant 2011	[0.013]	[0.020]	[0.060]	[0.021]	[0.035]	[0.012]	[0.005]
GDP per capita growth	−0.143***	−0.012**	0.008	−0.002	0.021***	−0.022***	0.008***
	[0.009]	[0.006]	[0.014]	[0.002]	[0.006]	[0.003]	[0.001]
WDI legal rights index	0.005***	−0.007**	0.018***	0.013***	0.141***	−0.011***	−0.002
	[0.002]	[0.003]	[0.007]	[0.002]	[0.018]	[0.003]	[0.003]
Real interest rate	–	−0.009***	0.001	−0.001	−0.028***	–	0.001
		[0.002]	[0.009]	[0.001]	[0.001]		[0.001]
Housing affordability index	0.583***	0.133***	0.039*	0.113***	0.619***	0.037***	0.001
	[0.017]	[0.036]	[0.020]	[0.014]	[0.088]	[0.010]	[0.010]
Outstanding mortgage	0.035***	0.016	0.052***	0.033***	0.022	0.058	0.054***
	[0.012]	[0.012]	[0.012]	[0.012]	[0.014]	[0.038]	[0.008]
Has any account	0.138***	0.056***	0.101***	0.115***	0.051***	0.087***	0.096***
	[0.023]	[0.007]	[0.021]	[0.008]	[0.006]	[0.015]	[0.006]
Male	−0.003	0.006	0.008	0.026***	−0.006	−0.007	0.006
	[0.010]	[0.004]	[0.007]	[0.007]	[0.011]	[0.016]	[0.004]
Urban region	−0.040**	0.004	−0.029***	−0.002	0.005	0.011	0.013**
	[0.020]	[0.007]	[0.010]	[0.009]	[0.007]	[0.016]	[0.006]
Education: Tertiary	0.014	0.032***	0.058***	0.032***	0.028***	0.013	0.033***
	[0.042]	[0.012]	[0.009]	[0.012]	[0.006]	[0.012]	[0.009]
Education: Secondary	0.026*	0.001	0.065***	0.025***	−0.001	0.024*	0.014**
	[0.015]	[0.011]	[0.014]	[0.009]	[0.003]	[0.012]	[0.006]
Age: 65 or more	0.267***	0.175***	0.206***	0.101***	0.083***	0.096***	0.099***
	[0.063]	[0.026]	[0.031]	[0.024]	[0.011]	[0.013]	[0.011]
Age: 56 to 65	0.251***	0.132***	0.228***	0.087***	0.083***	0.073***	0.078***
	[0.077]	[0.029]	[0.026]	[0.017]	[0.008]	[0.018]	[0.011]

Age: 46 to 55	0.189***	0.078***	0.169***	0.071***	0.054***	0.052***	0.049***
	[0.051]	[0.026]	[0.023]	[0.016]	[0.004]	[0.015]	[0.011]
Age: 36 to 45	0.156***	0.037	0.145***	0.061***	0.024*	0.054***	0.027***
	[0.055]	[0.026]	[0.024]	[0.015]	[0.013]	[0.011]	[0.008]
Age: 26 to 35	0.071**	−0.003	0.079***	0.033**	0.001	0.028	0.01
	[0.032]	[0.019]	[0.021]	[0.014]	[0.010]	[0.018]	[0.008]
Married	0.066***	0.040***	0.055***	0.014*	−0.004	0.027***	0.023***
	[0.023]	[0.009]	[0.011]	[0.008]	[0.013]	[0.010]	[0.007]
Widowed/divorced/separated	0.005	0.034***	−0.009	0.021	−0.013*	0.064***	0.017**
	[0.029]	[0.010]	[0.013]	[0.020]	[0.008]	[0.023]	[0.008]
Single	[Ref.]	[Ref.]	[Ref.]	[Ref.]	[Ref.]	[Ref.]	[Ref.]
Has children under 15	0.030**	−0.023	0.025***	−0.004	0.019	0.006	0.008*
	[0.012]	[0.015]	[0.009]	[0.008]	[0.013]	[0.011]	[0.005]
Household income per capita	0.016**	0.024**	0.050***	0.049***	0.024***	0.02	0.040***
centile by country:	[0.007]	[0.012]	[0.013]	[0.010]	[0.004]	[0.015]	[0.006]
4th centile	−0.006	0.007	0.030**	0.027**	0.013**	0.003	0.024***
	[0.004]	[0.011]	[0.014]	[0.013]	[0.006]	[0.009]	[0.006]
2nd centile	−0.087***	0.001	−0.056***	−0.019**	−0.016**	−0.017*	0.001
	[0.018]	[0.013]	[0.012]	[0.009]	[0.007]	[0.010]	[0.008]
bottom centile	−0.143***	−0.025**	−0.083***	−0.010	−0.033***	−0.030***	−0.01
	[0.036]	[0.012]	[0.012]	[0.011]	[0.013]	[0.010]	[0.007]
Self-employed	0.059***	0.025**	0.104***	0.043***	0.043***	0.038***	0.029***
	[0.023]	[0.013]	[0.019]	[0.007]	[0.010]	[0.012]	[0.006]
In paid employment	0.073***	0.002	0.124***	0.040**	0.025***	0.067***	0.061***
	[0.016]	[0.010]	[0.013]	[0.016]	[0.008]	[0.014]	[0.008]
Unemployed	−0.019	−0.003	−0.039*	−0.014	−0.028*	0.060**	−0.016*
	[0.057]	[0.020]	[0.021]	[0.012]	[0.017]	[0.024]	[0.009]
Out of workforce	[Ref.]	[Ref.]	[Ref.]	[Ref.]	[Ref.]	[Ref.]	[Ref.]
Predicted probability	0.3470	0.1129	0.3627	0.1399	0.0667	0.0916	0.0901
No. of observations	11,184	21,040	30,119	15,536	9,069	9,132	33,042
Pseudo R^2	0.139	0.153	0.115	0.128	0.170	0.133	0.216
Log-likelihood	−6,505.2	−6,281.5	−17,458.3	−5,485.0	−1,844.9	−2,426.4	−7,844.8

Note: * p<0.10, ** p<0.05, *** p<0.01.

Source: Authors' calculations from Global FINDEX data 2015—weighted averages.

LAC, and South Asia. The effect is much higher in OECD^{HI}, but it is negative in EAP, ECA, and MENA. Higher GDP per capita and higher per capita growth both are positively linked to saving for old age in the MENA and Sub-Saharan Africa, but there is no significant effect in OECD^{HI} countries. (It is mixed in the remaining regions.) The probability of old age saving is higher in countries with higher legal-rights indexes in EAP, OECD^{HI}, LAC, and MENA. Higher real interest rates are positively linked to old age saving in Sub-Saharan Africa, but negatively in ECA. A greater housing affordability index is positively related to saving for old age in the majority of regions, with the exception of Sub-Saharan Africa, where there is no association.

We also examine additional factors associated with old age saving around the world, by region. Our results (see Table 7A.3, in the Appendix) indicate that deposit insurance schemes are positively related to saving for old age in ECA but negatively related in MENA. Moreover, higher benefits are only negatively related to saving for old age in MENA countries. Contribution rates are negatively related to saving for old age only in EAP. In sum, our results largely confirm the view of limited substitutability between regular retirement savings and other forms of conventional financial saving.

Conclusion

The looming worldwide retirement crisis has policymakers scrambling to better understand how adults prepare financially for old age. This chapter offers the first detailed global inquiry into patterns of old age saving around the world and across country groups, drawing on new and rich micro-data. We find that 24.8 percent of individuals around the world save for old age, with large regional differences: rates are above 35 percent in OECD^{HI} and EAP, 11.8 percent in ECA, 10.6 percent in LAC, and below 10 percent in Sub-Saharan Africa, South Asia, and MENA. We also found a small gender gap in saving for old age overall, which is larger in developing counties. Most regions exhibit patterns of higher saving for old age among those with higher education, with EAP standing out as the sole exception. In every region except South Asia, employed adults are more likely to save for old age than unemployed adults. Saving for old age also rises sharply among the 36–45 age group. Our findings also reveal large income disparities: adults in the top income centiles are far more likely, while the lowest income are much less likely, to save for old age. Adults who have an account at a bank or a financial institution are about 40 to 50 percent more likely to save for old age.

On the country level, we also uncover a significant and positive relationship between old age saving and the country's generic saving propensity, English legal origin, and GDP per capita. Institutional arrangements also help when they enable greater trust in the financial system. Finally, we find a significantly positive relationship between the probability of saving for old age and pension coverage, the size of contributions, and contribution ratios. More affordable housing is positively related to saving for old age everywhere except Sub-Saharan Africa. We interpret this as evidence suggesting little substitution between pension system provisions and contribution rates, other forms of financial saving, and saving for old age.

Appendix

TABLE 7A.1. Summary statistics by region

		EAP	ECA	OECD[HI]	LAC	MENA	South Asia	Sub-Saharan Africa
	Units							
Male	(%)	49.2	47.7	48.5	48.6	49.8	50.3	49.2
Urban region	(%)	31.4	35.7	44.7	38.7	62.0	14.9	23.1
Education: Tertiary	(%)	10.2	13.9	21.1	12.2	8.1	3.4	3.0
Education: Secondary	(%)	49.3	72.2	82.5	63.2	53.1	37.1	34.3
Education: Primary or less	(%)	50.4	27.3	15.8	36.5	46.7	62.9	65.3
Age: 65+	(%)	7.0	11.9	17.5	8.2	3.8	5.9	5.0
Age: 56 to 65	(%)	11.1	12.7	15.6	9.0	7.3	9.5	6.6
Age: 46 to 55	(%)	16.0	16.1	17.6	13.0	11.9	11.1	10.3
Age: 36 to 45	(%)	20.8	17.5	17.2	17.3	17.5	16.6	16.4
Age: 26 to 35	(%)	21.8	18.3	15.7	22.5	23.9	23.4	24.7
Age: 18 to 25	(%)	17.5	16.3	12.0	22.0	26.9	25.3	25.9
Married	(%)	69.5	60.3	57.6	51.8	54.3	67.8	51.3
Widowed/divorced/ separated	(%)	5.7	13.3	12.9	10.3	4.6	6.4	10.6
Single	(%)	24.8	26.4	29.6	38.0	41.1	25.8	38.1
Has children under 15	(%)	48.9	40.4	28.8	38.9	45.9	69.6	66.3
HH income per capita centile by country:	(%)	13.2	12.6	15.0	10.8	10.9	15.0	12.0
4th centile	(%)	18.5	15.2	16.9	12.0	13.7	17.6	15.1
3rd centile	(%)	19.9	17.5	18.7	13.2	15.0	20.0	17.5
2nd centile	(%)	18.5	18.9	20.8	14.6	18.1	22.2	19.7
bottom centile	(%)	22.6	21.6	25.2	16.0	20.2	25.2	21.1
missing centile	(%)	7.3	14.3	3.4	33.3	22.2	0.0	14.7
Self-employed	(%)	38.8	17.7	10.5	23.1	16.7	27.9	38.8
Employed	(%)	28.9	32.2	45.3	30.2	21.5	19.1	18.2
Unemployed	(%)	29.9	43.2	38.7	37.8	51.0	48.0	34.0
Inactive	(%)	2.5	6.9	5.6	8.9	10.7	5.0	8.9
Has any account	(%)	62.4	45.8	93.5	44.5	33.0	40.6	30.0
	(%)	67.0	37.1	70.1	47.4	38.6	39.1	58.0

(continued)

TABLE 7A.1. Continued

		EAP	ECA	OECD^{HI}	LAC	MENA	South Asia	Sub-Saharan Africa
Any savings last year (country average)								
Outstanding mortgage	(%)	9.9	11.2	27.6	10.4	9.6	5.4	5.2
Log (GDP per capita—PPP divided)		9.15	9.23	10.51	9.15	9.22	8.37	7.89
GDP per capita growth		6.47	4.42	0.76	3.65	1.71	5.27	5.22
WDR legal rights index		4.43	5.90	5.87	4.49	1.23	5.54	5.15
Legal origin: English	(%)	14.6	0.0	20.0	6.1	0.0	89.1	38.2
Legal origin: French	(%)	29.2	71.3	30.1	93.9	89.0	11.0	55.9
Legal origin: German	(%)	48.8	24.0	26.6	0.0	0.0	0.0	0.0
Legal origin: Other	(%)	7.4	4.8	23.3	0.0	11.0	0.0	5.9
Real interest rate		3.96	8.10	1.12	5.56	3.94	5.08	5.09
Missing real interest rate	(%)	15.9	19.0	59.9	12.1	22.7	11.5	55.9
Deposit insurance	(%)	47.2	95.3	90.0	69.7	44.1	77.9	32.4
Safety net/moral hazard index‡		0.59	0.81	1.07	−2.32	−0.07	−0.52	−0.34
Life expectancy		72.68	72.50	80.68	74.16	72.19	67.66	57.90
Benefit in PPP US$‡		34.13	86.84	614.85	144.21	62.00	9.25	95.86
Benefit as % of GDP per capita‡	(%)	4.2	11.7	20.3	13.5	21.0	4.7	14.9
Benefit as % of $1.25/day pov. line‡	(%)	90.0	228.6	1,617.2	379.2	162.0	24.9	252.1
Cost of pension spending as % GDP‡	(%)	0.09	1.07	1.48	0.27	0.06	0.10	0.70
% population 60+ covered‡	(%)	31.1	33.4	30.6	25.4	10.0	20.7	65.5
Age of eligibility‡		62.29	62.16	64.85	64.38	60.00	62.77	62.14
Employer/employee contribution ratio‡		1.91	7.63	1.94	2.70	3.33	3.03	4.01
% contribution rate	(%)	16.9	26.6	28.3	23.0	24.0	26.6	16.9

Note: Variables marked with the symbol (‡) have missing observations. For region definitions, see text.

Source: Authors' calculations from Global FINDEX data 2015—weighted averages.

TABLE 7A.2. Summary statistics by old age (OA) saving status

	(1) All countries	(2) SavingOA	(3) Not SavingOA	(4) Diff.	[Sig.]
#of Observations	147,692	30,395	117,297		
Male	49.0%	52.3%	48.3%	0.0397	***
Urban region	37.3%	41.8%	36.2%	0.0561	***
Education: Tertiary	12.4%	21.8%	10.2%	0.1160	***
Education: Secondary	59.9%	73.0%	56.9%	0.1614	***
Education: Primary or less	39.4%	26.2%	42.5%	−0.1626	***
Age: 65+	9.8%	14.6%	8.7%	0.0590	***
Age: 56 to 65	10.7%	16.8%	9.2%	0.0756	***
Age: 46 to 55	14.1%	19.1%	13.0%	0.0610	***
Age: 36 to 45	17.5%	20.7%	16.8%	0.0387	***
Age: 26 to 35	21.0%	17.8%	21.8%	−0.0399	***
Age: 18 to 25	19.4%	9.3%	21.8%	−0.1241	***
Married	57.7%	68.8%	55.1%	0.1370	***
Widowed/divorced/separated	10.5%	11.4%	10.3%	0.0116	***
Single	31.8%	19.8%	34.6%	−0.1486	***
Has children under 15	45.6%	36.8%	47.7%	−0.1094	***
Household income per capita centile:	12.8%	18.6%	11.5%	0.0711	***
4th centile	15.4%	19.4%	14.4%	0.0493	***
3rd centile	17.3%	18.9%	16.9%	0.0203	***
2nd centile	18.9%	16.4%	19.5%	−0.0312	***
bottom centile	21.4%	15.6%	22.8%	−0.0715	***
missing centile	14.2%	11.1%	15.0%	−0.0380	***
Self-employed	23.3%	22.3%	23.5%	−0.0114	***
Employed	30.1%	43.5%	26.9%	0.1657	***
Unemployed	39.8%	31.3%	41.8%	−0.1053	***
Inactive	6.9%	2.9%	7.8%	−0.0490	***
Has any account	55.5%	83.9%	48.8%	0.3509	***
Any savings last year (country average)	54.6%	64.4%	52.3%	0.1212	***
Outstanding mortgage	13.2%	25.0%	10.5%	0.1453	***
Log(GDP per capita—PPP divided)	9.22	9.80	9.08	0.7150	***
GDP per capita growth	3.75	3.22	3.88	−0.6596	***
WDR legal rights index	5.00	5.39	4.91	0.4846	***
Legal origin: English	24.4%	27.4%	23.7%	0.0366	***
Legal origin: French	52.8%	37.1%	56.4%	0.0412	***
Legal origin: German	14.7%	22.5%	12.9%	0.0963	***
Legal origin: other	8.1%	13.0%	7.0%	−0.1926	***
Real interest rate	4.34	3.15	4.62	−1.4614	***
Deposit insurance	66.5%	73.3%	64.9%	−0.0014	**
Moral hazard index‡	0.17	0.71	0.03	0.6808	***
Life expectancy	71.11	75.11	70.19	4.9177	***
Benefit in PPP US$‡	256.36	353.02	227.06	125.9557	***
Benefit as % of GDP per capita‡	13.7%	14.3%	13.5%	0.0075	***
Benefit as % of $1.25 a day pov. line‡	674.4%	928.6%	597.3%	331.3	***
Cost of pension spending as % GDP‡	0.68%	0.89%	0.61%	0.2808	***
% population 60+ covered‡	31.1%	34.1%	30.1%	0.0403	***
Age of eligibility‡	63.52	63.59	63.50	0.0960	***
Employer/employee contribution ratio‡	3.42	2.94	3.53	−0.5902	***
% contribution rate‡	23.5%	24.6%	23.3%	0.0136	***

Note: Weighted averages in columns 1–3. Weighted mean differences in column 4 and levels of significance of the differences are from a t-test for weighted mean differences with unequal variances produced using the parmby and metaparm commands in Stata. Variables marked with the symbol (‡) have missing observations. Asterisks denote the following levels of significance: * $p < 0.10$, ** $p < 0.05$, *** $p < 0.01$.

Source: Authors' calculations from Global FINDEX data 2015—weighted averages.

TABLE 7A.3. Additional models of saving for old age and regional differences, probit regressions

	EAP	ECA	$OECD^{HI}$	LAC	MENA	South Asia	Sub-Saharan Africa
Panel A: Saving for old age by region and deposit insurance							
	(1)	(2)	(3)	(4)	(5)	(6)	(7)
Deposit Insurance dummy	–	0.176***	−0.031	−0.004	−0.212***	–	0.006
		[0.027]	[0.053]	[0.018]	[0.005]		[0.008]
Predicted probability	0.3470	0.1129	0.3627	0.1399	0.0667	0.0916	0.0901
No. of observations	11,184	21,040	30,119	15,536	9,069	9,132	33,042
Pseudo R^2	0.139	0.145	0.115	0.127	0.170	0.133	0.215
Panel B: Saving for old age by region and pension-system characteristics							
	(9)	(10)	(12)	(13)	(14)	(15)	(16)
Log benefit in PPP US$	0.026*	2.626***	−0.004	0.011***	−0.082***	−0.031	0.012***
	[0.015]	[0.053]	[0.010]	[0.001]	[0.004]	[0.078]	[0.004]
% population over 60 covered	0.091	216.423***	0.003	−0.320***	–	0.304	−0.042
	[0.103]	[6.358]	[0.059]	[0.029]		[0.614]	[0.035]
Contribution rate (%)	−0.195***	25.968***	0.709***	1.147***	5.905***	0.090	0.144
	[0.070]	[0.535]	[0.163]	[0.088]	[0.267]	[0.350]	[0.099]
Predicted probability	0.3753	0.1294	0.3557	0.1393	0.0702	0.0969	0.0908
No. of observations	5,000	14,036	26,114	14,528	8,069	6,112	27,040
Pseudo R^2	0.141	0.148	0.12	0.136	0.168	0.118	0.225

Note: * $p < 0.10$, ** $p < 0.05$, *** $p < 0.01$.

Source: Authors' calculations from Global FINDEX data 2015—weighted averages.

Endnotes

1. The literature does offer contrary views on retirement and wellbeing, such as Charles (2002).
2. The author reviews how designing public policy toward retirement security must recognize both the heterogeneity among households saving for retirement, as well as the multiple policy objectives that are served by various policy instruments.
3. In a similar vein, the Future of Retirement report (HSBC 2013), which surveyed 1,050 respondents in the UK and more than 16,000 people across 15 countries, revealed that almost two-fifths of retired UK respondents (39%) said that they had not prepared adequately or at all for a comfortable retirement.
4. Moreover, one-third of respondents said that they had foregone some form of medical treatment in the preceding year due to the treatment's expected cost. Not surprisingly, the decision not to seek treatment was more common for those without savings, those indicating that they were struggling with their finances, or had no insurance.
5. For a detailed investigation on the heuristics and the biases that emerge in the area of retirement savings, see Benartzi and Thaler (2007). Other studies on retirement planning strategies involving relevant considerations include Ameriks and Zeldes (2004) and Brown (2007).
6. See Holzmann (2012) and Pallares-Miralles et al. (2012) for reviews of international pension systems.
7. The rationale is that by separating the redistributive function from the savings function, the public pillar, as well as the size of the payroll tax needed to support it, can be kept relatively small, thus avoiding many of the growth-inhibiting problems associated with a dominant public pillar (World Bank 1994).
8. Such incentives involve tax exemptions and subsidies. These might require changes in fiscal policy that can be socially costly because they increase distortions. Moreover, such schemes might suffer from limited or lower coverage as well as volume of savings, particularly among the poor, compared to the remaining pillars. Valdés-Prieto (2002a) suggests that most third-pillar fiscal incentives are regressive because the incentives are taken up mostly by higher-income workers while the increase in general tax rates fall to some degree upon middle- and lower-income workers. There is a rich literature on the effects of social security incentives and provisions on labor market distortions (e.g., Gruber and Wise 1998, 2002; Coile 2015), on the strong connections between subjective retirement expectations and future work behavior (e.g., Chan and Stevens 2004), on the role of financial incentives on retirement choices (e.g., Kingston 2000; Belloni and Alessie 2009), and on the role of fluctuations on the business cycle, financial markets, and the housing market on retirement choices (e.g., Crawford and Lilien 1981; Coile and Levine 2010).
9. The complete database is available at: <http://datatopics.worldbank.org/financialinclusion>.

10. The survey is conducted in the major languages of each country. The target population is the entire civilian, non-institutionalized population age 15 and above. Data weighting is used to ensure a nationally representative sample for each economy. Final weights consist of the base sampling weight, which corrects for unequal probability of selection based on household size, and the poststratification weight, which corrects for sampling and nonresponse error. Poststratification weights use country-level population statistics on gender and age and, where reliable data are available, education or socioeconomic status. In some large economies, such as China and Russia, sample sizes of at least 4,000 are collected. Detailed country-level information about the data collection dates, sample sizes, excluded populations, and margins of error can be found at <http://go.worldbank.org/IGRTPHK660>.
11. We do not exclude from the sample individuals older than 65 years old, following the evidence in Alessie et al. (1999), who find little evidence of decumulation among the elderly, and only at an advanced age. The authors find that precautionary savings, bequest motives, and health are among the reasons why some elderly do not decumulate in the pattern predicted by the life-cycle model.
12. All summary statistics are weighted country averages.
13. Data on real GDP per capita, PPP (constant 2011 international dollars) are from the World Development Indicators.
14. Out of the total 146 countries in the Global Findex 2014 data, Liberia, Paraguay, and South Sudan are excluded from these specifications due to missing data on saving for old age.
15. Across the developing world, only about 4% of adults—160 million people—are unbanked but save by using a savings club or a person outside the family, while in Sub-Saharan Africa the share is three times that size. On average, in the region's economies, 13% of adults are unbanked and save semi-formally (Demirgüç-Kunt et al. 2015).
16. The housing affordability index is from Numbeo (2015). The data and description are available at: <http://www.numbeo.com/property-investment/rankings_by_country.jsp?title=2014>.
17. The data and detailed description are available at: <http://www.pension-watch.net/pensions/about-social-pensions/about-social-pensions/social-pensions-database>.
18. The data are described by Pallares-Miralles et al. (2012) and are available at: <http://www.worldbank.org/en/topic/socialprotectionlabor/brief/pensions-data>.
19. Descriptive statistics for the main variables in the analysis of old age saving around the world appear in Tables 7A.1 and 7A.2 in the Appendix. Column 1 presents weighted averages for the pooled sample of all countries (147,692 individuals), while columns 2 and 3 present averages for individuals who save for old age (24.8% of the weighted sample, or 30,395 individuals) and those who do not (75.2% of the weighted sample, or 117, 297 individuals), respectively. Column 4 also presents the mean difference and significance levels for tests of

differences in the means of the variables across the two samples. Weighted mean differences are computed and a t-test for weighted mean differences with unequal variances produced using the parmby and metaparm commands in Stata.

20. It is worth noting that the magnitude of the effects with respect to the income variables does not differ much when overall equivalized household income centiles are used, instead of centiles by country (results available upon request).
21. Indeed, there is limited empirical evidence in favor of downsizing housing adjustments on retirement, such as Ermisch and Jenkins (1999).

References

Alessie, R., A. Lusardi, and A. Kapteyn (1999). 'Saving after Retirement: Evidence from Three Different Surveys,' *Labour Economics*, 6: 277–310.

Ameriks, J. and S. P. Zeldes (2004). *How do Household Portfolio Shares Vary with Age?* Working Paper. New York: Columbia University. <https://www0.gsb.columbia.edu/mygsb/faculty/research/pubfiles/16/Ameriks_Zeldes_age_Sept_2004d.pdf>.

Andersen, T. M. (2008). 'Increasing Longevity and Social Security Reforms: A Legislative Procedure Approach,' *Journal of Public Economics*, 92(3): 633–46.

Banks, J. and Z. Oldfield (2007). 'Understanding Pensions: Cognitive Function, Numerical Ability and Retirement Saving,' *Fiscal Studies*, 28(2): 143–70.

Bardasi, E., S. P. Jenkins, and J. A. Rigg (2000). *Retirement and the Economic Well-Being of the Elderly: A British Perspective*, ISER Working Paper No. 2000-33, Colchester: Institute for Social and Economic Research, University of Essex.

Belloni, M. and R. Alessie (2009). 'The Importance of Financial Incentives on Retirement Choices: New Evidence for Italy,' *Labour Economics*, 16(5): 578–88.

Benartzi, S. and R. H. Thaler (2007). 'Heuristics and Biases in Retirement Savings Behavior,' *Journal of Economic Perspectives*, 21(3): 81–104.

Bernheim, D. B., J. Skinner, and S. Weinberg (2001). 'What Accounts for the Variation in Retirement Wealth among U.S. Households?,' *American Economic Review*, 91(4): 832–57.

Board of Governors of the Federal Reserve System (2014). *Report on the Economic Well Being of U.S. Households in 2013*. Washington, DC: Federal Reserve Board. <http://www.federalreserve.gov/econresdata/2013-report-economic-well-being-us-households-201407.pdf>.

Bonsang, E. and T. J. Klein (2011). *Retirement and Subjective Well-Being*, IZA Discussion Paper No. 5536. Bonn: IZA.

Brown, J. R. (2007). *Rational and Behavioral Perspectives on the Role of Annuities in Retirement Planning*, NBER Working Paper, 13537. Cambridge, MA: National Bureau of Economic Research.

Chan, S. and A. H. Stevens (2004). 'Do Changes in Pension Incentives Affect Retirement? A Longitudinal Study of Subjective Retirement Expectations,' *Journal of Public Economics*, 88(7–8): 1307–33.

Charles, K. K. (2002). *Is Retirement Depressing? Labor Force Inactivity and Psychological Well-Being in Later Life,* NBER Working Paper, 9033. Cambridge, MA: National Bureau of Economic Research.

Chen, M. K. (2013). 'The Effect of Language on Economic Behavior: Evidence from Savings Rates, Health Behaviors, and Retirement Assets,' *American Economic Review,* 103(2): 690–731.

Clark, R. L. and J. F. Quinn (1999). *Reform of Retirement Programs and the Future Well-Being of the Elderly in America,* Boston College Working Papers in Economics, 423. Chestnut Hill, MA: Boston College.

Coile, C. C. (2015). *Disability Insurance Incentives and the Retirement Decision: Evidence from the U.S.,* NBER Working Paper, 20916. Cambridge, MA: National Bureau of Economic Research.

Coile, C. C. and P. B. Levine (2010). *Reconsidering Retirement: How Losses and Layoffs Affect Older Workers.* Boston, MA: Brookings Institution Press.

Crawford, V. P. and D. M. Lilien (1981). 'Social Security and the Retirement Decision,' *Quarterly Journal of Economics,* 96(3): 505–29.

Crystal, S. and D. Shea (1990). 'The Economic Well-Being of the Elderly,' *Review of Income and Wealth,* 36(3): 227–47.

Demirgüç-Kunt, A., E. Kane, and L. Laeven (2014). *Deposit Insurance Database,* IMF Working Paper, 14/118. Washington, DC: International Monetary Fund.

Demirgüç-Kunt, A., L. Klapper, D. Singer, and P. Van Oudheusden (2015). *The Global Findex Database 2014,* World Bank Policy Research Working Paper, 7255. Washington, DC: World Bank.

Duflo, E. and E. Saez (2002). 'Participation and Investment Decisions in a Retirement Plan: The Influence of Colleagues' Choices,' *Journal of Public Economics,* 85 (1): 121–48.

Duflo, E. and E. Saez (2003). 'The Role of Information and Social Interactions in Retirement Plan Decisions: Evidence from a Randomized Experiment,' *Quarterly Journal of Economics,* 118(3): 815–42.

Ellis, C. D., A. H. Munnell, and A. D. Eschtruth (2014). *Falling Short: The Coming Retirement Crisis and What to Do About It.* Oxford: Oxford University Press.

Ermisch, J. F. and S. P. Jenkins (1999). 'Retirement and Housing Adjustment in Later Life: Evidence from the British Household Panel Survey,' *Labour Economics,* 6(2): 311–33.

Fridson, M. S. (2015). 'Book Review: Falling Short: The Coming Retirement Crisis and What to Do about it,' *CFA Institute Book Reviews,* 10(1). <http://www.cfapubs.org/doi/full/10.2469/br.v10.n1.10>.

Galasso, V. (2008). 'Postponing Retirement: The Political Effect of Ageing,' *Journal of Public Economics,* 92(10–11): 2157–69.

Gratton, B. (1996). 'The Poverty of Impoverishment Theory: The Economic Well-Being of the Elderly, 1890–1950,' *Journal of Economic History,* 56(1): 39–61.

Gruber, J. and D. Wise (1998). 'Social Security and Retirement: An International Comparison,' *American Economic Review,* 88(2): 158–63.

Gruber, J. and D. Wise (2002). *Social Security Programs and Retirement around the World: Micro Estimation,* NBER Working Paper, 9407. Cambridge, MA: National Bureau of Economic Research.

Holzmann, R. (2012). '*Global Pension Systems and their Reform: Worldwide Drivers, Trends, and Challenges,* World Bank, Social Protection & Labor Discussion Paper, 1213. Washington, DC: World Bank.

HSBC (2013). *The Future of Retirement: Life After Work?* London: HSBC. <https://investments.hsbc.co.uk/myplan/files/resources/130/future-of-retirement-global-report.pdf>.

James, E. and X. Song (2001). *Annuities Markets around the World: Money's Worth and Risk Intermediation,* Center for Research on Pensions and Welfare Policies Working Paper, 16/01. Moncalieri, Italy: CeRP.

Kingston, G. H. (2000). 'Efficient Timing of Retirement,' *Review of Economic Dynamics,* 3(4): 831–40.

La Porta, R., F. Lopez-de-Silanes, and A. Shleifer (2008). 'The Economic Consequences of Legal Origins,' *Journal of Economic Literature,* 46(2): 285–332.

Lusardi, A. (2003). *Planning and Saving for Retirement.* Hanover, NH: Dartmouth College. <http://www.dartmouth.edu/~alusardi/Papers/Lusardi_pdf>.

Lusardi, A. and O. S. Mitchell (2011). 'Financial Literacy around the World: An Overview,' *Journal of Pension Economics and Finance,* 10(4): 497–508.

Lusardi, A. and O. S. Mitchell (2014). 'The Economic Consequences of Financial Literacy,' *Journal of Economic Literature,* 52(1): 5–44.

Numbeo (2015). 'Property Prices Index by Country 2014.' <http://www.numbeo.com/property-investment/rankings_by_country.jsp?title=2014>.

Pallares-Miralles, M., C. Romero, and E. Whitehouse (2012). *International Patterns of Pension Provision II: A Worldwide Overview of Facts and Figures,* World Bank: Social Protection & Labor Discussion Paper, 1211. Washington, DC: World Bank.

Papke, L. E. (2004). 'Individual Financial Decisions in Retirement Saving Plans: The Role of Participant-Direction,' *Journal of Public Economics,* 88(1–2): 39–61.

Poterba, J. M. (2014). 'Retirement Security in an Aging Population,' *American Economic Review,* 104(5): 1–30.

Poterba, J. M., S. F. Venti, and D. A. Wise (1995). 'Do 401(k) Contributions Crowd out Other Personal Saving?,' *Journal of Public Economics,* 58(1): 1–32.

Sabelhaus, J. and J. Manchester (1995). 'Baby Boomers and their Parents: How does their Economic Well-Being Compare in Middle Age?,' *Journal of Human Resources,* 30(4): 791–806.

Valdés-Prieto, S. (2002a). *Improving Programs that Mandate Savings for Old Age,* Background Paper for the Regional Study on Social Security Reform. Washington, DC: World Bank.

Valdés-Prieto, S. (2002b). *Justifying Mandated Savings for Old Age,* Background Paper for the Regional Study on Social Security Reform. Washington, DC: World Bank.

World Bank (1994). *Averting the Old Age Crisis.* Oxford: Oxford University Press.

8

Retirement Replacement Rates: What and How

Andrew G. Biggs

Replacement rates are a common measure of retirement income adequacy used by households to gauge their own saving for retirement, and by policymakers to assess the effectiveness of government and private pensions in providing income for the retired population. Replacement rates represent retirement income as a percentage of pre-retirement earnings and thus assess households' ability to maintain their pre-retirement levels of consumption once they have ceased working. A replacement rate of 100 percent is not necessary, as retirees face lower taxes and work-related costs, and they often have paid off their mortgages and completed their saving for retirement. Nevertheless, the ratio provides an intuitive yardstick for retirement income adequacy.

While seemingly simple, replacement rates can be measured in different ways based on different concepts of retirement income adequacy. These differences have important implications for our assessment of Americans' retirement saving. Discussion of the methodology of replacement rates was ignited when, in 2014, the Social Security Trustees opted to remove from their annual report tables that represented Social Security replacement rates for stylized workers with different levels of lifetime earnings (Social Security Trustees 2014). The replacement rate data in earlier annual Trustees reports had informed how many policymakers thought about retirement policy. Yet the Social Security Trustees warned in 2013 that replacement rates figures in their report produced 'percentages that may differ significantly from those that would be produced by comparing benefits to these representative workers' recent average earnings levels or to other, more common measures of pre-retirement income' (2013: 143). Those figures were deleted entirely in 2014, and it is not clear when and in what form they might reappear.

This chapter discusses three topics pertaining to replacement rates calculations. First, I ask whether policymakers should continue to rely upon stylized hypothetical earnings patterns in illustrating replacement rates, or whether they should turn to administrative data and microsimulation models whose output is, while more complex, capable of producing a more realistic and nuanced view of retirement income adequacy. Second, I address the question of how pre-retirement earnings should be represented in the replacement rate calculation. Most analysts agree that career-average earnings are a better measure of the pre-retirement standard of living than earnings in a single year immediately prior to retirement. Yet there is disagreement on whether pre-retirement earnings should be adjusted for growth in the cost of living or for growth in national average wages. This disagreement is based upon conceptual differences in how analysts view the purpose of retirement saving. Third, I examine the question of how children affect parents' need to save for retirement. Adjustments for differences in family size and composition have a significant impact upon measured retirement income adequacy. Indeed, several prominent studies that find undersaving for retirement to be a modest problem utilize family-size adjustments, while studies concluding that retirement undersaving is a much larger problem fail to adjust for the presence of children.

Finally, I illustrate the effects of different methods of calculating replacement rates using a microsimulation model of Social Security and employer-sponsored pensions. The Policy Simulation Group models are used to project Social Security benefits and pension incomes for members of the 1940 birth cohort.

While replacement rates are a seemingly simple concept, analysts face a range of choices regarding the type of pre-retirement earnings to be illustrated, how those earnings should be adjusted for changes in the cost or the standard of living, and how household size and composition should be accounted for in replacement rate calculations. There are many plausible combinations of such choices, such that a given level of retirement income could be characterized as wholly inadequate to overgenerous, depending upon the way in which the replacement rate is structured. How replacement rates are defined and calculated is crucial for assessing Americans' preparedness for retirement. In other words, the question on Americans' retirement security is not simply 'How much income will retirees have?' but 'How much is enough?' It would be impossible to review here every possible combination of choices for calculating replacement rates. In what follows, however, I review the focal points of current policy discussions and illustrate the range of possible outcomes.

The Use of Stylized Earners versus Microsimulation

Probably the best-known replacement rate figures are published by the US Social Security Administration, which administers the Old Age and Survivors Insurance program that is commonly referred to as 'Social Security.' The SSA is the source of the well-known statistic that, for an average earner, Social Security retirement benefits will replace only about 40 percent; moreover, SSA states that, according to most financial advisors, retirees need 70 percent of their pre-retirement earnings to sustain their pre-retirement standard of living (SSA 2014). This leads to the conclusion that Social Security benefits provide roughly 40/70ths, or 57 percent, of what a typical individual requires to maintain his standard of living in retirement.[1]

The SSA's replacement rates figure for its 'medium earner,' along with those for 'low' and 'high' earners, are calculated using stylized earnings patterns rather than directly from administrative data. The evolution of these stylized earnings patterns is worth analyzing. The SSA initially illustrated replacement rates using so-called 'steady earners,' who in each year of their working lives were assumed to earn a stated percentage of the Average Wage Index (AWI). For instance, the medium steady earner always earned 100 percent of the AWI, the low earner 45 percent, and the high earner 160 percent. Replacement rates were calculated by comparing benefits at the normal retirement age (then 65) to nominal earnings in the year prior to retirement.

Over time, however, it became clear that these steady earnings patterns failed to match the inverted U-shaped age-earnings profile typical of actual workers. As Munnell and Soto put it, these steady earnings patterns 'bore little relation to reality' (2005: 8). In response to such concerns, SSA introduced in 2011 its so-called 'scaled earners' with more representative earnings patterns. The broad age-earnings profiles were derived from administrative data, but the level of annual earnings was calibrated such that, in combination with a change in calculation methods, replacement rates for the hypothetical scaled earners would equal those calculated using the prior steady earners. Thus, while the new scaled earnings patterns are more realistic than the previous SSA steady earners, the methodology was structured to maintain the results calculated under the previous steady earner approach.[2]

The new SSA scaled earners are used to illustrate benefits payable under current law, such as in the annual Trustees Report, as well as in reform proposals that would change the benefits to which retirees become entitled. One problem with these improved scaled earners is that they are still not particularly representative of the typical earner. For instance, scaled earners are assumed to work every year from age 21 to age 65, when most real-world individuals take at least some time away from the workforce and tend to claim benefits before the Full Retirement Age of 66. Individuals at risk of poverty in retirement are most likely to have had a short working life than a long working life at low wages as per SSA's scaled low earner. Likewise, even the scaled medium earner has annual earnings that are substantially higher than those of a typical individual in the workforce (Mitchell and Phillips 2006).

A second problem is that these stylized earners are most informative for illustrating benefits for never-married workers, whereas most Social Security participants are married, divorced, or widowed. This is important because households tend to make saving and consumption decisions as a unit, and also because a significant portion of Social Security benefits is paid to spouses and widows. Roughly 23 percent of female retirees in 2012 received a benefit that was in part or whole based upon their spouse's earnings record (SSA 2013). If marital benefits are not accounted for, the effects of Social Security's auxiliary benefits are understated.

It is not that replacement rates have never been calculated using real-world data. Both Nichols (1977) and Grad (1990) used Social Security administrative data to calculate benefit replacement rates for retirees. Yet the use of administrative and microsimulation data has become increasingly common in recent years. The SSA Office of Disability and Retirement Policy utilizes a microsimulation model known as MINT (Modeling Income in the Near Term) as its principal tool for benefit analysis. The Congressional Budget Office uses the CBOLT (CBO Long-Term) model, and the Government Accountability Office uses the PSG models that are used in this chapter. More recently, SSA's Office of the Chief Actuary has published replacement rate figures based upon administrative data. Analysts outside the government can now utilize public use earnings and benefits data made available by SSA.

The better data allow for a much more realistic view of individual workers, capturing differences in years in the workforce, age-earnings profiles, age of retirement, and other factors that affect Social Security benefits and retirement income. Moreover, microsimulation data allow analysis of households, calculating the interactions of peoples' earnings in determining Social Security benefits. This approach provides a much more accurate representation of the replacement rates payable to female retirees, who are the main recipients of Social Security auxiliary benefits.

The ability to group individuals into households is extremely important in overcoming some of the limitations of replacement rates as a measure of retirement income adequacy. For instance, a spouse who stays home to care for the couple's children may receive an extremely high (or even infinite) replacement rate relative to her own earnings, but her earnings are not representative of the standard of living she enjoyed prior to retirement. Combining spouses into a single household unit that shares earnings and benefits equally provides a better picture of the role Social Security plays in the household's retirement preparation. A similar point can be made when pensions and other retirement savings enter the picture.

There seems little reason for policymakers or analysts to continue to rely principally upon stylized workers when administrative data or microsimulation models are increasingly available, particularly as the latter provide a more detailed and nuanced view of Social Security and retirement income than previously available. They also allow potential Social Security reforms to more accurately target individuals who, due to having earnings patterns or other characteristics not typical of a stylized full-career earning, may not be well-served by the current benefit formula.

How Should Prior Earnings Be Expressed?

A replacement rate expresses retirement income as a percentage of pre-retirement earnings. There is a debate over how the denominator of the calculation—pre-retirement earnings—should be measured.

Traditionally, replacement rates have expressed retirement income as a percentage of workers' pre-retirement earnings. This was how the SSA calculated replacement rates for its stylized 'steady earners.' Moreover, traditional defined benefit (DB) pension plans still continue to calculate replacement rates in such a way, since benefits under such plans are calculated relative to some measure of final earnings.

Yet many policy analysts argue today that replacement rates are better calculated relative to a longer-term average of pre-retirement earnings. Earnings in a single year can fluctuate significantly and hence may not be representative of the standard of living that pre-retirement earnings provided over the longer term.

Due in part to the Social Security Trustees removing replacement rates from their annual report, there has recently been significant discussion of how career-average pre-retirement earnings should be represented. SSA calculates replacement rates by comparing Social Security benefits in the first year of retirement to the average of the highest 35 years of pre-retirement earnings, indexed for the growth of average economy-wide wages. This so-called 'wage indexing' increases past nominal earnings by the ratio of SSAs' Average Wage Index (AWI) in the year the individual turned age 64 to the AWI in the year the earnings took place.

Since the AWI generally rises about one percentage point faster than the Consumer Price Index, this process will produce higher measured pre-retirement earnings, and lower replacement rates of pre-retirement earnings, than a replacement rate calculation that utilizes nominal or inflation-indexed earnings. The wage-indexed average of lifetime earnings is generally about one-fifth higher than inflation-indexed earnings, leading to a proportional reduction in measured replacement rates. In its National Retirement Risk Index (NRRI), the Center for Retirement Research applies a replacement rate calculation very similar to SSA OACT's to overall retirement income, concluding that a majority of working-age Americans are 'at risk' of falling below target levels of retirement income.[3]

The theory underlying 'wage-indexed replacement rates' is that retired households want their standard of living to increase in step with the standard of living of active workers. Literally speaking, the replacement rate for SSA's stylized 'scaled medium earner' is equal to the benefit received by this earner in retirement divided by the AWI at the time he retires.[4] That is, wage-indexed replacement rates effectively compare income for retirees to the earnings of contemporaneous workers.

Munnell, one of the co-authors of the CRR's NRRI, states that 'When constructing the NRRI targets, my colleagues and I made a conscious decision to assume that households had a preference for a standard of living that increased during their working lives at the rate of economy-wide wage growth. This assumption reflected our belief that households care not only about their absolute standard of living, but also about their relative standard of living' (2014). One can think of this as a 'keeping up with the Joneses,' relative-income approach reminiscent of Duesenberry (1949) or, more recently, Frank (2005).

Nevertheless, a number of commentators have expressed concern that indexing pre-retirement earnings for economy-wide wage growth, rather than merely for the growth of prices, overstates what households consider to be an adequate retirement income. Steuerle et al. observe that 'many retirees may be satisfied just to maintain their ability to purchase: They want the same purchasing power they've had all along. If this is the case, replacement rates could be derived from individual wages adjusted for inflation instead of wage growth. Since prices usually rise more slowly than wages, this would result in lower past wages and higher replacement rates' (2000: 1–2). Or, as the Congressional Budget Office recently stated, 'Indexing earnings to prices better captures the real amount of resources available to a worker over his or her lifetime, whereas indexing earnings to wages may overstate those amounts' (2014: 16).[5]

Thus, a more plausible approach may be to compare retirees' Social Security benefits or total retirement incomes to the purchasing power of their pre-retirement earnings. This approach is more reminiscent of a simplified life-cycle model in which individuals seek to consume more or less the same amount from year to year. For instance, the financial planning program 'ESPlanner,' which applies the life-cycle model to retirement planning, seeks to calculate the highest level of steady, inflation-adjusted consumption that an individual or household can maintain over its lifetime.[6] A replacement rate calculated relative to inflation-adjusted pre-retirement earnings is a simple approximation of such an approach.[7]

The differences between these two measures can be substantial. For instance, the Congressional Budget Office (2014) recently projected that Social Security will provide the average retiree born in the 1960s with a wage-indexed replacement rate of 46 percent, versus a price-indexed replacement rate of 58 percent.[8]

Neither price-indexed nor wage-indexed replacement rates fully capture all the factors that affect saving and consumption, such as time preferences, precautionary saving, borrowing constraints, and uncertainty regarding future earnings. But this should not be a disqualification, given replacement rates' role as a simplified rule-of-thumb that is accessible to savers and policymakers lacking specialized knowledge. At a minimum, offering replacement rates calculated using both inflation-indexed and wage-indexed pre-retirement earnings, as in CBO (2014), makes readers more aware of the importance of these definitional choices.

Adjusting Replacement Rates for Household Size and Composition

Another area of disagreement pertains to how measures of retirement income adequacy should account for the effects of children on their parents' need to save for retirement. The justification for such an adjustment is that households with children need not save as much for retirement as households without children, because part of parents' income during their working years is consumed by their children. Skinner describes the logic in humorous terms:

> Parents are already used to getting by on peanut butter, given that a large fraction of their pre-retirement budget has been devoted to supporting children, so it's not difficult to set aside enough money to keep them in peanut butter through retirement. By contrast, childless households with the same income accustomed to caviar and fine wine must set aside more assets to maintain themselves in the style to which they have become accustomed. (2007: 69)

In this context, the costs of raising children are akin to the costs of paying off a mortgage or saving for retirement: they represent foregone consumption during the household's working years that need not be replaced once the household has retired. Put simply, parents do not need to replace consumption they never had. Notably, studies that find higher levels of retirement saving adequacy, such as Gale et al. (2009) and Hurd and Rohwedder (2011, 2014), use a family-size adjustment. By contrast, the Center for Retirement Research's NRRI adjusts target replacement rates for single individuals versus couples, but it makes no adjustment for whether retirees had children. The NRRI's designers argue that, once children leave home, parents 'take over' their children's share of household consumption and wish to maintain this higher standard of living through retirement.

This remains an open area for research. Some research focuses on household wealth accumulation. For instance, Engen et al. (1999) find that households with high saving rates and above-average wealth tend to have fewer children than low-saving households. Likewise, Scholz and Seshadri (2007) show that households with children hold less average wealth than similar households that did not have children. From these results, Scholz and Seshadri conclude that parents tend to save to replace their own pre-retirement consumption, implying that analysis of retirement saving adequacy should account for household size. Another research path focuses on how household saving patterns change when children leave the home. If children depress household saving, then one might expect saving to increase once children have left the nest. There are a number of reasons why such a change may not be apparent. For instance, inertia may cause households to leave contribution rates to employer-sponsored pension plans unchanged even after children leave, at least delaying changes to saving rates. Likewise, college tuition or loan payments for children may continue even after children have technically left home, making measurement of saving changes more difficult. Also, parents may wish to enjoy a temporary splurge in spending after children have left home.

Coe and Webb (2010) follow households in several waves of the Health and Retirement Study, concluding that parents do not appear to reduce their consumption once children leave home. However, that study has been criticized for relying upon a sample of only 36 households whose parents were unusually old at the time their children left home. Klos and Rottke use a larger German dataset to analyze how parents respond to children leaving home. They find that 'household consumption drops and saving rises significantly within four years after a child moves out of a household' (2013: p. ii). However, for college-educated parents, who are more likely to have children attending college and thus continuing college-related costs, the transition to higher saving takes longer than four years. Klos and Rottke conclude that 'Assuming that household consumption remains constant after a child's move-out would overstate the problem of inadequate saving' (2013: 20).

Analysts taking an alternate approach rely on subjective assessments of retirement income adequacy. As already noted, households with children appear to have lower average wealth than childless households. This result implies either that parents save to replace their own pre-retirement consumption rather than the household's total consumption, or that households with children undersave for retirement compared to similar childless households. If the latter is true, then having children can be seen as detrimental to parents' retirement planning. In the latter case one would expect that retirees who had children would express greater reservations than non-parents about their income security and quality of life. Rohwedder (2006) used Health and Retirement Study data to analyze respondents' answers to questions including, 'All in all, would you say that your retirement has turned out to be very satisfying, moderately satisfying, or not at all satisfying?'; 'Would you say the retirement years have been better, about the same, or not as good?'; and 'Please tell me if you worry a lot, somewhat, a little, or not at all [about] not having enough income to get by.' She found no significant difference in how retired parents answered these questions versus similar non-parents, buttressing the notion that having children affects parents' retirement saving in predictable and rational ways.

To illustrate the effects of adjusting replacement rates for household size and composition, the following sections will use the framework established in Citro and Michael (1995) to calculate the number of 'adult equivalents' living in a household. It takes the form

$$\text{Adulte quivalents} = (A + PK)^F$$

where A is the number of adults in the family, K is the number of children, P is the cost of a child relative to an adult, and F is a factor reflecting economies of scale in household size. Following common usage, I assume a of value 0.7 for both P and F. Lower values of P will result in relatively lower costs of living for a child versus an adult household member, while lower values of F will result in larger economies of scale as household size increases. I assume that children are counted as part of households until age 21.

In any given year, an individual's earnings are taken to equal total household earnings divided by the number of adult equivalents in the household. Career-average earnings are based on the annual family-size adjusted earnings. Thus, this process accounts for earnings when the respondent is single, married, divorced, or remarried; and when childless, when children are living at home, and when children have left home. Similarly, the respondent's total household Social Security or other retirement income is divided by the number of adult equivalents at the time the replacement rate is calculated. For the small number of retiree households who have children living at home, the family-adjustment is applied to Social Security and pension benefits.

Illustrating Social Security Replacement Rates

We develop replacement rates using a suite of microsimulation models developed by the Policy Simulation Group (PSF).[9] These models simulate the US population's participation in the Social Security program and employer-sponsored DB and defined contribution (DC) pension plans. Used by the Social Security Administration, the Department of Labor, and the Government Accountability Office, these models are calibrated to reproduce both system-level and distributional outcomes similar to those generated by Social Security's Board of Trustees and the Social Security Administration's Office of the Chief Actuary.

The denominators used in the replacement rate calculations are based upon the present value of individual or household earnings from ages 21 through 65, calculated using the historical or projected yield on the Social Security Trust Funds. This present value is converted to a steady earnings path that increases annually either with the AWI or the Consumer Price Index (CPI). These figures are qualitatively similar to the indexed average of pre-retirement earnings used in other studies, but they are designed to include earnings-years and to be consistent with the present value of lifetime earnings.[10]

I illustrate the results using individuals born in 1940 who survive to age 70. Age 70 is chosen because practically all eligible individuals will have claimed Social Security benefits by then.[11] Social Security replacement rates equal the individual's total scheduled Social Security benefit including any auxiliary supplement, as a percentage of the average of the individual's own highest 35 years of earnings. A couple's replacement rate equals the couple's total Social Security benefit divided by the couple's average pre-retirement earnings. Combined replacement rates include Social Security benefits, DB pensions payments, and the value of employer-sponsored DC pensions expressed as an inflation-indexed annuity payment. Retirement saving outside of employer-sponsored plans is not included in these calculations, nor is the value of home equity.

The median individual Social Security replacement rate measured relative to AWI-indexed earnings is 60 percent. This is substantially higher than the 40 percent commonly discussed. As mentioned earlier, the SSA states that an average earner will receive a benefit replacement rate of 40 percent. Likewise Goss et al. (2014) present replacement rates for individuals claiming benefits in the year 2011, finding a median replacement rate relative to wage-indexed average earnings of 39 percent. The difference between my results and those of the SSA and Goss et al. arises due to differences in how replacement rates are calculated, as well as in the beneficiaries and the benefits that are included in the replacement rate calculation.

The denominator used in my figures is the wage-indexed average of all earnings between the ages of 21 and 62, whereas SSA's figures use the individual's highest 35 years of earnings. Lifetime earnings used here are therefore lower than SSA's calculations, and so this produces higher measured replacement rates. Yet it also provides a better measure of how individuals with different total lifetime earnings are treated by the Social Security program.

In addition, the calculation here for the 1940 birth cohort includes all Social Security beneficiaries who survive to age 70, including those who collect only an auxiliary (spousal or widow) benefit. Goss et al. (2014), by contrast, include only those who are eligible for benefits based upon their own earnings records. Likewise, for individuals eligible for benefits based upon their own earnings, the calculations here include all benefits they receive, including spousal or widow benefits. Goss et al. (2014) measure only the benefits received based upon the beneficiary's own earnings. This approach significantly understates total benefits for those retirees, generally women, who receive a spousal or widow supplement. Approximately one-fifth of all retirees in 2012 received an auxiliary benefit, and for such retirees, the auxiliary payment increased their total benefit by 78 percent (Biggs et al. 2015).

The individual Social Security replacement rates presented here are a more complete picture of the Social Security beneficiary population and the Social Security benefits they receive, nevertheless these are difficult to interpret. For instance, what does it *mean* for retirement preparedness if a spouse who worked little outside the home receives a high benefit relative to her own earnings, when her standard of living prior to retirement depended on her spouse's earnings? We believe this justifies calculating replacement rates on a household basis. By doing so, we avoid interpretive problems while still including the full Social Security beneficiary population and all the benefits they receive.

When we calculate wage-indexed Social Security replacement rates on a household basis, the median value for the 1940 birth cohort falls from 60 to 54 percent. Perhaps more important, the number of very low and very high replacement rates is reduced. For instance, at the couple level, 10 percent of beneficiaries receive a replacement rate above 100 percent; at the individual level, the top 10 percent of beneficiaries receives replacement rates higher than 165 percent.

Nevertheless these figures are calculated relative to AWI-indexed earnings, which effectively compares their benefits not to their *own* pre-retirement earnings, but to the earnings of active workers. A CPI-indexed denominator in the replacement rate calculation provides a better picture of how households' Social Security or pension benefits compared to the purchasing power of their own average pre-retirement earnings. The median individual replacement rate relative to CPI-indexed pre-retirement earnings for the 1940 birth cohort is 72 percent, versus 60 percent of wage-indexed earnings. The median couple replacement rate is 65 percent, versus 54 percent for couples relative to wage-indexed earnings.

Next we consider how an adjustment for family size and composition alters replacement rates. The family-size adjustment increases the median household Social Security replacement rate for the 1940 birth cohort from 65 to 82 percent of inflation-indexed average pre-retirement earnings. Not surprisingly, the family-size adjustments are smallest for those who were never married, where median replacement rates rose only from 67 to 68 percent. These individuals' replacement rates can be affected by accounting for children. For married individuals, the effect of the family-size adjustment is much larger, raising median replacement rates from 61 to 82 percent. The difference is more modest but still important for divorced individuals, where median replacement rates rise from 64 to 75 percent. For widows and widowers, the effect depends importantly upon gender: widowers see increased replacement rates through a family-size adjustment, as their share of household pre-retirement earnings is generally lower than their own pre-retirement earnings. Replacement rates for widowers rise from 78 to 87 percent when family-size adjusted. For widows, however, the opposite is true: median replacement rates decline from 88 to 81 percent, reflecting the loss of economies of scale when living alone versus as a couple.

The PSG models also simulate benefits from employer-sponsored retirement plans, allowing for the calculation of replacement rates covering a greater share of total retirement income. The PSG models also simulate pension rollovers to Individual Retirement Accounts, but they do not model IRAs or other individual retirement saving that is funded independently of rollovers. The approach assumes that DC pension accounts earn a return equal to the yield on the Social Security Trust Funds. At retirement, households are assumed to convert DC pension accounts to an inflation-adjusted annuity.

Nevertheless, the PSG models do not simulate the full range of retirement income sources including housing equity, income from non-retirement assets, and government transfer programs other than Social Security. For the 1940 birth cohort, combined Social Security, DB, and DC pension income amounts to about two-thirds of retired households' total non-earnings income, implying that total retirement income would be higher than the combined Social Security and employer-sponsored pension benefits simulated here.[12]

When we include income from employer-sponsored pensions along with Social Security benefits, combined family-size adjusted replacement rates relative to CPI-indexed pre-retirement earnings rise to 126 percent at the median. Seventy-five percent of households have replacement rates above 85 percent of career earnings, and 90 percent of households have replacement rates above 50 percent. As a result, it appears that most households at age 70 would have a higher standard of living—after accounting for economies of scale in living costs, household income consumed by children, and work-related costs—than their *average* during their pre-retirement years.

By contrast, if replacement rates are calculated relative to wage-indexed earnings without a family-size adjustment, 43 percent of the 1940 cohort fall short of a combined Social Security and pension replacement rate of 75 percent. Thus, much of the difference of opinion regarding whether Americans face a retirement 'challenge' or a retirement 'crisis' is attributable to differing definitions of income adequacy, rather than projections of what Americans' actual retirement incomes will be in dollars and cents.

Conclusion

Replacement rates are a commonly-used measure of retirement income adequacy by individuals, financial advisors, and policymakers, but until recently little attention was paid to *how* replacement rates are calculated. Replacement rates began with simple calculations that compared retirement income to retirees' earnings immediately preceding retirement, using stylized workers with unrealistic earnings patterns and ignoring the interaction of spouses' earnings and savings. More recently however, methods have improved through access to administrative data and microsimulation models, and replacement rate calculations have been applied to career-long average earnings rather than earnings in a single year preceding retirement.

Even so, there remain key conceptual disagreements about how to index pre-retirement earnings in a replacement rate calculation. Price-indexed replacement rates measure a household's ability to replace its own average pre-retirement consumption, while wage-indexed replacement rates effectively compare the incomes of retirees to those of working-age households. To the degree that retired households wish to maintain their own prior levels of consumption rather than chase contemporary workers' living standards, replacement rates calculated relative to inflation-adjusted earnings may be a better shorthand measure of retirement income adequacy.

There is also disagreement about how replacement rates should consider the effects of children on retirement saving needs. Research in this area is continuing, but households with children do save less for retirement than similar households without children. Despite this, they seem not to suffer in terms of subjective assessments of retirement income adequacy. Thus an adjustment for family size and composition seems a reasonable way to analyze households with and without children in a more comparable way.

Applying these different methods of calculating replacement rates to simulated populations shows how important the definitional issues are. Many models are used to project the earnings, Social Security benefits, and pension income of future cohorts of US retirees. Nevertheless, differences in how retirement income adequacy is conceived of, defined, and measured, appear to have greater impacts on perceptions of retirement preparedness than do differences in the dollar values that different models project. For this reason, it is extremely important that analysts and policymakers step back and ask what households are trying to do when they save for retirement. Are they trying to maintain their own personal pre-retirement consumption, or are they trying to match the amount that they and their children consumed together? Likewise, are they concerned with matching their pre-retirement consumption, or are they more concerned with 'keeping up with the Joneses,' in the form of maintaining a standard of living in retirement that matches that of contemporaneous workers? These conceptual questions are as important in gauging retirement income adequacy as are the more technical issues of projecting Americans' future earnings, Social Security benefits, and pension incomes. While government agencies such as the Social Security Administration, the Congressional Budget Office, the Department of Labor, and others have expended significant resources in projecting how much income future retirees will have, the most fruitful step going forward may be to focus research attention more closely on how much income future retirees will need.

Endnotes

1. This discussion draws on Biggs et al. (2015).
2. In addition to calibrating the scaled earnings patterns, SSA OACT adjusted its approach for calculating replacement rates. Under the steady earner methodology, replacement rates expressed Social Security benefits to earnings in the year immediately prior to benefit claiming. Once the scaled earner approach was adopted, replacement rates were calculated by comparing Social Security benefits to the average of the highest 35 years of pre-retirement earnings, where earnings were adjusted through age 64 to the growth of overall earnings in the economy. This new method of calculation replacement rates, along with the calibration of pre-retirement earnings levels, allowed SSA OACT to maintain the same measured replacement rates for the low-, medium-, and high-earning scaled workers as were produced using the previous steady earners.
3. See Munnell et al. (2006).
4. This can be demonstrated using data from table V.C7 of the 2014 Trustees Report, which includes annual benefit amounts for the hypothetical scaled earners retiring in a given year along with the annual wages paid to workers in that year. The stylized medium earner retiring in 2014 receives an annual benefit of $19,477, which is equal to 41.6% of the $46,787 Average Wage Index in 2014. Clingman and Nichols (2004) calculate a wage-indexed replacement rate for a medium-scaled relative to wage-indexed career average earnings of 41.1%, indicating that the medium-scaled earner's average prior earnings are almost precisely equal to the AWI in the year he retires.
5. Also see MacDonald and Moore (2011).
6. For instance, see Bernheim, et al. (2000) and <www.ESPlanner.com>.
7. Calculating replacement rates relative to some truncated measure of the individual's pre-retirement earnings might be taken to account for borrowing constraints early in life. For instance, it is common to calculate replacement rates relative to the highest thirty-five years of earnings, though the full working life from age 21 through Social Security's normal retirement age now covers forty-five years.

8. These figures, and others produced here, assume that scheduled Social Security benefits will continue to be paid. Under current projections the combined Social Security trust funds will become exhausted around the year 2030. Under current law, at that point benefits would be reduced across the board by approximately 25%. No observers expect such an outcome, but these issues illustrate that future Social Security benefit levels are uncertain.
9. Background on the models is available in Holmer et al. (2015). See <www.polsim.com>.
10. This method of calculating the denominator of the replacement rate calculation has relatively little distributional impact in any given year. However, changes in interest rates can alter average replacement rates over time as the present value of pre-retirement earnings changes.
11. Measured replacement rates at age 70 will be altered somewhat by mortality between ages 62 and 70, which may disproportionately reduce the number of low-earning retirees with above-average replacement rates while increasing the number of widows, who also tend to have higher replacement rates.
12. See Butrica et al. (2012), table 6.

References

Bernheim, B. D., L. Forni, J. Gokhale, and L. J. Kotlikoff (2000). 'How Much Should Americans Be Saving for Retirement?' *American Economic Review*, 101(3): 288–92.

Biggs, A. G., G. Pang, and S. J. Schieber (2015). 'Measuring and Communicating Social Security Earnings Replacement Rates,' *Journal of Retirement*, 2(4): 69–85.

Butrica, B. A., K. E. Smith, and H. M. Iams (2012). 'This is Not Your Parents' Retirement: Comparing Retirement Income across Generations,' *Social Security Bulletin*, 72(1): 37–58.

Citro, C. and R. Michael (1995). *Measuring Poverty: A New Approach*, Washington, DC: National Academy Press.

Clingman, M. and O. Nichols (2004). *Scaled Factors for Hypothetical Earnings Examples under the 2004 Trustees Report Assumptions*, Actuarial Note Number 2004.3. Baltimore, MD: Office of the Chief Actuary, Social Security Administration.

Coe, N. B. and A. Webb (2010). *Children and Household Utility: Evidence from Kids Flying the Coop*, Center for Retirement Research Working Paper, 2010-16. Chestnut Hill, MA: Center for Retirement Research. <http://crr.bc.edu/wp-content/uploads/2010/11/wp_2010-16-508.pdf>.

Congressional Budget Office (CBO) (2014). *CBO's 2014 Long-Term Projections for Social Security: Additional Information*. Washington, DC: CBO.

Duesenberry, J. S. (1949). *Income, Savings and the Theory of Consumer Behavior*. Cambridge, MA: Harvard University Press.

Engen, E. M., W. G. Gale, C. E. Uccello, C. D. Carroll, and D. I. Laibson (1999). 'The Adequacy of Household Saving,' *Brookings Papers on Economic Activity*, 1999(2): 65–187.

Frank, R. H. (2005). 'Positional Externalities Cause Large and Preventable Welfare Losses,' *American Economic Review*, 95(2): 137–41.

Gale, W. G., J. K. Scholz, and A. Seshadri (2009). *Are All Americans Saving 'Optimally' for Retirement?* Working Paper. Madison, WI: University of Wisconsin–Madison. <http://www.ssc.wisc.edu/~scholz/Research/Are_All_Americans_v6.pdf>.

Goss, S., M. Clingman, A. Wade, and K. Glenn (2014). *Replacement Rates for Retirees: What Makes Sense for Planning And Evaluation?* Actuarial Note Number 155. Washington, DC: Social Security Administration.

Grad, S. (1990). 'Earnings Replacement Rates of New Retired Workers,' *Social Security Bulletin*, 53: 2.

Holmer, M., A. Janney, and B. Cohen (2015). *PENSIM Overview.* Washington, DC: DOL. <http://www.polsim.com/doc/overview.pdf>.

Hurd, M. D. and S. Rohwedder (2011). *Economic Preparation for Retirement*, NBER Working Paper, 17203. Cambridge, MA: National Bureau of Economic Research.

Hurd, M. D. and S. Rohwedder (2014). *More Americans May Be Adequately Prepared for Retirement than Previously Thought*, RAND Corporation RB-9792. Santa Monica, CA: RAND Corporation.

Klos, A. and S. Rottke (2013). 'Saving and Consumption When Children Move Out,' Paper presented at Beiträge zur Jahrestagung des Vereins für Socialpolitik 2013: Wettbewerbspolitik und Regulierung in einer globalen Wirtschaftsordnung—Session: Household Behavior, No. C12-V3. <http://hdl.handle.net/10419/79786>.

MacDonald, B. J. and K. D. Moore (2011). *Moving beyond the Limitations of Traditional Replacement Rates*, Society of Actuaries Working Paper. Washington, DC: Society of Actuaries. <http://www.soa.org/research/research-projects/pension/default.aspx>.

Mitchell, O. S. and J. W. R. Phillips (2006). 'Social Security Replacement Rates for Alternative Earnings Benchmarks,' *Benefits Quarterly* (Fourth Quarter), 22(4): 37–47.

Munnell, A. H. (2014). 'Yes, There is a Retirement Savings Shortfall,' *Market Watch.* July 16. <http://blogs.marketwatch.com/encore/2014/07/16/yes-there-is-a-retirement-savings-shortfall>.

Munnell, A. H. and M. Soto (2005). *What Replacement Rates do Households Actually Experience in Retirement?* Center for Retirement Research Working Paper, 2005–10. Chestnut Hill, MA: Center for Retirement Research

Munnell, A. H., A. Webb, and L. Delorme (2006). *A New National Retirement Risk Index*, CRR Issue Brief #48. Chestnut Hill, MA: Center for Retirement Research.

Nichols, O. (1977). *Actual Replacement Rates for Retiring Workers*, Actuarial Note Number 93. Washington, DC: Office of the Chief Actuary, Social Security Administration.

Rohwedder, S. (2006). *Self-Assessed Retirement Outcomes: Determinants and Pathways*, MRRC Working Paper, 2006–141. Ann Arbor, MI: Michigan Retirement Research Center.

Scholz, J. K. and A. Seshadri (2007). *Children and Household Wealth*, MRRC Working Paper, 2007–158. Ann Arbor, MI: Michigan Retirement Research Center.

Skinner, J. (2007). 'Are You Sure You're Saving Enough for Retirement?,' *Journal of Economic Perspectives*, 21(3): 59–80.

Social Security Administration (SSA) (2013). *Annual Statistical Supplement to the Social Security Bulletin, 2012.* Washington, DC: Social Security Administration.

Social Security Administration (SSA) (2014). 'Social Security Retirement Planner: Decide When to Retire.' <http://www.ssa.gov/retire2/>.

Social Security Trustees (2013). *The 2013 Annual Report of the Board of Trustees of the Federal Old-Age and Survivors Insurance and Federal Disability Insurance Trust Funds.* Washington, DC: Social Security Administration.

Social Security Trustees (2014). *The 2014 Annual Report of the Board of Trustees of the Federal Old-Age and Survivors Insurance and Federal Disability Insurance Trust Funds.* Washington, DC: Social Security Administration.

Steuerle, C. E., C. Spiro, and A. Carasso (2000). *Measuring Replacement Rates at Retirement*, Straight Talk on Social Security and Retirement Policy, 24. Washington, DC: Urban Institute.

9

Fundamentals of Cost and Risk that Matter to Pension Savers and Life Annuitants

Catherine Donnelly, Montserrat Guillén, and Jens Perch Nielsen

This chapter seeks to increase a pension saver's certainty about the amount of wealth available at retirement. To achieve this, we show how to design new, transparent investment strategies to be followed prior to the anticipated retirement date. Since reducing uncertainty about the amount of retirement wealth has a financial cost, we analyze this cost/risk tradeoff.

To determine one such investment strategy, the pension saver begins by choosing an upper bound for his retirement wealth. The surprising consequence of this approach is that wealth is more likely to attain this bound than if there were no such bound. For example, suppose an investor chooses an upper bound of $100,000, and following the resultant optimal investment strategy means that the probability of retiring with exactly $100,000 is 70 percent. Following this strategy means that the investor will never end up with more than $100,000 at retirement. On the other hand, throwing away the constraint of the upper bound gives a different optimal investment strategy that has a probability of 50 percent of producing a retirement wealth of $100,000 or higher.

Our proposed investment strategies are fully described. They can be implemented through a customized investment product, such as a managed account or a target date fund, or by a sophisticated individual. They may enable pension savers to plan better for their retirement, since there is more certainty about how much money will be available at retirement.

We consider a pension saver who makes a one-off contribution and intends to retire in 30 years' time. (The results can be easily extended to allow for additional contributions.) The single contribution is invested in line with one of the investment strategies that incorporate either an upper bound and/or a lower bound on the wealth at the retirement date. The distribution of retirement wealth is analyzed.

Background and Motivation

At least four factors threaten the understanding of pension savers and annuitants:

(1) duration: there is always uncertainty about the retirement date and for how long the individual will live;
(2) return with risk-adjusted measures: while there is no widespread agreement on how best to measure investment performance, we believe both risk and return should be measured as quantiles rather than, for example, as expected values;
(3) volatility: volatile investment returns imply uncertainty about the accumulated amount of wealth at retirement, which is anathema to some savers and many pension savers are averse to losing money;
(4) fees: the main problems of investment management costs are a lack of pricing transparency and the pension saver's ignorance about the amount of investment returns lost due to portfolio administration fees.

Our approach to the study of retirement savings relies on three concepts. First, any comparison of investment strategies must adjust for performance risk. By performance risk, we mean the possibility of large losses. Most studies on the performance of savings plans lack such a risk-adjustment component (Gerrard et al. 2014; Guillén et al. 2013, 2014; De Franco and Tankov 2011; Benartzi and Thaler 1999). Second, the management of longevity risk is usually done by a risk transfer to a third party at a very large cost. We claim that pooling longevity risk can potentially produce significant cost savings to the pensioner (Donnelly et al. 2014). Third, management fees have an important effect on wealth at retirement. Many authors show that the fees paid for managing investment funds and for mitigating longevity risk produce a substantial decrease to the wealth of pensioners (Guillén et al. 2014; MacKay et al. 2015).

A sensible investment strategy for a pension saver to retirement and beyond requires analyzing the stochastic distribution of retirement wealth (Basu et al. 2011; Greninger et al. 2000; Browne 1999; Grossman and Zhou 1996). The accumulated wealth during savings and consumption at a given point of time depends on individual decisions and market conditions that investment assets have been through over time. A consumer living during a decade of economic expansion can have a different retirement wealth compared to another pensioner who may have lost most of his assets living through bubbles and recessions. Their lifetime investment experiences correspond to two trajectories with opposite consequences (Jin and Zhou 2008; Bodie et al. 1992).

We consider the problem of setting a dynamic investment strategy to invest initial wealth or, alternatively, periodic amounts, in order to reach a target capital sum at the intended retirement date. Many studies have introduced constraints on the portfolio or the terminal wealth (Bouchard et al. 2010; Van Weert et al. 2010; Gaibh et al. 2009; Boyle and Tian 2007; Cuoco 1997; Korn and Trautmann 1995; Zariphopoulou 1994). Ours is a different formulation of one of the problems described in Dhaene et al. (2005), in which an investor wishes to find the optimal constant-proportion portfolio that attains the highest target capital with a fixed probability. We introduce a different vision of risk, since we consider both upper and lower targets. We constrain the investor to have *at most* a target capital at the time of retirement, whereas Dhaene et al. (2005) focuses on ensuring that at least the target capital is attained with maximum probability. We also propose a more general setting in which we have both an upper and a lower target, so that the pensioner can ensure that the wealth at retirement lies between these bounds.

In proposing this mechanism, we seek to promote transparent and automatic products where pension savers can obtain guaranteed bounds on their potential final wealth, and where their portfolios are automatically rebalanced to the chosen strategy. As noted by Leshno and Levy (2002) and von Gaudecker et al. (2011), there is much heterogeneity regarding risky choice behavior in the population. Thus, if decision-making is made automatic, this reduces uncertainty and cost. Our ultimate aim is to combine the proposed strategies in the savings phase with financial management after retirement, in order to design annuity schemes where the longevity risk is also inexpensive. For instance, in some annuity schemes, the risk is shared among fund participants instead of being transferred to the insurance market (Donnelly et al. 2013, 2014).

Innovations in the design of pension products are rare in Europe, where there is generally a subsistence (or higher) level of income provided by public or occupational pensions. The private pension sector uses mostly classical products, namely, pure financial investments before retirement with some tax saving rewards, and, after retirement, the purchase of an annuity, with not much more to be offered to customers.

The importance of investment performance for lifetime investors is widely recognized (Milevsky and Huang 2011). Pension savers invest their savings for long periods of time, often for several decades. Small deviations in performance are magnified hugely as returns are compounded over decades. Current performance evaluation methods are usually too myopic and they overlook persistence in performance, for example, the role of time that we also discuss here.

Foundations of our Model and the Proposed Strategy

Our analysis sets limits on the level of wealth at the retirement date; we call this the restricted case. These limits constrain the stochastic distribution of retirement wealth and result in a risk-return profile that is significantly different from the unrestricted situation. We set limits on the level of wealth at the retirement date and compare the restricted and unrestricted situations.

Figures 9.1 and 9.2 compare those two scenarios. Figure 9.1 presents the unrestricted case, showing two pension savers over 30 years with no restrictions on their retirement wealth. One saver is very unlucky to have much less than the initial investment, as shown by the grey line, and another is fortunate and ends up with a very successful investment, as shown by the

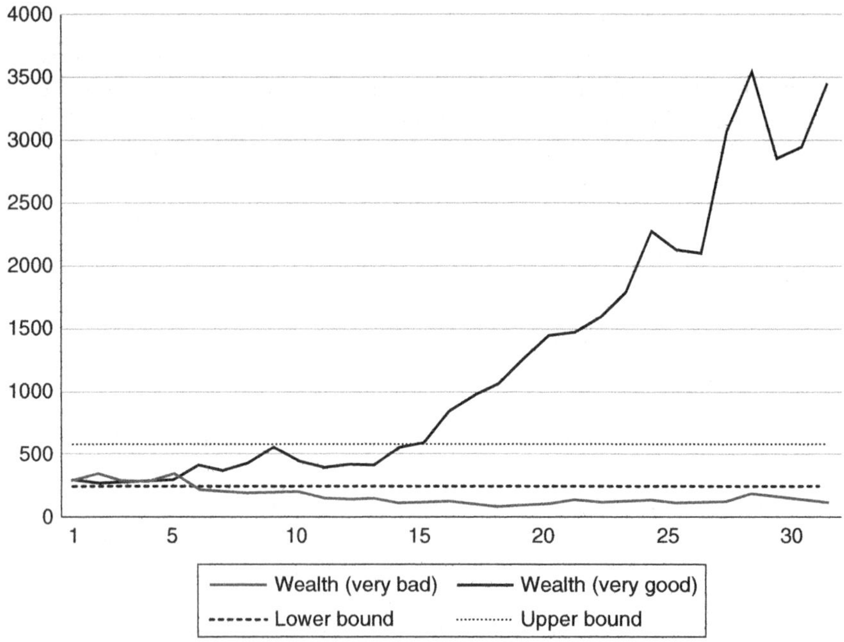

Figure 9.1 Sample paths of accumulated wealth for a one-off contribution during the 30 years for which it is invested

Note: The strategy followed does not incorporate any bounds on the wealth at retirement. The light grey path shows a pension saver who ends with less than the initial contribution. The black path shows a pension saver who accumulates large gains. The horizontal dotted and dashed bounds are included to allow comparison with Figure 9.2.

Source: Authors' computations.

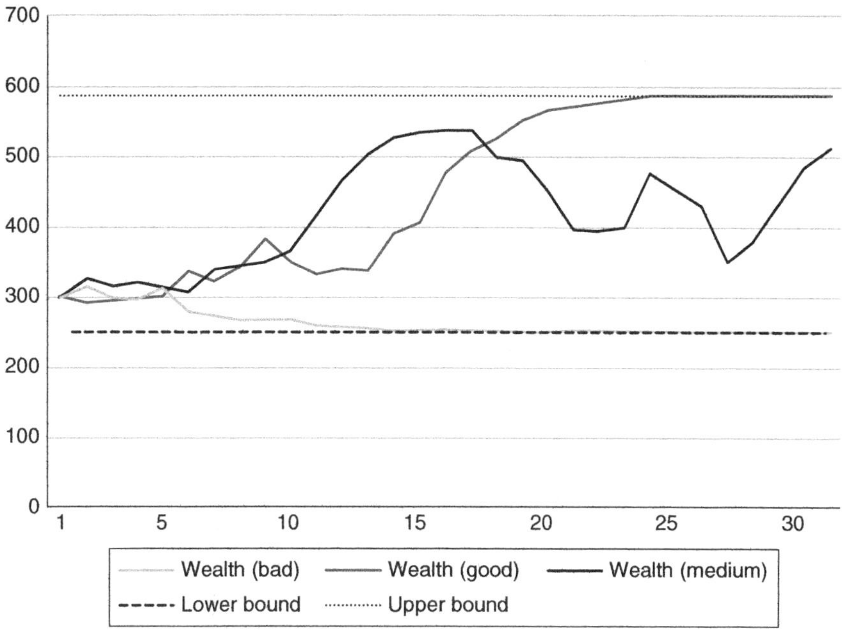

Figure 9.2 Sample paths of accumulated wealth for a one-off contribution during the 30 years for which it is invested, with bounds

Note: Here the strategy incorporates both a lower bound (dashed horizontal line) and an upper bound (dotted horizontal line) on the wealth at retirement. The light grey path shows a pension saver who accumulates the minimum amount at retirement, which was set equal to the chosen lower bound. The dark grey path shows a pension saver who accumulates the maximum level, as fixed by the upper bound. The black path shows a pension saver who accumulates wealth in between the fixed bounds.

Source: Authors' computations.

solid black line. For comparison with the restricted case, the bounds for the latter are also shown in Figure 9.1. The bounds happen to be each crossed by the unrestricted simulations.

Figure 9.2 shows an upper and a lower bound on retirement wealth, indicated by the horizontal dashed and dotted lines, for the restricted case. This means that the trajectories of the accumulated wealth are constrained to stay between the bounds. In particular, wealth cannot fall below the lower bound at retirement: this is the case for the light gray path. This means that whenever the discounted value of the lower bound is reached, the investor chooses to invest only in bonds (in these simulations, the annual discount factor equals one and so the bounds are constant across the 30 years). The second path, shown by the dark gray line, is the situation where the discounted value of the upper bound is crossed before retirement. It is very similar to the case with a lower bound: once the discounted value of the upper bound is reached, all wealth is invested in the risk-free bond. In the third case, shown by the solid black line, the investor has both an upper and a lower bound. Accumulated wealth must not fall below the lower level, or exceed the upper level. While, potentially, better gains could have been obtained, it is guaranteed that the investor is accumulating at least a minimum value and at most a maximum value.

Technical details of the calibrating strategy are given in the Appendix, and more detail appears in Donnelly et al. (2014, 2015a, 2015b).

Numerical Illustration

Here we investigate the optimal strategy for the constrained strategy. We use the unrestricted strategy as the benchmark strategy. Our initial investment is 300 units[1] and the time horizon is 30 years. Table 9.1 shows the distribution of the terminal wealth under the restricted strategy for combinations of the lower and upper bounds. The probabilities are expressed by the first column on the left as a percentage. The subsequent columns refer to the corresponding percentiles under each of the scenarios.

The unrestricted case appears in the second column. Here, one investor has 300 units at the beginning and after 30 years has a 1 percent chance of having at most 82.09 units. There is a 40 percent chance of having at most 473.87 units. Following the unrestricted strategy means that there is just over a 20 percent chance of ending up with less than the initial investment. There is slightly less than a 50 percent chance of at least doubling the initial investment after 30 years. Note that we do not allow for inflation and the risk-free interest rate is zero. We assume only that the risky stock has a larger expected return than a risk-free bond, and we have computed these examples with realistic scenarios of volatility.

The third column in Table 9.1 shows the case where we set only a lower bound of 250. That means that the investor loses at most 50 units from the original investment of 300, by the end of the 30 years, which happens 30 percent of the time. Imposing the lower bound means that the chance of at least doubling the initial investment falls to just under 30 percent. In other words, the cost of having a guaranteed floor is the loss of potential high gains.

In the fourth column, we set only an upper bound of 587.10, which is close to being double the original investment; the upper bound is attained 50 percent of the time. The effect of imposing the upper bound is to raise the lower quantiles, in comparison to the unrestricted case. However, there is a 1 percent chance that the investor ends up having accumulated

TABLE 9.1. Distribution of wealth after 30 years for an initial investment of 300 units and various choices of the terminal lower and upper bounds

Probability (%)	Unrestricted (no bounds)[a]	Only lower bound equal to 250[b]	Only upper bound equal to 587.10[c]	Both bounds, lower equal to 250 and upper equal to 587.10[d]
1	82.09	250.00	100.86	250.00
2.5	111.91	250.00	137.49	250.00
5	146.08	250.00	179.48	250.00
10	198.62	250.00	244.03	250.00
20	288.14	250.00	354.02	250.00
25	331.88	250.00	407.76	256.80
30	376.80	250.00	462.95	291.56
40	473.87	312.82	582.22	366.68
50.	587.10	387.57	587.10	454.28
60	727.38	480.17	587.10	562.82
70	914.77	603.88	587.10	587.10
75	1038.57	685.60	587.10	587.10
80	1196.24	789.69	587.10	587.10
90	1735.38	1145.59	587.10	587.10
95	2359.53	1557.63	587.10	587.10
97.5	3080.05	2033.27	587.10	587.10
99	4198.77	2771.78	587.10	587.10

Notes:
[a] This column indicates the maximum level of terminal wealth that is obtained with the probability in the first column and no restriction on the terminal wealth.
[b] This column indicates the maximum level of terminal wealth according to the optimal strategy that restricts terminal wealth to be no smaller than 250.
[c] This column indicates the maximum level of terminal wealth according to the optimal strategy that restricts terminal wealth to be no larger than 587.10.
[d] This column indicates the maximum level of terminal wealth according to the optimal strategy that restricts terminal wealth to lie between 250 and 587.10.
Source: Authors' computations.

only 100.86 units, which means that he would have lost two-thirds of the initial investment.

The last column in Table 9.1 is our fully restricted case, with the two bounds. The main result here is that in 20 percent of the future scenarios, pension savers get exactly the lower bound of 250 units. In comparison, the unrestricted case has a similar percentage of scenarios in which the investor ends up with less than 250 units. On the other hand, in the fully restricted case only 30 percent of the investors approximately double the initial investment, and they never get above the ceiling of 587.10. In fact, 50 percent of the investors stay within those two bounds.

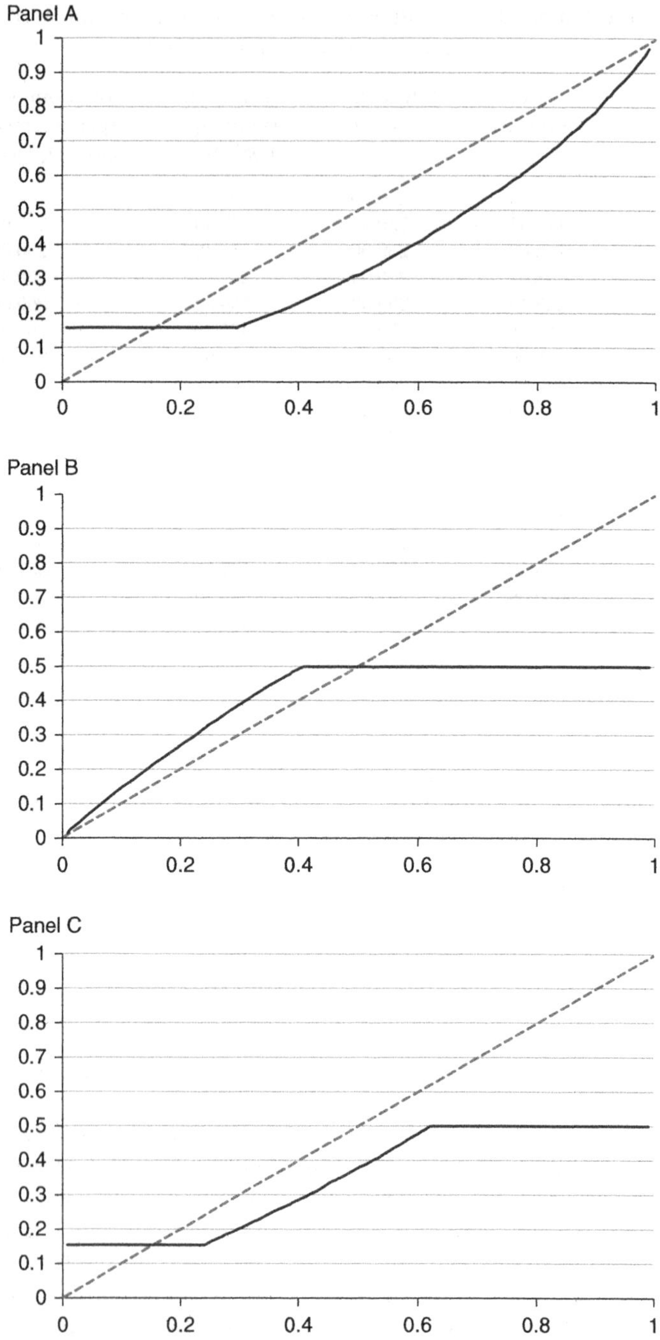

Figure 9.3 Wealth distribution quantile plots after 30 years

Note: The dashed diagonal line corresponds to the unrestricted case. Panel A considers only a lower bound (solid black line), Panel B considers only an upper bound (solid black line) and Panel C includes both upper and lower bounds (solid black line).

Source: Authors' computations.

Let us use $F_{(L,U)}(\cdot)$ to represent the statistical distribution function of the terminal wealth for a given lower bound L and upper bound U. The interpretation is that the terminal wealth is at most equal to the value x with probability$F_{(L,U)}(x)$. Note that as the unrestricted case is equivalent to the restricted case with the bounds $L = 0$ and $U = \infty$, its distribution function is $F_{(0,\infty)}(\cdot)$. As before, we consider the unrestricted case as the benchmark.

Figure 9.3 shows three probability plots which allow us to compare visually the terminal wealth distributions of the restricted and unrestricted cases. In Panel A, the solid black line is a plot of $F_{(0,\infty)}(x)$ against $F_{(250,\infty)}(x)$—corresponding to a lower bound of 250 and no upper bound—as x varies. Each point on the line corresponds to a possible terminal wealth value, although the value is not explicitly shown on the plot. Instead, the x and y coordinates give the probability of the terminal wealth being at most that value under the restricted and unrestricted case, respectively. In all diagrams, the dashed line corresponds to a plot of $F_{(0,\infty)}(x)$ against itself, which we consider as the benchmark line.

The solid black line beneath the dashed line indicates that the quantiles of the restricted case are below those of the unrestricted, and vice versa. For example, part of the horizontal segment of the solid black line is above the dashed line, indicating that the very lowest quantiles of the restricted case are above those of the unrestricted case. This corresponds to an investor's terminal wealth hitting the lower bound in the restricted case.

In Panel B in Figure 9.3, the solid black line is a plot of $F_{(0,\infty)}(x)$ against $F_{(0,587.10)}(x)$—corresponding to no lower bound and an upper bound of 587.10—as x varies. Here the lower quantiles for the restricted case are above those for the unrestricted case, and it is only when the upper bound bites that they start falling below. In Panel C, the restricted case has a lower bound of 250 and an upper bound of 587. This gives quantiles for the restricted case that generally lay below those of the unrestricted case and are in a shorter range. Figure 9.3 illustrates the ability of our proposed method to restrict the distribution of the terminal wealth to a limited domain.

Conclusion

The puzzle of retirement plan investment decisions in savings or in consumption phases is largely due to a weak comprehension of risk. We believe that it is much easier to communicate the extent of uncertainty using bounds on the desired income. By letting pension savers fix an upper and a lower wealth bound, we can produce an automatic method that fixes the amount of current wealth that should be invested in risky stock. This method produces an embedded guarantee that accumulated wealth is never smaller than the lower bound fixed by the pension saver, and it is never larger than the upper bound fixed by the pension saver. The investment strategy can be implemented by individuals or by fund managers.

Comparing strategies based only on their expected returns neglects the most dangerous part of the potential outcome, and we argue that decision-makers should look at the extremes of the distribution instead. This is why we concentrate on quantiles, to set up target bounds so that the investment is restricted to remain within the limits and be able to compare distributions by means of a risk-adjusted judgment. The visualization of probability plots summarizes the power of investment strategies that can be implemented in practice.

When we study the effect of administration costs on the expected or the median rate of return as in Guillén et al. (2014), we fix the level of risk in the wealth distribution. The level of risk in the wealth distribution can be measured by a (low) percentile in the distribution (i.e., a Value-at-Risk measure). We then compare two distributions, one with no administration costs, and a second with positive administration costs, which has the same risk as the given baseline. Accordingly, we find the reduction in return due to administration costs exclusively such that the percentile of the wealth distribution with administration costs and without administration costs are the same. This method allows for risk-adjusted evaluations of the return lost due to the presence of managerial costs. Here we have seen that risk of terminal wealth in a pension saver setting can be bounded using suitable investment strategies. Therefore, our proposed mechanism does not need to implement and to pay for the fund manager to reduce risk.

Acknowledgments

Montserrat Guillén thanks ICREA Academia and the Spanish Ministry grant ECO2013-48326-C2-1-P.

Appendix

We assume investment in a continuous-time market model over a finite time horizon $[0,T]$ for an integer $T>0$. We also refer to t as the *terminal time*. The market consists of one risky stock and one risk-free bond. The price of the stock is driven by a one-dimensional, standard Brownian motion $W=\{W(t);t\in[0,T]\}$. The risk-free bond has price process $\{S_0(t);t\in[0,T]\}$ and the risky stock has price process $\{S_1(t);t\in[0,T]\}$ with dynamics

$$dS_0(t)=rS_0(t)dt, \qquad dS_1(t)=S_1(t)\left(\mu dt+\sigma dW(t)\right),$$

with $\sigma > 0$, $S_0(0) = 1$ and $S_1(0)$ being a fixed, strictly positive constant. We assume that $\mu > r$.

The information F_t available to investors at time t is generated by the Brownian motion up to time t. The market price of risk is $\theta := (\mu - r)/\sigma$.

An investor starts with a fixed non-random initial wealth $x_0 > 0$ and plans to make a sequence of known future savings $a > 0$. Define $C(t)$ to be the sum from time 0 to time t of the investor's planned discrete savings, with

$$dC(t) = \begin{cases} a & \textit{if } t = 1,2,\ldots,T-1 \\ 0 & \textit{otherwise.} \end{cases}$$

In other words, at the end of each unit time period, the investor pays an amount $a > 0$ into their fund.

A portfolio process $\pi = \{\pi(t); t \in [0,T]\}$ is a square-integrable, $\{F_t\}$-progressively measurable process. The investor follows a self-financed strategy, investing at each instant $t \in [0,T]$ a monetary amount $\pi(t)$ in the stock such that $\pi = \{\pi(t); t \in [0,T]\}$ is a portfolio process.

The wealth process $X^\pi = \{X^\pi(t); t \in [0,T]\}$ corresponding to a portfolio process is the F_t- adapted process given by the *wealth equation*

$$dX^\pi(t) = \left(rX^\pi(t) + \pi(t)\sigma\theta\right)dt + \pi(t)\sigma dW(t) + dC(t), X^\pi(0) = x_0.$$

Define the *savings plan* g of the investor, which is the discounted sum of the future savings by the investor by

$$g(t) := \int_t^T e^{-r(s-t)} dC(s), \forall t \in [0,T].$$

Then the set of *admissible portfolios* for the investor's initial wealth $x_0 > 0$ is defined to be

$$A := \{\pi : \Omega \times [0,T] \rightarrow R : X^\pi(0) = x_0, \ \textit{and} \ \ X^\pi(t) + g(t) \geq 0, t \in (0,T]\}.$$

We say that a portfolio process π is *admissible* if $\pi \in A$.

Define the state price density process H as $H(t) := exp\left(-\left(r + \frac{1}{2}\theta^2\right)t - \theta W(t)\right)$, for each $t \in [0,T]$. A portfolio π must satisfy the *budget constraint* that

$$\mathrm{E}\Big(H(T)X^\pi(T)\Big) \leq x_0 + g(0).$$

The utility function of the investor is the power utility function

$$v(x) := \frac{1}{\gamma} x^\gamma, \ x > 0,$$

for a fixed constant $\gamma \in (-\infty,1)\ \{0\}$. The investor seeks to maximize the expected utility of their terminal wealth, subject to constraints on the range of values of the terminal wealth.

Define the constant $A := \theta/(\sigma(1-\gamma))$ and the process

$$Z(t) = exp\left(\left(r + \theta\sigma A - \frac{1}{2}\sigma^2 A^2\right)t + \sigma A W(t)\right), \forall t \in [0,T].$$

Problem with a Lower and an Upper Bound

The problem with only an upper bound U was introduced and solved in Donnelly et al. (2015a). Here we extend the problem to include a lower bound $L \in (0,U)$, below which the terminal wealth must not fall. Combined with the upper bound U, this means that the investor's terminal wealth lies in the range$[L,U]$.

The addition of a lower bound has already been well studied in the literature (Basak 1995) and this is logical as pension savers are usually afraid of their wealth falling below a certain minimum level.

In order to avoid both the uninteresting case that the investor can immediately be assured of maximizing the terminal utility and the breaching of the non-arbitrage condition, we assume that $L < \left(x_0 + g(0)\right)e^{rT} < U$.

Problem 1

Find $\pi^\theta \in A$ such that

$$E\left(v(X^{\pi^\theta}(T))\right) = \sup_{\pi \in A}\{\mathrm{E}\left(v(X^{\pi}(T))\right)\},$$

and $X^{\pi^\theta}(T) \in [L,U]$, almost surely.

The optimal terminal wealth with a lower and upper bound

The next proposition gives an expression for the optimal terminal wealth for Problem 2, when there is both a lower and upper bound constraint on the terminal wealth.

Proposition 1

A solution to the restricted problem at the terminal time T is

$$\begin{aligned} X^\theta(T) = \quad & (z_0 + g(0))Z(T) - \max\{0,(z_0 + g(0))Z(T) - U\} \\ & + \max\{0, L - (z_0 + g(0))Z(T)\}, \end{aligned}$$

with $z_0 > 0$ chosen so that the budget constraint is satisfied with equality by X^θ, given the investor's initial wealth $X^\theta(0) = x_0$, and savings plan g.

Proof

The proof is an adaption of the proof of a proposition in Donnelly et al. (2015a).

Proposition 2

An optimal investment strategy for Problem 2 is to invest the amount

$$\pi^\theta(t) := A[1 - \Phi(d_+\left(t,P(t);U\right) - \Phi(-d_+\left(t,P(t);L\right))]P(t)$$

in the risky stock and the amount $X^{\pi^\theta}(t) - \pi^\theta(t)$ in the risk-free bond, in which $P(t) = \left(z_0 + g(0)\right)Z(t)$ and the function d_+ is defined for each $K>0$ by

$$d_+(t,y;K) := \frac{1}{\sigma A\sqrt{T-t}}\left(\ln\left(\frac{y}{K}\right) + \left(r + \frac{1}{2}\sigma^2 A^2\right)(T-t)\right), \forall y > 0.$$

Proof

The proof follows trivially from the previous results. Details can be found in Donnelly et al. (2015b).

Lemma 1 (p-quantiles)

Suppose an investor has initial wealth $x_0 > 0$ and follows the savings plan g. Define

$$\beta_p := \sigma A\sqrt{T}\Phi^{-1}(p) + \left(r + \theta\sigma A - \frac{1}{2}\sigma^2 A^2\right)T.$$

If the investor follows the optimal constrained strategy, that is the terminal wealth is constrained to lie in the range $[L,U]$, then the p-quantile of the investor's terminal wealth $X^\theta(T)$is

$$Q_p\left(X^\theta(T);(L,U)\right) = max\left\{L, min\left\{U, \left(z_0 + g(0)\right)e^{\beta_p}\right\}\right\}.$$

Proof

The proof can be found in Donnelly et al. (2015b).

Endnotes

1. Following the notation in the Appendix, we fix the parameter values: $r = 0,\ \mu = 0.0343,\ \sigma = 0.1544,\ A = 1,\ T = 30,\ g \equiv 0,\ x_0 = 300.$

Note that the choice of the parameters implies that the investor's risk aversion constant is $\gamma = -0.44$. We use parameters similar to those proposed in Donnelly et al. (2015a) and Guillén et al. (2014).

References

Basak, S. (1995). 'A General Equilibrium Model of Portfolio Insurance,' *Review of Financial Studies*, 8(4): 1059–90.

Basu, A., A. Byrne, and M. Drew (2011). 'Dynamic Lifecycle Strategies for Target Date Retirement Funds,' *Journal of Portfolio Management*, 37: 83–96.

Benartzi, S. and R. Thaler (1999). 'Risk Aversion or Myopia? Choices in Repeated Gambles and Retirement Investments,' *Management Science*, 45(3): 364–81.

Bodie, Z., R. Merton, and W. Samuelson (1992). 'Labor Supply Flexibility and Portfolio Choice in a Life Cycle Model,' *Journal of Economic Dynamics and Control*, 16(3): 427–49.

Bouchard, B., R. Elie., and C. Imbert (2010). 'Optimal Control under Stochastic Target Constraints,' *SIAM Journal on Control and Optimization*, 48(5): 3501–31.

Boyle, P. and W. Tian (2007). 'Portfolio Management with Constraints,' *Mathematical Finance*, 17(3): 319–43.

Browne, S. (1999). 'Reaching Goals by a Deadline: Digital Options and Continuous Time Active Portfolio Management,' *Advances in Applied Probability*, 31(2): 551–77.

Cuoco, D. (1997). 'Optimal Consumption and Equilibrium Prices with Portfolio Constraints and Stochastic Income,' *Journal of Economic Theory*, 72(1): 33–73.

De Franco, C. and P. Tankov (2011). 'Portfolio Insurance under a Risk-Measure Constraint,' *Insurance, Mathematics and Economics*, 49(3): 361–70.

Dhaene, J., S. Vanduffel, M. Goovaerts, R. Kaas, and D. Vyncke (2005). 'Comonotonic Approximations for Optimal Portfolio Selection Problems,' *Journal of Risk and Insurance*, 72(2): 253–300.

Donnelly, C., R. Gerrard, M. Guillén, and J. P. Nielsen (2015a). 'Less is More: Increasing Retirement Gains by Using an Upside Terminal Wealth Constraint,' *Insurance, Mathematics and Economics*, 64: 259–67.

Donnelly, C., M. Guillén, and J. P. Nielsen (2013). 'Exchanging Uncertain Mortality for a Cost,' *Insurance, Mathematics and Economics*, 52(1): 65–76.

Donnelly, C., M. Guillén, and J. P. Nielsen (2014). 'Bringing Cost Transparency to the Life Annuity Market,' *Insurance, Mathematics and Economics*, 56: 14–27.

Donnelly, C., M. Guillén, J. P. Nielsen, and A. M. Pérez-Marín (2015b). *On the Practical Implementation of Retirement Gains by Using an Upside and a Downside Terminal Wealth Constraint*, UB Riskcenter Working Papers Series 2015-07. Barcelona: University of Barcelona.

Gaibh, A., J. Sass, and R. Wunderlich (2009). 'Utility Maximization under Bounded Expected Loss,' *Stochastic Models*, 25(3): 375–407.

Gerrard, R., M. Guillén, J. P. Nielsen, and A. M. Pérez-Marín (2014). 'Long-Run Savings and Investment Strategy Optimization,' *Scientific World Journal*, 2014, article ID 510531, 13 pages. doi:10.1155/2014/510531

Greninger, S. V. Hampton, K. Kitt, and S. Jacquet (2000). 'Retirement Planning Guidelines: A Delphi Study of Financial Planners and Educators,' *Financial Services Review*, 9(3): 231–45.

Grossman, S., and Z. Zhou (1996). 'Equilibrium Analysis of Portfolio Insurance,' *Journal of Finance*, 51(4): 1379–403.

Guillén, M., S. F. Jarner, J. P. Nielsen, and A. M. Pérez-Marín (2014). 'Risk-Adjusted Impact of Administrative Costs on the Distribution of Terminal Wealth for Long-Term Investment,' *Scientific World Journal*, 2014, article ID 521074, 12 pages. doi: 10.1155/2014/521074

Guillén, M., J. P. Nielsen, A. M. Pérez-Marín, and K. Petersen (2013). 'Performance Measurement of Pension Strategies: A Case Study of Danish Life-Cycle Products,' *Scandinavian Actuarial Journal*, 2013(1): 49–68.

Jin, H. and X. Zhou (2008). 'Behavioral Portfolio Selection in Continuous Time,' *Mathematical Finance*, 18(3): 385–426.

Korn, R. and S. Trautmann (1995). 'Continuous-Time Portfolio Optimization under Terminal Wealth Constraints,' *Mathematical Methods of Operations Research*, 42(1): 69–92.

Leshno, M. and H. Levy (2002). 'Preferred by "All" and Preferred by "Most" Decision Makers: Almost Stochastic Dominance,' *Management Science*, 48(8): 1074–85.

MacKay, A., M. Augustyniak, C. Bernard, and M. R. Hardy (2015). 'Risk Management of Policyholder Behavior in Equity-Linked Life Insurance,' *Journal of Risk and Insurance*. Published online Sept. 24 (doi 10.111/jori.12094).

Milevsky, M. A. and H. Huang (2011). 'Spending Retirement on Planet Vulcan: The Impact of Longevity Risk Aversion on Optimal Withdrawal Rates (Corrected July 2011),' *Financial Analysts Journal*, 67(2): 45–58.

Van Weert, K., J. Dhaene, and M. Goovaerts (2010). 'Optimal Portfolio Selection for General Provisioning and Terminal Wealth Problems,' *Insurance, Mathematics and Economics*, 47(1): 90–7.

von Gaudecker, H. M., A. van Soest, and E. Wengström (2011). 'Heterogeneity in Risky Choice Behavior in a Broad Population,' *American Economic Review*, 101(2): 664–94.

Zariphopoulou, T. (1994). 'Consumption-Investment Models with Constraints,' *SIAM Journal on Control and Optimization*, 32(1): 59–85.

10

Pension Fund Investment in Infrastructure and Global Financial Regulation

Javier Alonso, Alfonso Arellano, and David Tuesta

A topic attracting attention in recent global regulatory discussions is the possibility that private pension funds should invest in alternative assets, particularly infrastructure projects.[1] As defined by the OECD, this refers to

> the system of public works in a country, state or region, including roads, utility lines and public buildings. Infrastructure is typically used for performing long term capital activities which provide essential services to the public. Infrastructure investments are expected to produce predictable and stable cash flows over the long term. Infrastructure assets normally operate in an environment of limited competition as a result of natural monopolies, government regulation or concessions. Investments are usually capital intensive and include a tangible asset that must be operated and maintained over the long term. (Della Croce et al. 2011: 15–16)

Although there are relevant pros and cons to be considered by pension funds when investing in infrastructure, there have been at least three alluring factors that make it interesting for pension funds to invest in alternative assets. First, these assets are attractive in terms of profitability and risk, and many pension funds have had apparently successful experiences with them. Second, there are arguments about the suitability of such long-maturity assets, given institutional investors' long-term horizons. Third, there are perceived needs to fund infrastructure when governments have budgetary limitations and banks are forced to disinvest from these assets due to financial regulation.

Against this backdrop, countries around the world are introducing regulatory changes to allow or increase pension fund investments in infrastructure. Generally speaking, this means allowing pension funds to invest more in specific projects and, at the same time, designing specific financial vehicles to balance the investment criteria of pension fund members in terms of profile, risk, returns, and portfolio diversification. Our goal in this chapter is to assess the role of regulation on pension fund decisions to invest in this specific financial asset. We carry out a quantitative analysis with the aim of shedding some light on the different explanatory variables which might affect whether or not pension funds invest in infrastructure, among them financial regulatory factors. In what follows, we first highlight the elements encouraging pension funds to invest in infrastructure projects. Next, we analyze the pros and cons of pension investments in this alternative asset. We then focus on financial regulatory factors that interact with pension fund investments in infrastructure in different regions. We also offer an econometric analysis to assess which factors are currently the most influential on pension funds investing in infrastructure. We close with our key conclusions.

Factors Accelerating the Trend for Pension Funds to Invest in Infrastructure

We have constructed a database for 72 pension funds across 21 countries, where their investment menu includes investing in infrastructure (see Table 10.1). For those countries currently investing in infrastructure, this averages 5.6 percent. This average is influenced by two countries that actively invest in infrastructure, namely Canada (6.6 percent) and Australia (8.6 percent). Interestingly, in our sample, there are a dozen pension funds which invest between 10 and 31 percent of their portfolios in unlisted infrastructure assets. Moreover, Della Croce (2012) estimates that, between 2010 and 2013, the world's ten largest pension funds boosted their allocation to alternative assets from 17.6 to 19.5 percent. Several factors have contributed to this trend.

The financial crisis

The straitjacketing of public spending in the wake of the financial crisis has suppressed much infrastructure funding vital to economic growth.

The European Commission (2014c) suggests that Europe will need to raise €1.5–2.0 trillion in funds for infrastructure investment by 2020, and the US will seek $1.7–3.0 trillion by the same date. Several groups including the European Commission (2014a, 2014b) seek formulas for co-financing by the private sector. One reason is that banks, which had fulfilled this role in the past, are now facing problems in providing funding, owing to the restrictions imposed under Basel III, specifically under the Capital Requirement Regulation (CRR). Given this, the Commission has suggested that the insurance and pension fund industry may be the ideal candidate to step in.

Pension funds and their role in the economy

There has been increasing support for pension funds investing in infrastructure, as a win-win situation for pension funds and macroeconomic stability (Escrivá et al. 2010). Figure 10.1 shows the interaction between pension

TABLE 10.1. Pension fund investment in infrastructure

	Actual (%)	Target (%)	Year
Aust-Ausfund	0	10.0	2010
Aust-BUSS (Q)	17.9	0.0	2010
Aust-Care	6	0.0	2010
Aust-Catholic	0	5.0	2010
Aust-Cbus	14.1	0.0	2010
Aust-Firstsuper	0	7.5	2010
Aust-First State SA	3.5		2011
Aust-Future	8	0.0	2013
Aust-Health Super	4.6		2009
Aust-AusGov Superfund	6.7		
Aust-Hesta	0.8	10.0	2010
Aust-Hosplus	0	4.0	2009
Aust-Military	9	0.0	2010
Aust-MTAA	31.1	25.0	2010
Aust-Q Super	6.2		2011
Aust-QIC	4	0.0	2010
Aust-State Super	1.9	0.0	2010
Aust-Sun Super	5.1	5.0	2013
Aust-Australian Super	9.8	14.0	2013
Aust-Retail Employees	13.8		2011
Aust-Reward	13.8		2011
Aust-Telstra	3	0.0	2010
Aust-Unisuper	4.4	6.5	2010
Aust-VIC	5.5	0.0	2010
Aust-West Schem	17.9	0.0	2010
Argentina-Sustainability Guarantee Fund	13.6	20.0	2013
Bras-Pension Funds	1.0	0.0	2010
Brasil-Previ	6.9	0.0	2013
Brasil-Funcef	6.9	0.0	2013
Brasil-Fapes	0.0	0.0	2013
Can-CPP Alberta	6.1		2012
Can-Caisse de Depo	1.4	8.8	2010
Can-CPP	6.1		2012
Can-CPPIB	5.5	0.0	2010
Can-OMERS	14.9	21.5	2013
Can-OTTP	8.4	8.5	2013
Can-PSP	6.1		2012
Can-Quebec Pension Plan	4.0	5.0	2013
Chil-AFP	1.2	0.0	2010
Chil-Provida	0.0	0.0	2013
Chil-Habitat	0.2	0.0	2013
Chil- Pension Reserve Fund	0.0	0.0	2013
Col-AFP	0.7	0.0	2010
Den-PFA	0.8	0.0	2013
Finland-Ilmarien	0.3	0.0	2013
Finland-Keva	0.0	0.0	2013
Israel-Menora-Mitvachim	2.9	0.0	2013
Japan-Pension Fund Association	0.1	0.0	2013

Mex-AFORE	4.8	0.0	2010
Mex-AFORE XXI Banorte	0.3	5.0	2013
Mex-Banamex	1.8	2.5	2013
Ned- ABP	1.5	3.0	2013
Ned- PFZW	2.4	3.0	2013
Ned-PGGM	0.8	0.0	2010
Ned-PMT	0.6	1.0	2013
New Zealand-Superannuation Fund	1.9	0.0	2013
Per-AFP	3.7	0.0	2010
Portugal-BPI Pension Fund	3.3	0.0	2013
Portugal-CGD Staff 's Pension Fund	1.6	1.6	2013
RSA-Gov Employees	0.1	0.0	2013
Swe- AP Fonden	0.8	0.0	2010
Swe- AP 4	0.0	0.0	2013
Swe- AP 3	1.4	2.0	2013
Spain-Endesa	0.0	0.0	2013
Spain-Fonditel	0.1	0.0	2013
Turkey -Oyak	4.4	0.0	2013
UK-USS	4.4	5.0	2013
USA-Alaska PFC	0.0	18.0	2010
USA-Calpers	0.0	3.0	2010
USA-MERS	0.0	5.0	2010
USA-Calsters	0.0	2.5	2010
USA-NYC Combined Retirement Service	0.0	0.0	2013

Sources: Derived by the authors from Inderst (2014), OECD (2014a), Tuesta (2013), Weber and Alfen (2010), Future Fund Board (2011), Infrastructure Partnerships Australia (2010), and Macquarie (2009).

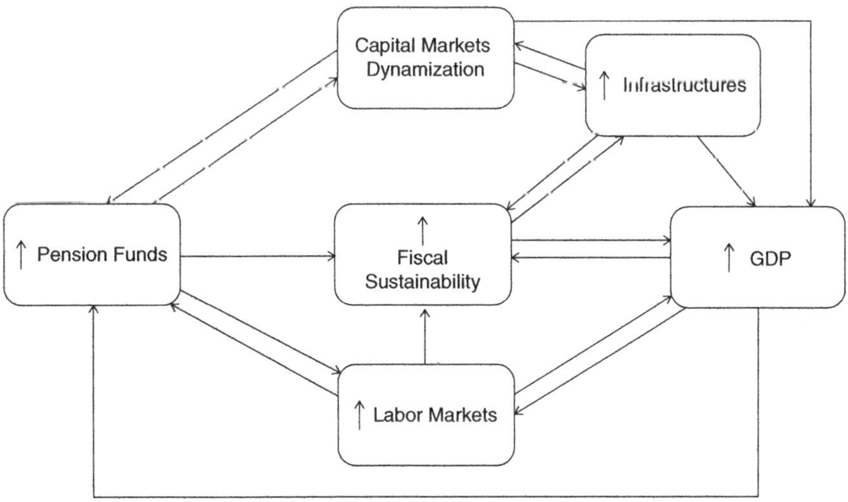

Figure 10.1 Pension funds and infrastructure: the theoretical virtuous circle

Source: Authors' depiction.

funds and economic growth through various channels of transmission, foremost among these being financial, fiscal, and labor market mechanisms. The same figure highlights the role fulfilled by infrastructure and its impact on growth, suggesting that pension funds could become the backers of infrastructure projects and their effects on growth. A study by Alonso et al. (2009) revealed that elasticity of growth with respect to infrastructure could be between 7.0 and 13.5 percent.

Also in Figure 10.1, it is important to focus on the fiscal channel. This could be positively affected, since the presence of the private sector means a lower public borrowing requirement, thus reducing its vulnerability and boosting growth. Likewise, capital markets play a major role through pension fund financing, by bringing more resources to economic agents, greater efficiency, and improving fiscal sustainability.

It should be pointed out that for such a 'virtuous circle' between pension funds and infrastructures to crystallize, there must be well-defined and sound projects, a good financing vehicle for them, and an institutional framework that enables the interests involved in carrying out infrastructure projects to be harmoniously aligned in pursuit of the success of the investment.

Ultra-low interest rates

Another important incentive for pension funds to think about investing in infrastructure projects is the low interest rate environment. This type of alternative asset could counterbalance the negative effects. In the case of defined contribution (DC) plans, the low interest rate scenario has a direct impact on the pension accumulation process, already threatened by rising longevity. Systems with defined benefit (DB) pensions will have difficulties in ensuring that their commitments comply with lower interest rates.

Why Might Pension Funds Invest in Infrastructure?

Beyond the forces that are driving forward the policy trends in favor of pension funds investing in infrastructure projects, it is important to take into account at least three relevant conceptual criteria.

The perspective of the pension fund member

Various reasons are cited by the literature as justification for greater pension fund investment in infrastructure (Alonso et al. 2009). These can be reduced to six basic concepts:

(1) there is a neat fit between the pension fund portfolio and the long-term time horizon for infrastructure projects to mature;
(2) infrastructure tends to operate like natural, regulated monopolies, or oligopolies, with reduced or non-market competition, resulting in a portfolio with more stable asset values;
(3) there is a low correlation between the assets in infrastructure projects and other financial asset classes, which normally track the vicissitudes of the economic cycle;
(4) infrastructure provides protection against inflation;
(5) it offers a good risk–return tradeoff; and
(6) infrastructure assets have greater cash-flow stability when the project has matured.

In a nutshell, infrastructure offers an improved portfolio efficient frontier (Andrews and Wahba 2007; Weber and Alfen 2010; Sawant 2010).

In spite of these attractive features of infrastructural investments, a lack of statistical data can thwart attempts to examine this issue in depth. One country that provides much information on this matter is Australia: Peng and Newell (2007), Bird et al. (2012), Connolly (2012), and Inderst (2014) all report high risk-adjusted returns and low correlations with other asset classes in this context. Inderst (2014) states that some aspects require deeper analysis, as many of these studies make their estimates using small samples and valuations of unlisted infrastructure assets based on expected values, which tends to underestimate volatility and correlations to listed instruments, while overestimating potential portfolio diversification.

Pension fund liabilities and their role in investment selection

A decision to include infrastructure investments in a pension fund's portfolio should also depend on the characteristics of the pension liabilities. The value of a liability is related to the expected benefit payments (the future cash outflows) and the discount rate, which implies inherent risks that could impose volatilities attributable to wages, inflation, and many non-market-related factors. They also exhibit growth attributable to future service costs and other non-market-related factors. Uncertainty in pension benefits varies greatly by demographic group, with exposures which are either market-related or not. During the recent financial crisis, many DB schemes did experience funding problems; considering that infrastructure projects are long-term investments, these could match the long duration of pension liabilities (Della Croce 2012; Della Croce and Yermo 2013). Accessibility has also proven to be a problem in the past, particularly for smaller pension schemes in the case of the UK (NAPF 2013).

Focusing on the characteristics of pension fund liabilities and the financial situation they are facing, it may be savvy for pension funds to increase their exposure to long-term infrastructure. For instance, healthcare infrastructure could be an interesting choice. Healthcare is poised to be the most significant growth industry of the century, one of the few asset classes that can generate consistently high returns according to Yun (2012). A declining, aging population is a demographic headwind for most investment assets, but for healthcare it is a tailwind. Thus investing in healthcare infrastructure could allow pension funds to isolate longevity risk, the variable that most imbalances their revenues and obligations. Investing in the healthcare sector may be a natural hedge for pension funds.

Limitations for investing in infrastructure

Investing in infrastructure is a very complicated endeavor, requiring the alignment of several different stakeholder interests: shareholders, financial institutions, regulators, insurance companies, constructors and operators of infrastructure projects, suppliers of raw materials, and end users (Tuesta 2015). Besides that, a Special Purpose Vehicle designed for this end needs to deal with different risks and coverages: construction (delays, extra costs, technical failures), operational (insufficient production, increase in costs, quality of the product), supply contract (deficit or supply, interruptions, price of supply), financial markets (rates of return, currency), market fluctuations (demand, price, delay in payments), and politics (expropriation, political turmoil, regulation).

Accordingly, it may be difficult for a pension fund to deal with all the issues and risks. In order to deal efficiently with an infrastructure portfolio, the pension funds need to invest important resources in human capital and develop a degree of expertise that interplays with the characteristic of the project, market functioning, and the institutional framework. This is probably the most important lesson learnt from Australia and Canada (Inderst 2014). From these country cases, there are at least three areas that must be reinforced to facilitate the participation of pension funds investing in infrastructure projects.

The availability of good projects

Pension funds face a combination of factors that disincentivize infrastructure investment. These are principally characterized by the relation of the concession (or project finance) process and the different conditions in each country's domestic financial market. Additionally, there may be other barriers more specific to the sector, related to their technical capacity to evaluate investment in this type of asset and country-specific regulation. Project financing also involves inherent risks (OECD 2014d). For greenfield projects, the risks are apparent at the time that the project is conceived, and the construction risk can cause deviations in the costs of the project. In the operational phase, there can be supply, operating, and market risks. The latter are the most recurrent and appear when the expectations of the use of the infrastructure fall to much lower levels than those initially estimated, which affect the profitability of the operation. There are also other risks, including regulatory, legal, and credit risk.

A more fundamental concern has to do with the scant availability of high-quality investment projects. Although estimates by international institutions indicate a broad availability of potential investment projects around the world, in reality, available opportunities are much more limited. Depending on the country, there are enormous differences in the tradition of private-sector financing. In Europe, the usual procedure is that local development companies themselves undertake domestic infrastructure projects. For instance, in Spain and Germany, most toll roads are financed by the public sector, while in other countries, such as Portugal and France, they are financed by the private sector. In addition, in developed countries, the more profitable infrastructure projects have already been completed, while those still pending tend to involve more risk and less certain profitability. In this context, one of the proposals made by the European Commission (2014a, 2014b) to mitigate this problem is the creation of a pipeline of infrastructure projects at a European level that makes the necessary information available, such that any potential institutional investor in any country can participate in financing a project.

Rule of law

Other equally important elements are those related to legal uncertainties regarding contracts. Investors in public infrastructure need clear and stable regulations, together with efficient contractual procedures (OECD 2014b). This has not always been the case, however, and some governments have changed the contractual terms of their concessions. For example, the Spanish government has not complied with the contracts signed in solar electricity generation and the developers have seen a cut in the price per kilowatt-hour generated. This type of failure to comply can have an enormous impact on a project's financial return.

Risk mitigation tools

The regulatory framework for the financial sector (Basel II and III and Solvency II) prioritizes the need to measure such risks and provide the necessary capital to cover them. Yet this presents a disincentive for some institutions to finance infrastructure. Moreover, traditional insurers such as monoline companies collapsed in the last financial crisis. Without such insurance support, many infrastructure projects would be poorly rated by the rating agencies. For example, the use of project bonds has shrunk since 2008, due to the lowered ratings on the monoline companies that had been insuring them (OECD 2014d).

Many argue that the participation of international financial institutions such as the World Bank, the International Development Bank, or the European Investment Bank (EIB) has become fundamental in the wake of the financial crisis. Nevertheless, public–private partnerships (PPPs) can be seen as helpful in incentivizing the participation of the private sector in financing infrastructure (World Bank 2011). Some projects might be unviable from a financial point of view but might nonetheless be socially viable or generate positive externalities. In such a case, the private sector would not undertake the project unless it had some kind of guaranteed minimum level of earnings that would ensure an appropriate return on investment. Yet governments must ensure that the conditions for the infrastructure investment provide value for money, in relation to construction costs and underwriting risks.

Global Financial Regulation and Pension Fund Investment in Infrastructure

When Basel II came into effect in 2004, it forced lending institutions to build up capital to cover operating risks and market risk. Basel II allows the entities to use internal models to calculate their risk-weighted assets. The financial crisis in 2008–10 revealed the weaknesses of the system due to the high leverage of the lending institutions, their liquidity problems, and the low level and quality of their capital. Basel III is the consequence of this, and it obliged the institutions to improve the quality and quantity of their capital, enhance their risk management systems, reduce leverage, increase liquidity, and take counter-cyclical measures.

Global financial regulation limits the participation of banks in infrastructure projects

The consequences for infrastructure finance were immediate. First, financing entities became more risk-averse. Some countries have established a Liquidity Coverage Ratio (LCR) of 50 percent, which practically eliminates infrastructure projects. Second, the degree of coverage depends on the time horizon: the longer the time horizon, the higher the consumption of capital. As financing infrastructure construction and operation is long-term, this has provided a further disincentive to continuing investment.

In addition to the global legislation, there are also local regulations that can have a negative impact on the development of products linked to infrastructure. For example, infrastructure funds have been unsuccessful in Spain because the solvency requirements for these funds when tendering for PPP projects present an obstacle, as they normally manage funds that are not in themselves corporate. These tenders are normally designed for construction companies (CEOE 2013).

Pension fund investment in infrastructure and its regulation

Infrastructure regulation is complex for several reasons. First, there is the problem of defining what infrastructure to launch. Second, historical data are insufficient to evaluate the possible impacts of this regulation. These assets are supported by physical installations, so their characteristics will determine the specific type of project finance. A project for investment in a toll road is not the same as for a photovoltaic electricity generating plant, or a hospital. Nor is a toll road connecting the two principal cities in a country directly comparable with one connecting relatively unpopulated areas, for example. In addition to the different types of infrastructure, the type of investment project must reflect whether it is a greenfield investment, or whether it is for the maintenance or improvement of a previously existing asset (brownfield). The financing project must also consider whether the investment is based on shares or debt, and also whether these instruments are traded in an organized market. Sometimes the investment is directly to build the infrastructure itself, while other times it is indirect through other financial vehicles. Investments that have a direct link include, for example, pension fund loans to the developer through project bonds, obligation bonds, or by taking an equity stake in one or several specific infrastructure assets through greenfield shares. Indirect investments would be made by buying shares in quoted companies involved in infrastructure development, or by buying into an infrastructure investment fund, whether quoted or not. Given this wide range of possibilities, the ideal would almost be to establish specific regulations for each project, although this is evidently impossible, and therein lies the difficulty of specifying general regulations.

In several countries, pension funds investing in infrastructure assets have done so within the limitations imposed by their respective financial investment regulations, the degree of sophistication of their respective capital markets that allow or forbid this type of investment, and the pension fund's technical possibility of accessing infrastructure financing, either direct or indirect. Individual countries also adopt different regulatory responses to this complexity, which varies between relying on total flexibility of pension funds' investment in infrastructure and imposing restrictions.

Geographies with extremely flexible financial regulation

Countries that have completely flexible regulations probably find that legislating for investment in this type of asset is too expensive, given the enormous diversity of the potential projects. They assume that the best entities to assess the risks of the project are the investors themselves, and as such, only establish that the investments should be 'prudent' and well planned (OECD 2014a). Adopting this model implies that the pension funds should have the necessary knowledge to successfully evaluate each project. This group typically comprises the Anglo-Saxon countries (UK, US, Australia, and Canada), plus Belgium and the Netherlands, all of which establish no quantitative limits on infrastructure investment.

Within this group, there is also a significant diversity in terms of the investment policy adopted. For example, in Canada and Australia, the instruments selected vary considerably. Canada has an interesting combination of direct investment in unlisted infrastructure asset projects; it has one of the most developed project bond markets and at the same time invests a significant proportion of its infrastructure portfolio abroad. Meanwhile, Australia has developed great expertise in packaging the risks in special financing vehicles managed by infrastructure funds, and it recently has invested more actively in unlisted assets. We also note that pension fund investment in Australian infrastructure was incentivized by the introduction of an obligatory DC pension system, while in Canada this boost came from very mature private DB pension funds (Inderst 2014).

Regulation of infrastructure investment by means of limits or conditionality

Some countries set limits on pension fund investment in infrastructure. For example, one-third of the countries analyzed by the OECD (2014a) did not allow investment in private investment funds or via direct loans. Yet a majority of the countries allow investment in private bonds (including infrastructure bonds), though the limit is almost always lower than for holdings of government bonds. Most countries do not allow investment in unlisted shares and have limits for quoted assets, as is exemplified by various Latin American countries. According to Tuesta (2015), Brazil, Chile, Colombia, Mexico, and Peru, the countries with the most important private pension schemes in the region, are investing around 2.6 percent of their total portfolios in infrastructure. Mexico is of particular note, which to date has invested an average of 4.8 percent of its portfolio in infrastructure projects.

The regulatory experience of these countries has been limited. The first infrastructure bonds were developed under the 1998 monoline scheme in Chile, which enabled the financing of that country's key infrastructure. Later on, this scheme had to be dropped, however, and current investments in such assets occur via infrastructure funds. Mexico is leading the way in developing packaged instruments for pension fund investment in such projects, with the so-called Fibra (Real Estate Investment Trusts) and CKD (Development Capital Certificate). Colombia, meanwhile, has developed infrastructure bonds with limited government financing. Peru has opted for trust funds to invest in infrastructure set up by the pension funds themselves; these take stakes in infrastructure funds where they play an active role on the board. Peru has also developed the so-called CRPI (Work in Progress Certificates) for mega infrastructure projects that are more like public works, as they have substantial guarantees from government tax revenues.

All the Latin American infrastructure investments have some type of quantitative limitation, either direct, in the case of identifying the special vehicle itself, or indirect, such as the general quantitative cap for debt or equity instruments. Countries such as Colombia and Mexico have set limits on their infrastructure investment vehicles that vary depending on the risk profiles of the workers participating in the pension funds and of the portfolios in which the funds are invested (Tuesta 2015). In the case of Mexico, these can be up to 12 percent, while in Colombia the limit is 7 percent of certain portfolios.

The case of Europe

Several efforts have been made to encourage institutional infrastructure investment in Europe in recent years (European Commission 2014a, 2014b). Nonetheless, the enormous diversity of pension systems has so far prevented regulation of a common infrastructure investment market. Within the EU, national legislation predominates, with significant differences between the least restrictive countries regarding such investments (Belgium, with 10.58 percent) and the strictest (Spain, 6.06 percent) (see Appendix and results in Table 10.2).

In 2009, the European Commission proposed a directive on Alternative Investment Fund Managers (AIFMs) with the objective of creating a regulatory and supervisory framework for AIFMs at a European level, which would make the management of these funds more transparent for both the

TABLE 10.2. Index of regulatory liberalization for the investment of pension funds in infrastructure

Country	Index	Country	Index	Country	Index	Country	Index
Belgium	10.58	Sweden	7.93	Iceland	6.01	Zambia	4.91
Canada	10.58	Germany	7.93	Jordan	6.01	Nigeria	4.57
Ireland	10.58	South Korea	7.78	Switzerland	5.68	Nigeria	4.57
Netherlands	10.58	Portugal	7.61	Brazil	5.68	Romania	4.57
Gibraltar	10.58	United States	7.59	Malta	5.66	Czech Republic	4.33
Malta	10.58	Hungary	7.22	Poland	5.50	Albania	4.18
Malawi	10.22	Greece	6.80	Bulgaria	5.50	Colombia	4.18
Australia	9.86	Mauritius	6.79	Slovak Republic	5.32	China	4.18
United Kingdom	9.86	Austria	6.74	Armenia	5.31	Pakistan	4.18
Israel	9.85	Italy	6.47	Armenia	5.31	Russian Federation	3.98
New Zealand	9.83	Turkey	6.47	Costa Rica	5.29	Maldives	3.79
Norway	8.71	France	6.43	Slovenia	5.29	Egypt	3.74
Japan	8.41	Thailand	6.10	Tanzania	5.29	Dominican Republic	3.38
Estonia	8.36	Trinidad and Tobago	6.07	Peru	5.29	Chile	3.07
Jamaica	8.31	South Africa	6.07	Kenya	4.93	Uganda	3.02
Luxembourg	7.95	Spain	6.06	Republic of Macedonia	4.93	India	2.30
Finland	7.94	Mexico	6.04	Namibia	4.91	Ukraine	2.25

Source: Derived by the authors from OECD (2014a).

authorities and investors (European Commission 2014a, 2014b). The body responsible for regulating pension funds in Europe (EIOPA) proposed the IORP and IORP II directives to homogenize national legislation on occupational pension funds with the requirements of Solvency II. In other words, the European focus prioritizes solvency and active risk management through models that allow the appropriate evaluation of the associated risks, not forgetting the required pillar of control and reporting.

Although EIOPA has recognized the importance of infrastructure for economic growth and its potential advantage for pension funds, it cautions that more work needs to be done and consultations carried out before any common legislation can be passed. In this respect, EIOPA proposed a discussion paper which first establishes how the various infrastructure and other long-term assets should be treated within the Solvency II framework, and for what type of financial investor (2013). EIOPA considers that the preferred type of investment for insurance companies in long-term assets would be direct project finance (bonds, loans, or equity), infrastructure investment funds (listed and unlisted), and infrastructure loan securitization vehicles.[2]

The most advanced initiative that tries to mitigate the problems noted is the Europe 2020 project bond initiative under the auspices of the EIB. The EIB plays a role like the former monoline insurers, covering greenfield infrastructure risks and providing the projects with an adequate credit rating. More specifically, the principal characteristics would be as follows: limiting loss coverage below 20 percent; aiming for an 'A' rating for the project (the minimum requirement for pension funds and insurance company asset portfolios); the possibility of subordinated loans from the EIB based on their financial situation and rating; and selecting the project finance or PPP projects available for audit by the EIB itself. In 2015, EIOPA created a working group to define what types of infrastructure investment offer predictable cash flows in the long term with well-identified risks. This group is also evaluating criteria for new types of infrastructure assets including transparency and standardization.

What Variables Have Influenced Pension Fund Investment in Infrastructure? The Empirical Evidence

As we have noted, both regulatory and non-regulatory factors may encourage or discourage the participation of pension funds in infrastructure funding. In this section we propose a model to quantify which factors are most empirically relevant.

Data

Our data come from several sources. Information on pension investment regulation and aspects of the institutional and business environment is available in several OECD publications and the World Economic Forum USA's report. To determine which variables could affect the investment of pension funds in infrastructure, we use three sets of variables.

A first group of variables was collected from the OECD (2014a), with data as of December 2013. This report contains information about all forms of restriction and legal regulation for pension funds to invest in infrastructures. Variables refer to the limits on OECD and selected non-OECD pension funds investment in several asset categories (equity, real estate, bonds, retail investment funds, private investment funds, loans, and bank deposits). Information is also available on whether the assets are domestic or foreign.

A second set of variables is taken from the World Economic Forum USA (2012), with data on institutional and business environments, financial stability, non-banking financial services, and financial access. One subset focuses on the capital account liberalization and the quality of overall infrastructure, both standardized on a scale from one (least) to seven (most).

A second subset is formed by an index of the strength of legal rights, the strength of investor protection index, and a financial strength indicator. These three factors take values from zero (worst) to 10 (best). The third subset includes the number of procedures to enforce a contract (in number of days) and the share of total number of securitization deals (as a percentage of total deals).

A supplementary group of variables is available in OECD (2014c) which tracks trends in pension fund financial performance (assets, investments, and industry structure). In particular, variables selected refer to the importance of pension fund assets as a share of GDP, the percentage of non-financial corporate bonds with respect to total bonds, and the amount of DB pension plans' assets as a percentage of total assets.

As the dependent variable we use the investment of pension funds in infrastructure (OECD 2014b). Here the total investment in infrastructure includes assets belonging to sectors such as transport, telecommunications, utilities, and energy. Pension funds can access infrastructure through different channels and the infrastructure investment (as a percentage of total investment) can be distinguished by three different categories: unlisted equity, listed equity, and debt. In this study, we consider the total amount of infrastructure investment (total infrastructure investment = unlisted equity + listed equity + debt). Table 10.3 provides further details on all variables.

Our unit of observation is the pension fund, not the country. Given the legislation of several countries (in alphabetical order, Armenia, Bulgaria, Czech Republic, Estonia, Finland, Germany, Luxembourg, Malta, Nigeria, Poland, the Russian Federation, Slovak Republic, and South Korea), these countries have different types of pension funds with different conditions of financial regulation and levels of investment. To study the effect of financial regulation and the institutional framework on the weight of the investment of pension funds in infrastructure, we use a Tobit model. The use of this model is conditioned by the particular characteristics of the dependent variable. The dependent variable is observed only over some interval, so we see a mixture of observations with zero and positive values. Therefore, the likelihood function has to take into account this particularity and involves additional computational complications.

The financial regulation is associated to the financial product considered. The high number of variables compared to the small number of observations and the limitations derived from the information of the variables require the use of principal components methodology. This procedure allows aggregating the information into two indicators: the portfolio limit in domestic asset categories and the portfolio limit in foreign asset categories (see Appendix).

TABLE 10.3. Variable descriptions

Variable	Description	Source
Portfolio limit in domestic asset categories	Relying on the OECD's report about the restrictions and regulation of pension funds, this index is created to measure how easy it is to make investments in different types of domestic assets. The OECD's report includes seven categories: equity, real estate, bonds, retail investment funds, private investment funds, loans, and bank deposits. Different codes are used for each of them depending on the existent regulation or restrictions, the higher the value for this index, the higher degree of flexibility when investing.	BBVA Research, OECD (2014a)
Portfolio limit in foreign asset categories	Relying on the OECD's report about the restrictions and regulation of pension funds, this index is created to measure how easy it is to make investments in different types of foreign assets. Seven categories are also included in this variable: equity, real estate, bonds, retail investment funds, private investment funds, loans, and bank deposits. Different codes are used for each of them depending on the existent regulation or restrictions, the higher the value for this index, the higher degree of flexibility when investing.	BBVA Research, OECD (2014a)
Capital account liberalization	This index measures the degree of capital account liberalization within a country, standardized on a scale from 1 (least liberalized) to 7 (most liberalized). This variable includes the level of capital controls based on information from the IMF's *Annual Report on Exchange Arrangements and Exchange Restrictions*, the Legal and Regulatory Issues subpillar and the Bond Market Development subpillar of the Financial Development Index included in *The Financial Development Report 2012*.	World Economic Forum USA Inc. (2012)
Quality of overall infrastructure	It includes the assessment of general infrastructure in each country (e.g., transport, telephony and energy) on a scale from 1 (extremely underdeveloped) to 7 (extensive and efficient by international standards).	World Economic Forum USA Inc. (2012)
Strength of legal rights index	This index measures the degree to which collateral and bankruptcy laws protect the rights of borrowers and lenders and thus facilitate lending. The index ranges from 0 to 10 (the higher the score, the better are collateral and bankruptcy laws designed to expand access to credit).	World Economic Forum USA Inc. (2012)
Strength of investor protection index	This index is the average of the extent of disclosure index, the extent of director liability index, and the ease of shareholder suits index. The index ranges from 0 to 10, with higher values indicating more investor protection.	World Economic Forum USA Inc. (2012)

(continued)

TABLE 10.3. Continued

Variable	Description	Source
Number of procedures to enforce a contract	This variable is the number of procedures from the moment the plaintiff files a lawsuit in court until the moment of payment. A procedure is defined as any interaction between the parties, or between them and the judge or the court officer (e.g., steps to file the case, steps for trial and judgment, and steps necessary to enforce the judgment).	World Economic Forum USA Inc. (2012)
Importance of pension funds relative to the size of the economy in the OECD	This indicator measures the market value of pension funds' assets relative to the size of the economy: in this case, it is measured by the GDP.	OECD (2014c)
DB pension plans' assets as % of total assets	This indicator reflects the relation among total investment of DB plans and total investment.	OECD Stats (2015)
Financial strength indicator	This indicator is a weighted average of financial strength rating by bank assets. It is a measure of a country's banks' ability to meet obligations to depositors and other creditors. It incorporates quantitative and qualitative information on a country's banks' operating environment (only larger banks are included in each country).	World Economic Forum USA Inc. (2012)
Non-financial corporate bonds to total bonds and notes outstanding (%)	Total amount of domestic nonfinancial corporate bonds and notes outstanding to total amount of domestic bonds and notes outstanding, both corporate and noncorporate.	BIS (2015)
Share of total number of securitization deals	It is the three-year average of the sum of asset-backed securities (ABS), mortgage-backed securities (MBS), high-yield bonds, and highly leveraged loans deals as % of total deals.	World Economic Forum USA Inc. (2012)
Anglosphere countries	Countries in which English is the first language of the majority of the population and other countries which present possess substantial English knowledge dating back to the British Empire.	
EU countries	Countries corresponding to one of the 28 current member states of the European Union (from 2013 onwards).	
EFTA countries	Countries belonging to the European Free Trade Association (EFTA), an intergovernmental organization created for the promotion of free trade and economic integration. Its members are Iceland, Liechtenstein, Norway, and Switzerland.	
Latin American and Caribbean countries	Considering the following countries: Brazil, Chile, Colombia, Costa Rica, Dominican Republic, Jamaica, Mauritius, Mexico, Panama, Peru, and Trinidad and Tobago.	

Source: Authors' derivations from sources listed.

Geographic binary variables are also included in the model. Several areas are considered: Anglosphere countries in a broad sense (those countries in which English is the first language of the majority of the population and those countries with substantial English knowledge) dating back to the British Empire, EU countries, EFTA countries, and Latin American and Caribbean countries. Table 10.4 presents the main descriptive statistics of all the variables.

Pension funds can access infrastructure through different channels. We follow the OECD (2014b) in considering infrastructure investment in unlisted equity, listed equity, and debt, which we aggregate to obtain the fraction of infrastructure investment relative to total investment. The average value shows that the investment of pension funds in these assets represents a small part of the total, though this varies widely across countries. Several countries do not invest anything in infrastructure, whereas countries like Portugal, Canada, Brazil, and Australia have a significant pension fund participation in infrastructure.

Focusing on the portfolio limits in domestic and foreign asset categories, the results suggest that the investment of pension funds in domestic asset

TABLE 10.4. Descriptive statistics

	Mean	Standard Deviation	Min	Max
Total infrastructure investment (as % of total investments)	3.104	8.843	0	51.3
Portfolio limit in domestic asset categories	5.847	2.8	0	10.579
Portfolio limit in foreign asset categories	1.891	2.515	0	9.848
Capital account liberalization	5.199	2.026	1	7
Quality of overall infrastructure	5.033	1.042	2.83	6.64
Strength of legal rights index	6.456	2.105	3	10
Strength of investor protection index	5.825	1.368	3	9
Number of procedures to enforce a contract	32.93	5.454	21	46
Importance of pension funds relative to the economy in OECD	24.105	35.449	0	166.3
DB pension plans' assets as % of total assets	20.329	35.506	0	100
Financial strengths indicator	4.561	2.044	0	9
Non-financial corporate bonds to total bonds and notes outstanding (%)	6.722	11.297	0	36.21
Share of total number of securitization deals	2.13	7.27	0.02	53.63
Anglosphere countries (broad version)	0.123	0.331	0	1
EU countries	0.474	0.504	0	1
EFTA countries	0.018	0.132	0	1
Latin American and Caribbean countries	0.105	0.31	0	1

Sources: Derived by the authors from OECD (2014a, 2014b, 2014c) and World Economic Forum USA Inc. (2012).

categories overtakes the investment in foreign assets. Regulation for domestic categories is often more comprehensive than for foreign ones.

Regarding the capital account liberalization, which measures the degree of capital account liberalization within a country, the mean shows that the liberalization degree is quite high (a value of 5.2 with seven as the maximum value). However, there is high inequality, as shown by the value of the standard deviation.

The quality of overall infrastructure takes into account the business environment and assesses the infrastructure (transport, telephony, energy, etc.) in the country. An index standardized on a scale from one (extremely underdeveloped) to seven (extensive and efficient) is used. The mean shows that the infrastructure in the countries analyzed is developed (5.8, and 6.64 is the maximum value), but it does not reach high levels of efficiency. The countries with the best performance in this index are Switzerland and Finland. Least developed countries along this dimension are Romania, Tanzania, and Nigeria.

The strength of legal rights index refers to the degree to which collateral and bankruptcy laws protect the rights of borrowers and lenders and thus facilitate lending). In the case of the first variable, the protection of the rights of borrowers and lenders is similar to the average (6.5). Yet significant differences across the countries are observed. Countries like Kenya, South Africa, and the UK have a high level of protection and thus access to credit. By contrast, Brazil, Egypt, Indonesia, Italy, Portugal, and the Russian Federation present a low index, indicating vulnerability and difficulties in accessing credit.

In relation to investor protection, the average value shows that the majority of the countries are around the mean (6.0). We can highlight the position of some countries such as Canada, Colombia, and Ireland, where the protection index almost reaches the maximum, while other countries, such as Austria, Greece, and Switzerland, present low values of this index.

The number of procedures required to enforce a contract measures the number of procedures from the moment the plaintiff files a lawsuit in court until the moment of payment. The mean value shows that almost 33 procedures are needed. In general, countries range between 30 and 40 procedures except some extraordinary cases, such as Ireland, which only requires 21 procedures, versus Pakistan and India, which need 46 procedures.

Most pension funds are small relative to the size of the economy, though cross-country differences are remarkable. In most countries, pension funds represent less than 10 percent of the economy. But in a few, like Australia, Iceland, the Netherlands, and the UK, the relative size of pension funds to the economy exceeds 100 percent.

We also measure DB pension plan assets as a percentage of total assets. The mean value of this variable shows that DB pensions are not widespread, but the large standard deviation confirms notable differences among countries.

The indicator of financial strengths is the weighted average of the financial strengths rating by bank assets. The mean value is 4.6 and it ranges from four to six. Only a few countries such as Canada and Australia have higher values.

Concerning the share of non-financial corporate bonds relative to the total bonds and notes outstanding, the data indicate a very low percentage with high variability. In the Russian Federation and South Korea, these products represent 30 percent of the total, while for the other countries this percentage is much lower.

The share of the total number of securitization deals shows the three-year average of the sum of asset-backed securities, mortgage-backed securities, high-yield bonds, and highly leveraged loans deals, as a percentage of total deals. As the mean and the standard deviation suggest, there is a huge disparity among the countries analyzed because securitization deals represent less than 1 percent of total deals for most. This percentage reaches 53.63 percent in the US.

The model

To incorporate the information on these variables, the results of the regression models are presented in Table 10.5.

Model 1 includes as regressors only the financial regulation variables. Coefficient estimates on the portfolio asset limit suggest that a reduction of the limits in domestic assets significantly raises infrastructure investment as a percentage of the total, but this effect is not statistically different from zero in the case of foreign asset limits. Therefore, the main restriction for infrastructure investment by pension funds comes from domestic assets. These results indicate that much work remains to be done in the field of financial regulation.

Model 2 includes financial regulation variables as well as other variables associated with general regulation, legislation, institutional factors, and pension characteristics. The effect of financial regulation now becomes negative in both cases, but negligible in the domestic option and slightly significant for the foreign assets. The importance of other factors also determines the relationship between financial regulation and investment decisions, which do not exclusively depend on portfolio limits.

The degree of capital account liberalization, the strength of the legal rights index (measuring the degree to which collateral and bankruptcy laws protect the rights of borrowers and lenders), and the importance of pension funds relative to the size of the economy are all significant. The investor protection index has a negative and slightly significant effect on the percentage of infrastructure investment. A potential explanation comes

TABLE 10.5. Tobit model coefficient estimates[a]

	Model 1	Model 2	Model 3	Model 4
Portfolio limit in domestic asset categories	2.58[c]	−1.73	−2.79	−4.85
Portfolio limit in foreign asset categories	−0.40	−2.34[d]	−4.66[c]	−4.93
Capital account liberalization		6.40[c]	12.87[b]	49.61[c]
Quality of overall infrastructure		−5.96	−19.50[c]	−65.18[c]
Strength of legal rights index		4.24[d]	4.84[c]	15.04[c]
Strength of investor protection index		−5.96[d]	−11.73[b]	−38.67[c]
Number of procedures to enforce a contract		−0.23	−1.62	−5.55[c]
Importance of pension funds relative to the economy in OECD		0.19[d]	0.09	−0.07
DB pension plans' assets as % of total assets		0.04	0.01	0.39[c]
Financial strengths indicator			9.00[c]	32.41[c]
Non-financial corporate bonds to total bonds and notes outstanding (%)			0.94[c]	5.14[c]
Share of total number of securitization deals			0.34[d]	2.14[c]
Anglosphere countries (broad version)				47.65
EU countries				140.59[c]
EFTA countries				90.24[d]
Latin American and Caribbean countries				94.61[b]
Constant	−33.142[b]	0.628	69.281	29.45
No. of observations	57	57	57	57
Pseudo R^2	0.018	0.088	0.147	0.23
Log pseudolikelihood	−80.655	−74.884	−70.026	−63.68

Notes:
[a] Dependent variable: pension fund infrastructure investment (as % of total investments).
[b] Denotes estimates significant to 1%.
[c] Denotes estimates significant to 5%.
[d] Denotes estimates significant to 10%.
Source: OECD (2014a, 2014b, 2014c) and World Economic Forum USA Inc. (2012).

from the tradeoff between protection levels and pension fund investment opportunities, versus other investors in the context of infrastructure. Other variables considered are not statistically different from zero.

Further details relating to the financial system are included in Model 3, and results reinforce our observations from Model 2. Only the importance of pension funds relative to the size of the economy declines in significance. The financial system instruments variable has a positive and significant coefficient, establishing a direct relationship between flexibility, size, and development degree of the financial markets and the level of pension fund infrastructure investment.

A last group of variables is included in Model 4, related to geographic area. The results confirm the importance of all factors considered in Model 3. The geographic effects suggest that country characteristics affecting the percentage of pension fund infrastructure investments are especially important in the EU, EFTA, Latin American, and Caribbean countries.

Other results in Model 4 confirm the relevance of the development of financial protection, stability and fairness of legal rights, and the quality and strength of financial institutions. Financial market development also has positive and significant effects on the percentage of pension fund infrastructure investment.

Conclusion

This research explored factors driving pension fund investments in infrastructure projects. Pension investments in infrastructure could be attractive to the extent that these assets offer less correlation than other financial assets in their portfolios, better risk–return features, and long maturities. Yet investing in infrastructure projects is also risky and requires much expertise.

Pension regulations are adapting to allow pension funds to become more involved in infrastructure projects. Australia and Canada have a regulatory framework that allows them to invest with enormous flexibility, and apparently with success. Current discussions in Europe are taking place in the context of the development of a Capital Markets Union, as the EU seeks to deal with the different countries' regulatory issues. In Latin America, specialized financial vehicles have been developed for pension funds to invest in infrastructure, especially in Mexico.

Our empirical analysis also shows that the degree of development in the financial markets (i.e., capital account liberalization, non-financial corporate bonds as a share of the total bonds and notes outstanding, and the share of total number of securitization deals) is positively associated with infrastructure investment.

Acknowledgments

The authors are grateful to Ignacio Aparicio-Torices and Maria Rodriguez-Urbano for research assistance. The views expressed are those of the authors and do not necessarily reflect those of their respective academic affiliations.

Appendix: Measuring the Regulatory Flexibility of Pension Fund Infrastructure Investment through a Synthetic Index

In an attempt to homogenize and standardize the diversity of regulations on pension fund infrastructure investment, we create an index that measures how much of an opening or facility these funds have to make this kind of investment. We use principal component analysis (PCA), which is the statistical technique for data reduction. PCA uses an orthogonal transformation to convert a set of observations of possibly correlated variables into a set of values of linearly uncorrelated variables called principal components.

PCA is mathematically defined as an orthogonal linear transformation. This transformation is defined in such a way that the first principal component has the largest possible variance (and thus accounts for as much of the variability in the data as possible), and each succeeding component in turn has the highest variance possible under the constraint that it is orthogonal to the preceding components.

The OECD (2014a) reports details of the regulation for each financial product describing different forms of restriction and legal regulation on pension funds. The products are Equity, Real Estate, Bonds, Retail Investment Funds, Private Investment Funds, Loans, and Bank Deposits. We use four different codes for each product (not allowed to invest, allowed with restrictions, allowed with restrictions and with exceptions in some particular cases, and allowed with no limit). Therefore, a higher value of this indicator (for any product) implies a higher degree of flexibility. Each country's laws also distinguish between portfolio limits on pension fund investment in (_in) or outside (_out) the country using these seven asset categories.

The PCA procedure allows aggregating the information of the seven products in two indicators, the portfolio limit in domestic asset categories and the portfolio limit in foreign asset categories:

Portfolio limit in domestic asset categories = 0.3850 × Equity_in + 0.3640 × Real Estate_in + 0.3863 × Bonds_in + 0.3896 × Retail Investment Funds_in + 0.3832 × Private Investment Funds_in + 0.3603 × Loans_in + 0.3763 × Bank Deposits_in

Portfolio limit in foreign asset categories = 0.3992 × Equity_out + 0.3439 × Real Estate_out + 0.4142 × Bonds_out + 0.4113 × Retail Investment Funds_out + 0.3615 × Private Investment Funds_out + 0.3111 × Loans_out + 0.3927 × Bank Deposits_out

The values of the weights of these two formulas correspond to the results derived from the first principal component (eigenvector) for each set of products. The weights in both cases are similar among the financial products, although the differences seem to be higher in the foreign asset categories.

Results show that countries with regulations allowing pension fund investment in infrastructure are those of Anglo-Saxon origin, followed by those from northern Europe and Japan. Many developed countries have restrictive legislation including Spain, France, Italy, and Switzerland. In developing regions, especially in Africa and one or two in Latin America, very restrictive regulations are in place.

Endnotes

1. At the recent meeting of the International Organisation of Pension Supervisors (IOPS) and the International Organisation of Pension Funds Supervisory Authorities (AIOS) in San José, Costa Rica, on Feb. 2015, this topic took a starring role in the discussions.
2. It does not specify if this would also apply to pension funds.

References

Alonso, J., J. Bjeletic, C. Herrera, S. Hormazabal, I. Ordóñez, C. Romero, D. Tuesta, and A. Ugarte, (2009). *Projections of the Impact of Pension Funds on Investment in Infrastructure and Growth in Latin America,* BBVA Research Working Papers, 1002. Madrid. Spain: BBVA.

Andrews, A. and S. Wahba (2007). *Investing in Infrastructure: A Primer,* Infrastructure Paper Series, 2. New York: Morgan Stanley Partnership.

Bank of International Settlements (BIS) (2015). 'BIS Statistics.' <http://www.bis.org/statistics/index.htm>.

Bird, R., H. Liem, and S. Thorp (2012). 'Infrastructure: Real Assets and Real Returns,' *European Financial Management,* 20(4): 802–24.

CEOE (2013). *La inversión en infraestructuras públicas en España.* Madrid: CEOE. <http://www.ceoe.es/resources/image/inversion_infraestructuras_publicas_espana_propuesta_mejora_marco_legal_2013.pdf>.

Connolly, N. (2012). *Australians and Infrastructure Investments.* Seattle, WA: Russell Research.

Della Croce, R. (2012). *Trends in Large Pension Fund Investment in Infrastructure,* OECD Working Papers on Finance, Insurance and Private Pensions, 29. Paris: OECD Publishing.

Della Croce, R., P.-A. Schieb, and B. Stevens (2011). *Pension Funds Investment in Infrastructure: A Survey.* Geneva: OECD. <http://www.oecd.org/futures/infrastructureto2030/48634596.pdf>.

Della Croce, R. and J. Yermo (2013). *Institutional Investors and Infrastructure Financing,* OECD Working Papers on Finance, Insurance and Private Pensions, 36. Paris: OECD Publishing.

EIOPA (2013). *Discussion Paper on Standard Formula Design and Calibration for Certain Long-Term Investments.* Frankfurt: EIOPA. <https://eiopa.europa.eu/Publications/Reports/EIOPA_Technical_Report_on_Standard_Formula_Design_and_Calibration_for_certain_Long-Term_Investments__2_.pdf>.

Escrivá, J., E. Fuentes, and A. García-Herrero (2010). *Balance y Proyecciones de la Experiencia en Infraestructura de los Fondos de Pensiones en Latinoamerica,* Santiago, Chile: BBVA.

European Commission (2014a). *Long-Term Financing of the European Economy.* Brussels: EU. <http://eur-lex.europa.eu/legal-content/EN/TXT/PDF/?uri=CELEX:52013DC0150&from=EN>.

European Commission (2014b). *Communication on Long Term Financing of the European Economy.* Brussels: EU. <http://eur-lex.europa.eu/legal-content/EN/TXT/PDF/?uri=CELEX:52014DC0168&from=EN>.

European Commission (2014c). *Ad-Hoc Audit of the Pilot Phase of the Europe 2020 Project Bond Initiative.* Brussels: EU. <http://ec.europa.eu/economy_finance/financial_operations/investment/europe_2020/investment_needs_en.htm>.

Future Fund Board (2011). *Annual Report, 2011/2012.* Melbourne: Future Fund Board of Guardians. <http://www.futurefund.gov.au/__data/assets/pdf_file/0012/5106/FF_Annual_Report_2012_WEB.pdf>.

Inderst, G. (2014). 'Pension Fund Investment in Infrastructure: Lessons from Australia and Canada,' *Rotman International Journal of Pension Management,* 7(1): 40–8.

Infrastructure Partnerships Australia (2010). *The Role of Superannuation in Building Australia's Future.* Sydney: Infrastructure Partnerships Australia. <http://www.infrastructure.org.au/Content/TheRoleofSuperannuation.aspx>.

Macquarie Group (2009). *Infrastructure Sector Boosted by Government Spending.* Global Equity Research, Issue Brief. <http://www.macquarie.co.uk/dafiles/Internet/mgl/uk/mfg/docs/global-listed-infra-annual-sector-review.pdf>.

NAPF (2013). *Trends in Defined Benefit Asset Allocation: The Changing Shape of UK Pension Investment.* London: NAPF. <http://www.napf.co.uk/PolicyandResearch/DocumentLibrary/~/media/Policy/Documents/0314_Trends_in_db_asset_allocation_changing_shape_UK_pension_investment_NAPF_research_paper_July_2013_DOCUMENT.ashx>.

OECD (2014a). *Annual Survey of Investment Regulations of Pension Funds.* Paris: OECD. <http://www.oecd.org/finance/privatepensios/annualsurveyofinvestmentregulationofpensionfunds.htm>.

OECD (2014b). *Annual Survey of Large Pension Funds and Public Pension Reserve Funds. Report on Pension Funds' Long-Term Investments.* Paris: OECD. <http://www.oecd.org/finance/private-pensions/survey-large-pension-funds.htm>.

OECD (2014c). *Pension Markets in Focus 2014.* Paris: OECD. <http://www.oecd.org/finance/private-pensions/pensionmarketsinfocus.htm>.

OECD (2014d). *Private Financing and Government Support to Promote Long-Term Investments in Infrastructure.* Paris: OECD. <http://www.oecd.org/daf/fin/private-pensions/Private-financing-and-government-support-to-promote-LTI-in-infrastructure.pdf>.

OECD Stats (2015). 'Funded Pensions Indicators.' <https://stats.oecd.org/Index.aspx?DataSetCode=PNNI_NEW#>.

Peng, H. and G. Newell (2007). 'The Significance of Infrastructure in Australian Investment Portfolios,' *Pacific Rim Property Research Journal,* 14(4): 423–50.

Sawant, R. (2010). *Infrastructure Investing: Managing Risks and Rewards for Pensions, Insurance Companies and Endowments.* Chicago: Wiley Finance.

Tuesta, D. (2013). 'Uso de los Fondos de Pensiones en Obra Pública: Experiencia de los Países Latinoamericanos,' presented at Seminario: Acceso de los fondos de pensiones al financiamiento de obra pública, San José, Costa Rica.

Tuesta, D. (2015). 'Pension Funds' Experience Investing in Infrastructure,' presentation in IOPS/AIOS International Seminar on Pension Systems. San Jose de Costa Rica. <https://www.bbvaresearch.com/en/publicaciones/pension-funds-experience-investing-in-infrastructure>.

Weber, B. and H. Alfen (2010). *Infrastructure as an Asset Class: Investment Strategies, Project Finance and PPP.* Chicago: Wiley Finance.

World Bank (2011). *Best Practices in Public-Private Partnerships Financing in Latin America: Conference Report.* Washington, DC: World Bank. <https://einstitute.worldbank.org/ei/sites/default/files/Upload_Files/BestPracticesPPPFinancingLatinAmericaConferenceReport.pdf>.

World Economic Forum USA Inc. (2012). *The Financial Development Report.* New York. <http://www.weforum.org/issues/financial-development>.

Yun, J. (2012). 'Healthcare Sector is a Natural Hedge for Pension Funds' Investing,' Forbes. Dec. 12. <http://www.forbes.com/sites/joonyun/2012/12/25/healthcare-sector-is-a-natural-hedge-for-pension-funds>.

End Pages

The Pension Research Council

The Pension Research Council of the Wharton School at the University of Pennsylvania is committed to generating debate on key policy issues affecting pensions and other employee benefits. The Council sponsors interdisciplinary research on private and social retirement security and related benefit plans in the United States and around the world. It seeks to broaden understanding of these complex arrangements through basic research into their economic, social, legal, actuarial, and financial foundations. Members of the Advisory Board of the Council, appointed by the Dean of the Wharton School, are leaders in the employee benefits field, and they recognize the essential role of social security and other public sector income maintenance programs while sharing a desire to strengthen private sector approaches to economic security. For more information see <http://www.pensionresearchcouncil.org>.

The Boettner Center for Pensions and Retirement Research

Founded at the Wharton School to support scholarly research, teaching, and outreach on global aging, retirement, and public and private pensions, the Center is named after Joseph E. Boettner. Funding to the University of Pennsylvania was provided through the generosity of the Boettner family, whose intent was to spur financial wellbeing at older ages through work on how aging influences financial security and life satisfaction. The Center disseminates research and evaluation on challenges and opportunities associated with global aging and retirement, how to strengthen retirement income systems, saving and investment behavior of the young and the old, interactions between physical and mental health, and successful retirement. For more information see <http://www.pensionresearchcouncil.org/boettner>.

Executive Director

Olivia S. Mitchell, International Foundation of Employee Benefit Plans Professor, Department of Business Economics and Public Policy, Wharton School, University of Pennsylvania.

Advisory Board

Members of the Pension Research Council

Allianz Asset Management | Project M
The American College Bank of America Merrill Lynch

The Capital Group
Federal Reserve Employee Benefits System
William A. Frey
International Foundation of Employee Benefit Plans
Investment Company Institute
J.P. Morgan Chase & Co. Mercer Human Resource Consulting
MetLife
Mutual of America Life Insurance Company
Ontario Pension Board
Pensions & Investments
Pacific Investment Mgmt. Co. LLC (PIMCO)
Prudential
Retirement Made Simpler (FINRA)
Social Security Administration
Society of Actuaries
State Street Global Advisors
T. Rowe Price
TIAA Institute
Willis Towers Watson
The Vanguard Group

Recent Pension Research Council Publications

Reimagining Pensions: The Next 40 Years. Olivia S. Mitchell and Richard C. Shea, eds. 2016. (ISBN 978-0-19-875544-9.)

Recreating Sustainable Retirement. Olivia S. Mitchell, Raimond Maurer, and P. Brett Hammond, eds. 2014. (ISBN 0-19-871924-3.)

The Market for Retirement Financial Advice. Olivia S. Mitchell and Kent Smetters, eds. 2013. (ISBN 0-19-968377-2.)

Reshaping Retirement Security: Lessons from the Global Financial Crisis. Raimond Maurer, Olivia S. Mitchell, and Mark Warshawsky, eds. 2012. (ISBN 0-19-966069-7.)

Financial Literacy. Olivia S. Mitchell and Annamaria Lusardi, eds. 2011. (ISBN 0-19-969681-9.)

Securing Lifelong Retirement Income. Olivia S. Mitchell, John Piggott, and Noriyuki Takayama, eds. 2011. (ISBN 0-19-959484-9.)

Reorienting Retirement Risk Management. Robert L. Clark and Olivia S. Mitchell, eds. 2010. (ISBN 0-19-959260-9.)

Fundamentals of Private Pensions. Dan M. McGill, Kyle N. Brown, John J. Haley, Sylvester Schieber, and Mark J. Warshawsky. 9th edn, 2010. (ISBN 0-19-954451-6.)

The Future of Public Employees Retirement Systems. Olivia S. Mitchell and Gary Anderson, eds. 2009. (ISBN 0-19-957334-9.)

Recalibrating Retirement Spending and Saving. John Ameriks and Olivia S. Mitchell, eds. 2008. (ISBN 0-19-954910-8.)

Lessons from Pension Reform in the Americas. Stephen J. Kay and Tapen Sinha, eds. 2008. (ISBN 0-19-922680-6.)

Redefining Retirement: How Will Boomers Fare? Brigitte Madrian, Olivia S. Mitchell, and Beth J. Soldo, eds. 2007. (ISBN 0-19-923077-3.)

Restructuring Retirement Risks. David Blitzstein, Olivia S. Mitchell, and Steven P. Utkus, eds. 2006. (ISBN 0-19-920465-9.)

Reinventing the Retirement Paradigm. Robert L. Clark and Olivia S. Mitchell, eds. 2005. (ISBN 0-19-928460-1.)

Pension Design and Structure: New Lessons from Behavioral Finance. Olivia S. Mitchell and Steven P. Utkus, eds. 2004. (ISBN 0-19-927339-1.)

The Pension Challenge: Risk Transfers and Retirement Income Security. Olivia S. Mitchell and Kent Smetters, eds. 2003. (ISBN 0-19-926691-3.)

A History of Public Sector Pensions in the United States. Robert L. Clark, Lee A. Craig, and Jack W. Wilson, eds. 2003. (ISBN 0-8122-3714-5.)

Benefits for the Workplace of the Future. Olivia S. Mitchell, David Blitzstein, Michael Gordon, and Judith Mazo, eds. 2003. (ISBN 0-8122-3708-0.)

Innovations in Retirement Financing. Olivia S. Mitchell, Zvi Bodie, P. Brett Hammond, and Stephen Zeldes, eds. 2002. (ISBN 0-8122-3641-6.)

To Retire or Not: Retirement Policy and Practice in Higher Education. Robert L. Clark and P. Brett Hammond, eds. 2001. (ISBN 0-8122-3572-X.)

Pensions in the Public Sector. Olivia S. Mitchell and Edwin Hustead, eds. 2001. (ISBN 0-8122-3578-9.)

Available from the Pension Research Council website: <http://www.pensionresearchcouncil.org>.

Index

Diagrams, graphs and maps are given in italics.